HARD TIME BLUES

SASHA ABRAMSKY

HARD TIME BLUES

THOMAS DUNNE BOOKS

St. Martin's Press ≈ New York

THOMAS DUNNE BOOKS.
An imprint of St. Martin's Press.

www.stmartins.com

Design by Kathryn Parise

ISBN 0-312-26811-4

First Edition: January 2002

10   9   8   7   6   5   4   3   2   1

To my grandmother Mimi,
whose love I will never forget

and my wife, Julie Sze,
with whom I shall travel the highway of life

Acknowledgments

I started reporting and writing articles on America's criminal justice system five years ago. The idea for *Hard Time Blues* emerged out of stories I had published in newspapers and magazines in both the United States and England.

Numerous people have contributed to this book, both in terms of direct help given, and, more generally, through simply being part of my life, encouraging me and shoring up my confidence at those low moments that every writer sometimes falls prey to. Were I to thank everyone by name, I would have to publish an entire companion volume just devoted to this task. Instead of that, I would like to issue a blanket thank-you to the myriad editors who have supported my work over the years as well as to the Open Society Institute for their recent support of my work; to the library staffs in both California and New York who proved so cooperative during my research; to the public relations staff of the many departments of corrections and other government offices whom I badgered incessantly for information and for access; and to the numerous nongovernmental organizations, private foundations, and watchdog groups who have been studying the growth of America's prison system over the years, and who generously cooperated with me in my often exhausting search for information.

I would also like to thank the many friends and acquaintances who generously opened up their houses to me and allowed me to sleep in their spare bedrooms or living rooms while I was visiting prisons and interviewing sources across the country. And, of course, I am immensely grateful to the dozens of prisoners, ex-prisoners, and their family members who have, over the course of the years, shared the most intimate, and often painful, details of their lives with me, answered my questions, and helped me to develop an understanding both of the social conditions that lead so many into committing crimes, and also of what life inside prison is actually like. Similarly, my best wishes go out to the innocent victims of crimes—both to those who shared their thoughts with me during the course of my research, and to the myriad others whom I did not interview. This book, focused as it is on prisons and prisoners, is in no way intended to downplay the suffering that crimes of violence and of property inflict.

Beyond these groups, there are, however, many people whom I must thank individually.

The writing of this book would not have been possible without the cooperation of Billy Ochoa, his father, William, and his sisters, Gloria and Virginia. To them, I owe a debt of gratitude of the highest order.

Professor Sam Freedman, my mentor at the Columbia University Graduate School of Journalism and a faithful friend in the years since then, was instrumental in pushing me toward book writing. My dear friends Carolyn Juris and Jason Ziedenberg have been invaluable as companions, editors, and fonts of support and information in the years since journalism school. Likewise, Eyal Press, a fellow Brooklyn freelancer, has been a continual source of inspiration.

I would also like to express my gratitude to my agent, Paul Chung, and to my editors at St. Martin's—Melissa Jacobs for the first part of the book's genesis, and, in the later stages, Carin Siegfried.

More generally, I would like to thank my family. My parents, Jack and Lenore, who raised me to think for myself and to care about the world I live in. My brother, Kolya, with whom I sometimes argue but whom I admire and care for very much. My sister, Tanya, whose sense of humor never ceases to amaze me. My grandfather Chimen, in London, whose immense wealth of knowledge, love of books, and sense of humanity I have benefited from in a way too vast for words to describe. And my grandmother Mim, in Los Angeles, whose house has always been a home away from home for me, and with whom I stayed more times than I can recall while carrying out the Los Angeles–based research for *Hard Time Blues*. My grandmother Mimi and my grandfather Bob, both of whom are now deceased, were also most powerful influences on my life.

Above all, I would like to thank my wife, Julie Sze, who has exhibited remarkable patience during the years that this book has been in the works; who accepted, without complaint, the many months in which I had to travel away from home to research this book; who has borne my journalistic mood swings and frustrations; who has read my work line by line and given me invaluable comments and editing suggestions. I am extraordinarily lucky to have met, and married, such a loving, beautiful, and intelligent woman. Without Julie's presence, I doubt very much whether this book would ever have been completed. Thank you, Julie, for the Good Times.

Introduction

America, to me, is a land of dreams and a playground for the human imagination. When I was growing up in London, England, son to a British father and an American mother, I was always drawn to the world across the Atlantic; to a place that in almost every way seemed to me to be larger than life and fuller of spirit than the old, somewhat staid universe of Western Europe. I loved America, I longed to spend more than just my summers there, and—when I turned twenty-one—I realized that dream by moving to America and living as a newcomer in that ultimate city of newcomers, New York.

For someone interested in politics and history, what could be more wonderful than a young country pledged to democracy? What could be more inspiring than a land that has welcomed tens of millions of immigrants, including four of my eight great-grandparents, to its shores in the brief centuries of its existence? A place that considers happiness a right, freedom a necessity and political participation—from the PTA to the town council all the way through to the presidential elections—a festive civic virtue.

And yet, while America might seem to represent all that is good and noble in the human soul, over the years I have lived here and practiced journalism here, it has struck me that part of the American experience also represents something darker, more untamed and brutal that exists deep within the human psyche.

Hard Time Blues is my attempt to understand the flip side of the American Dream. It is an exploration of the popular forces and cultural trends that have helped institutionalize the largest prison system on earth—larger than the Russian and Chinese gulags we read so much about, more pervasive than the prison system in South Africa during the worst days of Apartheid oppression in the 1970s and 1980s. And it is a saga of how the ballot box itself—that most potent and elementary symbol of democracy—has, in the past quarter century, been used by electoral majorities to imprison an ever larger proportion of the country's population, and an ever greater number of people from within the Black and Latino minorities in that population.

Throughout its history, America has created for itself two unique intertwinings: the first being the use of the criminal justice system, and the sanction of punishment, to maintain its racial hierarchies; and the second being a conflation of the issues of drugs and crime—social problems that in many other countries are treated as separate issues demanding distinct political responses. In recent decades, despite the civil rights movement's massive strides toward a promise of equality, the prison population of America has not only ballooned, but its face has also gotten blacker and browner. How has a country usually so full of optimism, so committed to the rhetoric of equality, allowed this to happen? And what political trends made the recent expansion of the prison population, brought into being with a few legislative spasms in the 1980s and early-to-mid 1990s, such a tempting proposition?

Twenty-five years ago, under half a million people were imprisoned in the United States. In the year 2000, with crime rates roughly the same as they were in the mid-1970s—the result of a rise in crime being followed by a drastic fall in the 1990s—four times that number are doing hard time in the thousand-plus state and more than one hundred federal prisons dotted around the fifty states. In California alone, over 160,000 people live in the Golden State's burgeoning prison system. In Texas, with a prison population now above 163,000, close to 10 percent of adult African American men are now behind bars. In almost all states, those in prison cannot vote. And in twelve others, those convicted of a felony can *never* vote again. Thus in states such as Alabama and Florida, upwards of one quarter of Black men are now permanently denied that most basic right of citizenry: the right to vote.

Two thoughts strike me here: the first is that if crime rates fell throughout the 1990s, why the need to double, and then double again, the prison population? The second thought: if incarceration is so effective, why is the crime rate today still as high as it was twenty-five years ago, despite the soaring numbers behind bars?

Paradoxes abound in politics, and as a new century gets underway, I can think of nothing more paradoxical than the phenomenon of a populace reared on democratic values and committed to self-expression vociferously stamping its approval on changing approaches to crime and punishment that have resulted in two million fellow Americans being locked up behind bars and millions more being disenfranchised, oftentimes for minor crimes that other democracies would never deal with through the use of incarceration. True, a democracy degenerates into anarchy if nobody obeys the laws of the land. But, conversely, at some point a democracy collapses in on itself if a significant percentage of the population are imprisoned for crimes committed because of economic want and the lack of legitimate jobs.

Faced with a spiraling violent crime rate in the 1970s and 1980s, and arguably more important with a public fed ever more images of crime by the media and hence increasingly *fearful* of the perceived threat of a criminal underclass, politicians of all stripes rushed to become ever more "tough-on-crime." Only in the last few years have the broader political and cultural consequences of this strategy become visible.

In part, the toughening up of the criminal justice system was an understandable response to the violence and terror that racked America during the height of the crack-cocaine epidemic, during the latter part of the 1980s and the early 1990s. Yet, the carnage associated with this particular societal disaster only partly explains why so many people ended up behind bars. For the rush to incarcerate *predated* the influx of crack cocaine into inner city communities in the mid-1980s and it has continued for many years *after* the worst gang atrocities associated with the struggle for crack distribution rights abated.

Partly, I believe, the prison boom can be explained by a transformation in the political rhetoric away from a language of inclusion and hope and toward one of cynicism and fear. But I also believe it to be at least in part a deeply unfortunate by-product of America's greatest, most treasured, asset: its democratic culture. In a dictatorship, leaders can order their subordinates to imprison "enemies of the state," even to kill them, instantly and on a whim. In a democracy, due process must be observed. To change laws in response to something as intangible as "the fear of crime," bills must be crafted, popular support must be courted, debates must be enjoined, and committees of experts queried. By the time these bills become law, oftentimes the circumstances necessitating their existence have changed. Hence the peculiar spectacle, detailed in the pages to come, of the United States dramatically toughening up its criminal justice code in the mid-1990s, just at the moment when crime rates had actually begun *falling*.

Whatever the reasons, the result of a ratcheted-up political rhetoric has been a quarter century of domestic war—War on Crime and War on Drugs—and the remolding of America as a penal state, even as the crime rate stabilized and then fell.

What could be stranger than a country that continues to take in the world's beaten and brutalized at the same time imprisoning its own impoverished teenagers for ten, fifteen, even twenty or thirty years, for small-time drug crimes? And yet America has done so at the behest of its own populace. Mass imprisonment was born out of the popular will and has continued through popular demand.

Distract the mob with the blood of the gladiators, the Roman Caesars knew, and you could control an empire. Two thousand years later, our Supermax prisons should, perhaps, be considered the amphitheaters of a more complicated, more democratic age, the lives destroyed inside them serving largely to fuel the ambitions of demagogic politicians appealing to that which is base in the American soul.

There are three main characters in *Hard Time Blues*. The first is

Billy Ochoa, a repeat offender caught up in the web of history. Ochoa's crimes are numerous but nonviolent. However, in the new schema, Ochoa's actions are treated at least as severely as those of the murderers and rapists he shares a prison with. My second main protagonist is former California Governor Pete Wilson, a man who rode the crest of a wave — a large wave of popular fear based on an impression that the country was besieged by criminals — into the upper echelons of the United States' political elite. Wilson, and politicians like him, helped to create this wave of fear in the first place; and once the swell of wrath arose, they made sure that they were the ones who benefited. The third subject is more amorphous. It is that great phenomenon known as "the American public." It is the citizenry of this country, men and women who have themselves been victimized by criminals, or who have been bombarded, for decades, with sensational images of violent crime by a ratings-hungry media; who have been told by a generation of politicians that drugs and crime are larger social problems than poverty, unemployment, and despair; and who have reacted by battening down the hatches and supporting the building of ever-more prisons to house prisoners sentenced to ever-longer terms during a decade when those who studied the statistics knew that crime rates were actually falling.

Although most people I contacted during the writing of this book were gracious with their time and readily shared with me their memories, personal correspondence, and thoughts, one major character refused to participate. Despite repeated requests for interviews, delivered both over the telephone and in faxed correspondence with his office, and despite a cover letter from St. Martin's Press explaining the nature of the book and asking for cooperation, former Governor Pete Wilson never responded.

As a practical note to readers, a word on the structure of the book is in order. Rather than attempting a constant single narrative, I have chosen to create somewhat self-contained chapters. The book opens with Ochoa's story and then moves on to Pete Wilson. It expands to create an overview of America's prison population and then contracts again to the more particular narrative of Billy Ochoa's life. The alternation between characters and themes continues throughout the ten chapters. In this way, I have tried to paint vivid pictures without burdening my readers with too many areas on which to have to concentrate simultaneously.

I focus primarily on California because it is in California that so many of the nation's policies and attitudes coalesce, and because it is California—along with Southern states such as Texas—that has most visibly embraced the goals of punishment over rehabilitation, and imprisonment over alternatives to incarceration. The old adage, "where California goes, the nation follows," is particularly true in the area of contemporary crime and punishment. Nevertheless, because of the national scope of the subject, I have also included in my book the stories of prisoners incarcerated around the country. Their tales, gathered over the past four years during the course of face-to-face interviews in prisons, through telephone conversations and letters, and through meetings with family members on the outside, illustrate far better than mere statistics ever could how destructive America's prison policy has become.

It is my hope that in telling this story, in showing the faces behind the numbers, in showing prisoners in all their complex, often pathetic, often tragic, entirety, *Hard Time Blues* will help to stem the tide of incarceration. Perhaps the next generation will live in a country that not only fights crime, but also one that has learnt how to tackle social problems without imprisoning almost one percent of its entire population and a staggering ten percent of its young African American male population.

Prologue

Nobody but cousin Patty and Arthur Castaneda came to see Billy Ochoa off. Patty had always had a soft spot for Billy; and Arthur, Billy's nephew, was dying of muscular dystrophy and didn't know if he'd ever get a chance to see his uncle again.

The rest of Billy's family no longer cared enough to make the journey downtown to the courthouse. Ochoa had burnt his bridges long ago. His father, William Senior, gave him money every so often. But his father was old now, in his seventies, and he figured Billy had been around the block enough times to look after himself. Billy's mother, Josie, had doted on her eldest son, tolerated his foibles, stuck up for him when others bad-mouthed him; but Josie had died of kidney failure many years back. There was a brother, but he wanted nothing to do with Billy. And there were two sisters — Gloria and Virginia — who felt sorry for their wayward brother but also angry with him. So there Billy Ochoa was. Alone with his court-appointed lawyer, the prosecutor, and the judge. And cousin Patty sitting on the spectator benches looking on.

Of course, if Billy's family had realized what was about to happen, perhaps they'd have taken the trip downtown from the various suburbs to the east in which they now resided, despite the accumulated frustration of the years, despite the lying and cheating, the selfishness and the scheming. After all, it's one thing for a man to go to prison. It's quite another for him to be told he will never return.

The date was Friday September 20, 1996, a mild late summer day in Los Angeles, a full fourteen months after Billy had been arrested at his younger sister Virginia's bungalow in the small community of Arcadia. He had spent those months first at the L.A. County Jail, then the California Institute for Men, at Chino; and then, after he had failed to raise the $115,000 bail set by Judge Suzanne Person at his preliminary hearing, at the North County Correctional Facility in Wayside, near the roller coaster theme park of Magic Mountain. He shared a cell with another man, in module 911 — a sixteen-cell module within the jail. For exercise he played a little handball three times a week. Finally, for the duration of the trial and while he awaited sentencing, Ochoa had been kept at the Central Men's Jail, 441 Bauchet Street.

The court records listed him as five feet eight inches — an optimistic reckoning for the stocky, pot-bellied Ochoa — and 170 pounds.[1] His birthdate was given as 4/24/43. Ochoa was fifty-three years old and he looked it. His black hair was turning gray, his teeth were ragged, his chin was beginning to tuck itself down into his neck. Ochoa was, in all senses of the word, a *little* man, someone to whom things happened, someone unable to seize control of his own destiny. Even his attempts to represent himself during the lengthy maneuverings before the trial had backfired; Judge Alan Buckner had got so annoyed by the badly spelled letters that Ochoa had continuously fired off in his childish script to Buckner and to witnesses, and by the continuous barrage of ill-founded legal motions that Ochoa had crafted, that he had eventually forced the defendant to accept the sixty-five-year-old Baldwin Hills lawyer Ray Clark as his representative in court. "Even me receiving a sentence at minimum 25 years to life, is cruel and unjust," Ochoa had written to Buckner in a typical penciled letter. "But your [sic] the law and I imagin [sic] you are comfortable with this." Later on he wrote, "As you know I am a layman at law . . . If I am to loose [sic], I can spend the rest of my life in prison. Your honor, you may get mad and upset, but you get to go home every night." At one point Ochoa had even filed a motion asking the judge to dismiss himself from the bench.

And then, despite Clark's advice, Ochoa had insisted on taking the witness stand, thus giving the prosecutor an opportunity to inform the jury about all his prior convictions, about his whole sordid, drug-addicted past. After which Clark, who operated out of a run-down office in a dilapidated old shopping mall in one of the poorest parts of L.A. and who was billing the court fifty dollars per hour for his services, declined to call any more witnesses and rested his case.

The result was a foregone conclusion. Even Johnnie Cochran couldn't have saved Ochoa, Clark would later declare.[2] At 9:54 A.M. on the morning of June 11, the jury had filed back into court, and the foreman had read down the list, down all twenty-six charges, finding William Cruz Ochoa guilty on each and every count.

The summer had gone by since then. And now, in room 134 of this concrete monolith on the corner of Temple and Hope streets, just off the 101 freeway, the middle-aged jailbird with a prison-issued certificate stating his qualifications as an X-ray technician, with a heroin habit and a demonstrated lack of moral restraints, was about to be permanently removed from society.

"As to Counts 1, 3, 5, 7, 9, 11, 13, 15, 17, 19, 21, 23, and 25," Judge Buckner intoned, "the defendant is sentenced to twenty-five years to life, pursuant to Section 1170.12 a) to d) and 667 b) I) Penal Code, for a total of three hundred and twenty-five years. Each such count shall run consecutively to each other." He also found Ochoa guilty on the even-numbered counts, but didn't sentence him for those. Buckner paused. Then, for good measure, he added on one more year owing to the fact that Ochoa had been sentenced for a similar crime several years previously. "Total time is three hundred and twenty-six years to life."

Proceedings concluded. No emotion. No teary family. No dramatic outbursts, wails of remorse, sharp intakes of breath, or furious outcries from the defense bench. And Ochoa was led out, to begin a sentence that would keep him behind bars until he was 379 years old, in the year 2322.

Tamia Hope, the feisty, curly blond-haired District Attorney who had prosecuted his case, followed him with her eyes as he left the court. She had spent several weeks preparing for this case, and she felt that her reputation for thoroughness, for seeing a job through to the end, had been vindicated. Her colleagues considered her a "warrior," a "legend in the office," and Hope was glad not to have let them down. The fifty-year-old prosecutor felt a little sad for Ochoa, knowing he had just been sentenced to live out the rest of his days behind bars, but proud of the job she'd done. She knew her colleagues would approve and she believed that the city would be better off now that Ochoa was no longer around to commit his crimes. *Be a prosecutor*, her father—himself a private practice defense attorney—had urged her back in the early 1970s, when she graduated from Hastings Law School, San Francisco. And what was this, if not the ultimate prosecutorial success?[3]

Using California's new Three Strikes and You're Out law, Tamia Hope had just struck Billy Ochoa out not just once, but thirteen times, for $2,100 worth of welfare fraud.

PART 1

BUILDING THE BALLPARK

Take me out to the ball game,
Take me out with the crowd.
Buy me some peanuts and cracker jack,
I don't care if I never get back.
Let me root, root, root for the home team,
If they don't win it's a shame.
For it's one, two, three strikes, you're out,
At the old ball game.

—LYRICS BY JACK NORWORTH, 1908

ONE

Billy Ochoa had been living with his younger sister Virginia, her daughter, and her sick son Arthur, since he had been expelled from the Weingart Center halfway house on November 11, 1994, where he had lived after serving a couple of years in prison for welfare fraud in the early 1990s. Weingart had been a scary place to live, a shadowy home populated by ex-felons, many of whom were violent or sick. One time, Billy had seen a homeless guy just drop dead in the streets near the Center.[1] Not surprisingly, he had leapt at the chance of living with his sister. He was at Virginia's house, on Danbury Street, when he was arrested. It was shortly after one in the afternoon of July 7, 1995. Virginia was at work, and Evette was at school. Only Arthur and Billy were at home. Arthur was in an electric wheelchair and needed help getting around, going to the bathroom, getting dressed, even feeding himself. When Billy wasn't there, Virginia would have to come home during her lunch hour to wash him and feed him. He felt uncomfortable with most people, but his uncle he let help him. They could talk about things; about girls, about feelings, about the recent escapades of O.J. Simpson, about fear—emotions a twenty-five-year-old man whose life was ebbing away might harbor in his heart without knowing who to talk to.[2]

There was a knock on the door. Ochoa opened it. Outside was his parole agent, Paul Benedict—who knew Ochoa by the case number "D35968" and by the name of Richard Gutierrez, the alias Ochoa had been known by during his last stint in prison—along with several other parole office employees. The agents began searching the house while

Billy and Arthur watched. In a box in the living room, the room where Billy slept, next to a credenza, Benedict found the evidence he was looking for. It was in an envelope stuffed away in the box. The officials arrested Ochoa. They took him downtown and they began questioning him. Then they booked him for thirteen counts of welfare fraud and thirteen counts of perjury—for signing false statements on government documents: case number 4466580.[3]

When Benedict had first met Ochoa, at the parole office on Sixth Street, he had made him sign a "condition of parole" document, stating that Ochoa's place of residence could be searched by law enforcement officers at any time and without a warrant. Then he had taken a Polaroid photograph of the felon; this photo, when attached to a Department of Corrections identification form, would serve as Ochoa's I.D., for after spending several years in prison Billy no longer had a valid driver's license.

Shortly after that meeting, Ochoa whited out his name on the form and gave himself a new identity. He named himself Manuel Cortez. Between February and June, using copies of the original DOC letter, Ochoa created at least twelve more false identities. He would appear at Department of Public Social Services offices in northeastern suburbs of Los Angeles such as Pasadena, El Monte, and Pomona to apply for food stamps and emergency shelter vouchers using his many names—even at one point calling himself Kenneth Ochoa, the name of his kid brother. Ochoa was having heroin cravings. And since Virginia had made it absolutely clear that she would throw him out of the house if he brought his drugs anywhere near her family, Billy needed small sums of money every so often to rent flophouse rooms around Los Angeles' skid row, dingy little places in which he could inject the dope into his veins. That was why he was cheating the welfare department. For a man in his fifties, fraud was easier than his previous money-making pastime: burgling unoccupied houses and apartments and selling the loot to fences. He had switched over to welfare fraud sometime in the early 1990s, and had already served one term in prison for this activity.

Always, Ochoa would identify his parents as William and Josephine

Cata. William and Josephine Cata Luna. William and Josephine Cata Sola. To DPSS worker Om, in the Pomona office, he identified himself as Joe Mata, born in New York and recently released from a short spell in jail. To another welfare system bureaucrat, Sandra Walker, he was David Luna. To Mario Palacios he declared he was Robert Sola from New York. To Sylvia Zepeda he introduced himself as Joe Raya. To Jacqueline Glaspar he was one Ruben Paco. To Charles Perry, he sought emergency relief under the moniker of Ralph Garcia.[4] After the interviews, he would walk out of the offices with shelter vouchers worth up to $100, with food stamp vouchers ranging from $18 to $115. And then he would leave Arcadia for a couple days and disappear into the grotty netherworld of skid row. To find solace in heroin and women in the seedy, paint-cracked downtown hotels that catered to the city's lonely, destitute underclass.

With each application, Ochoa had to give his fingerprints — a recent DPSS innovation designed to catch people making multiple applications. He would sometimes cut his fingertips with a staple to try to smudge the print,[5] but eventually the welfare department's AFIRM Match Computer System made the connection. On July 5, welfare fraud investigator Brent Smith brought a copy of one of Ochoa's fake identity forms to Benedict's office. Two days later, when Benedict looked in the envelope, he found Ochoa's doctored DOC forms. And Ochoa was arrested.

For Billy Ochoa, being arrested was nothing new, and certainly nothing to get upset about. Ever since he was a juvenile, back in the 1950s, he'd been in and out of trouble. Sent to juvenile camp, sent to California Youth Authority reformatories, sent to jail, sent to prison. Arrested. Arrested. Arrested. His last stint had been in Chino state prison, for the exact same crime that Benedict had just caught him committing: welfare fraud. He'd entered into an agreement with the prosecutor, John Gilligan, in which he would plead guilty to welfare fraud and accept a fairly stiff prison term, in exchange for which Gilligan would ask the judge not to take all Ochoa's priors into account when determining sentence. It was the sort of plea bargain in which everyone benefited:

the judge's time wasn't taken up with a lengthy trial around a relatively petty crime, Gilligan got an easy conviction, and Ochoa avoided a potentially longer sentence. On June 8, 1993, Ochoa was sentenced to three years by Judge Jon M. Mayeda. He served just under two.[6]

When Benedict's team arrested Ochoa on July 7, the small man with the long rap sheet assumed the process would repeat itself. His family, none of whom paid close attention to the news, assumed the same. Here we go again, they thought, Billy's off to prison for a few years. But something had happened in the three years since his court appearance with Gilligan. And that something was a new law called Three Strikes.

If Billy Ochoa had followed politics, he might have known that California's Governor Pete Wilson had won reelection in 1994 largely because he had portrayed himself as the toughest, meanest crime buster around. He might also have been aware of the mood that California's, and more generally the United States', electorate had been in recently. A fearful mood; a siege mentality produced by a series of high-profile crimes, the ongoing chaos generated by drugs and by gangs fighting for turf, and news programs that were focusing ever more heartily on the blood-and-gore footage of the crime scene. If Ochoa had studied opinion polls, he might have known how presidents from Nixon onward had played the law-and-order card to gather public support for their administrations, how crime and drugs had surged to the top of the public's list of concerns toward the tail end of the Reagan presidency, and had remained high up that list ever since. How George Bush had destroyed Michael Dukakis's presidential hopes through portraying him as "soft on crime," and how politicians of all political persuasions since then had been doing everything in their power to avoid Dukakis's fate. But Ochoa was just a chronic small-time crook with an addiction he had carried with him all his adult life. He didn't know that in the new political equations around crime, his many relatively petty, nonviolent offenses would be treated as seriously as — no cancel that, *more seriously* than — those of the murderers and rapists and armed robbers who had traditionally drawn the long sentences in the maximum-security prisons. For, except for the rare cases in which a death sentence was handed down, even a murderer would only get one life sentence; whereas a chronic repeat offender such as Ochoa could now receive numerous life sentences under the new laws that California was embracing.

In the roiling national debates over crime, California was now leading the way, building more prisons, imprisoning more people, and introducing more draconian laws than any other state in the union. Two and a half years previously, a massive popular campaign had led the state legislature to sign the country's most sweeping Three Strikes and You're Out law into effect; this law stated that anybody with two "serious" prior convictions who committed any kind of felony, no matter how minor, would receive a sentence of twenty-five years to life. And since in California law burglary of an *unoccupied* house was considered a "serious" felony—the argument being that the *potential* for violence existed in the commission of such a crime, if, by chance the house being burgled turned out to be occupied at the time of the break-in— defendants who had committed two burglaries years in the past and who had then been arrested for mundane crimes such as small-time fraud, shoplifting, or drug possession were now facing life sentences in maximum-security prisons.

In November 1994, the state's voters had overwhelmingly reaffirmed their support for this particular brand of Three Strikes by passing Proposition 184, locking into place the new legislation. Governor Wilson, who had promised to veto any attempts to narrow the scope of this new law, and his attorney general Dan Lungren, had been touring the state arguing for a One Strike and You're Out law for certain criminals, and massively increased sentences for prisoners across the board.

This was the new reality into which Billy Ochoa had stepped.

Jean Robinson, the DPSS welfare fraud investigator who had looked at Ochoa's case, had estimated his actions had cost the welfare system $2,100. Examining his criminal record, the investigator recommended that Ochoa be returned to state prison. After all, Billy Ochoa had been arrested at least thirty-one times since his first brush with the law back in 1957. He'd been a joyrider as a teenager; a heroin addict from the early 1960s; a burglar convicted six times for breaking and entering, and a welfare conman. He did have a rather more serious crime in his juvenile record: he and a friend nicknamed Pinky had been convicted of kidnapping a girl from a party, and they had both done time in a youth authority camp. But even that crime was more serious on paper than in reality: in a fit of drunkenness, Pinky and Billy had promised to drive the girl home and had instead gone on a thrill ride along one of the newly opened L.A. freeways. It was stupid, but nothing had happened. The girl had gotten scared, had opened her window and begun screaming to passing drivers. A cop had heard her, had turned his siren on, and chased after the car. But that was thirty-five years previously — and because it occurred when he was a juvenile — it wasn't even one of the prior convictions held against Billy Ochoa during the Three Strikes trial. Since then, he had never been convicted of a violent crime.[7]

A probation officer had tried to visit Ochoa at the Correctional Facility in Wayside in order to evaluate him. But Ochoa, believing a prison sentence to be inevitable and not wanting to provide the probation officer any more personal information, had refused to see him. The parole board recommended that he "should be returned to the prison for as long a period as possible." Agent Kelly, who made the recommendation, was particularly outraged that Ochoa had violated their trust "by taking one of their identification letters that they had issued to him as a courtesy and altering it to use in his welfare fraud scams." The investigators for the D.A.'s office likewise concluded that Ochoa ought to face a long sentence. Summing up the various findings, probation officer Barry J. Nidorf wrote that the "defendant is a career criminal and if placed back on the streets he will just continue one type of illegal behavior or another. . . . All options for defendant were considered by this probation officer but there is in fact only one recommendation he can make and that is for state prison."

Because of Three Strikes, Ray Clark had felt from the start that his client was doomed. A Floridian who had migrated to California in the late 1950s, Clark had spent the first half of his working life as an audio engineer and music producer. He had enrolled in Southwestern Law School—the university that the one-time Mayor of Los Angeles, Tom Bradley, graduated from—when in his early forties, and he'd spent much of the next quarter century collecting small-change work as a court-appointed lawyer. "You never run short" of that kind of work, Clark believed. Recently, an awful lot of his clients, perhaps a couple dozen, mainly impoverished African American and Latino men from the inner city, seemed to be striking out on Three Strikes convictions.

For similar reasons, Tamia Hope had been confident that she would send Ochoa down for many years. In what she'd seen as a magnanimous gesture, Hope had offered Ochoa a single Three Strike prosecution in exchange for a guilty plea. Clark had practically begged his client to accept. But, since even that would have landed him a sentence of twenty-five-to-life, Ochoa had decided to chance it with a trial. And at that stage, Hope's boss, Don Eastman, who had set up the welfare fraud division of the D.A.'s office two years previously, had urged her to throw the book at the defendant.

Even though Ochoa's case was what Eastman described as "a wobbler,"[8] a minor crime that could be punished either as a felony or a high-level misdemeanor, Eastman felt that Ochoa was a classic recidivist, "a perfect example" of the kind of person the Three Strikes law was meant to stop in his tracks. In the sentencing memorandum that Hope had submitted to the court, the D.A. had urged the judge to impose a Three Strikes sentence, stating that "while the People do feel sympathy for the defendant, his prior record shows the type of criminal recidivist behavior that the Three Strikes law is intended to address." If, despite it all, the judge were to decide to ignore Ochoa's previous record, Hope urged that he be sentenced to the maximum possible term: ten years in a state prison.

But Hope needn't have worried. For Judge Alan Buckner as much as for the D.A.'s office, Three Strikes was an opportunity to rid Los Angeles of a troubling nuisance. So convinced was he of this that when Ray Clark asked him to use his discretion to ignore Ochoa's previous convictions, so as to be able to avoid giving Ochoa 325 years for a nonviolent crime that had cost the state only $2,100, Buckner responded with outrage. "Welfare is a sore subject in our society today," the judge informed the court-appointed lawyer. "I don't think that the Three Strikes law is absurd. And if it can be argued it is absurd in certain contexts, it is not absurd here, because what the prosecutor says is undeniably and very unfortunately true. 'This man is above the law. He is out for himself and he doesn't really care.' And he ran afoul of the fact that our society today doesn't look with favor on folks who rip off the welfare [sic]. I don't disagree with the Three Strikes law, and if I did, I would not disagree with it in this application to this case."[9]

Two months after Buckner handed down the sentence, the District Attorney's Association of Los Angeles held their monthly get-together in the Board of Supervisors room of the L.A. County Hall of Administration. Close to three hundred lawyers were present.

Each month, the association honors one of their own. That month, the board of directors had decided to declare Tamia Hope their D.A. of the month. The president, John Perlstein, rose from his seat to present the one-time Orange County resident with the award. "The defendant got three hundred and twenty-six years to life," Perlstein told his audience. And at that point, Hope recalled with pride three years later, "they all broke out in applause. To me it reflected people really just don't like welfare fraud anymore, thumbing your nose at the system. It was nice to get the applause; nice to feel the support of my colleagues."

By then, Ochoa was getting used to his new life in one of California's toughest prisons. Because of the length of his sentence, Department of Corrections guidelines mandated that he be sent to a level-four maximum-security prison; for an incoming inmate looking at a life sentence is thought to have nothing to lose, and thus to be a top-notch security risk. He might make a suicidal dash for freedom, try to attack a guard, even attempt to take some hostages. So, after spending three months at a prisoner "reception center" at San Quentin, Billy Ochoa had been put on a Department of Corrections bus late one night and driven to a top-security prison twenty miles east of Sacramento. On the way from L.A. to San Quentin, close to a four hundred-mile journey, Billy had stared out the windows, trying to soak up what he knew might be his last ever look at the farmlands and villages, the people and animals, of Central California. On the bus from San Quentin, Ochoa slept.

In the dead of night, the vehicle drove down Route 50 to the Folsom Boulevard exit. There, at the bottom of the off-ramp, was a sign welcoming visitors to Folsom Historic District. It touted the presence of a historic railroad, of a zoo and a city museum. What it didn't mention was the huge prison toward which the bus was now heading. Left on Folsom Boulevard a couple miles, then right on Natoma Street. Up a hill, past small suburban subdivisions—trim, but slightly run-down; past a glass and adobe town hall, a charmless little building that could serve as the administrative center for any number of anonymous small towns throughout America; past the rinky-dink fire station, a dentist's practice, a couple fast-food outlets, the town gas station, and a scrubby little park that played home to the annual Folsom rodeo. And then, while Ochoa slumbered, the vehicle made one more turn, left onto the prison access road, the tarmac cut through rolling, grass-covered hills dotted with windswept trees.

Had it not been so dark outside, the arriving prisoners would have been able to see the motivational signs attached to lampposts and tree trunks, posted at regular intervals along the side of the road. "We value our differences and use them as strengths." "Encourage exploration of new ideas." "Be recognized for our achievements." "Treatment of people." "Toward shared ideas." "Committed to working together." "Seek recognition of new ideas." "Working collaboratively toward shared goals."

And then the bus arrived, the first of many electronic security gates opened up, the prisoners, shackled, hobbled to their feet, and Ochoa looked around in the floodlit night to see the place he was supposed to call home from that day until whenever it was in the future that he eventually died.

Now, he was living in one of the gray concrete "pods" that formed the architectural centerpieces of the new prisons. He was sharing his eight-feet-by-eight-feet cell with a "cellie" and trying to keep up his spirits by picking up the odd game of handball out on the concrete yard. The grounds were surrounded by multiple electrified fences topped with layers of barbed wire, and the cell windows were nothing more than narrow slits covered over with bulletproof glass. Officially his institution was named California State Prison, Sacramento. Its acronym was simply CSP-SAC. Unofficially, everybody referred to the place as New Folsom. For it was just half a mile down the road from Old Folsom, the monumental nineteenth-century stone edifice that had long been known as one of the meanest, most dangerous prisons in the country. These days Old Folsom, overlooking the steep banks of the American River, was a medium-security facility, quaint-looking, somewhat like a neogothic castle; its flowery lawns, tended by the inmates, were almost pretty; and, with the wave of new prison construction in the 1980s and 1990s, most of the harder-core inmates had been removed to CSP-SAC, or to even tougher facilities such as Corcoran and Pelican Bay. Those who remained took part in work training, from an auto repair shop through to a woodwork center in which children's toys were made, to be distributed to needy kids across the state.[10]

At CSP-SAC, the inmates were categorized by race, and then sub-categorized again by point of origin. Ochoa was listed as a "Hispanic." He was also listed as a "southerner," one of the more than 25 percent of the institution's prisoners, or eight hundred-plus men,[11] who originated in Los Angeles, four hundred miles to the south. Because southern and northern Hispanic gangs had long-running vendettas against each other, because white gangs and black gangs loathed each other, because members of different street gangs from within the same race detested the very sight of each other, fights and stabbings in the prison yard were a dime a dozen. Young men would sneak up behind someone and stick him with an improvised shaft of metal. And then, in reprisal, the guards would put the warring groups into "lockdown," containing them within their tiny cells for over twenty-three hours a day. The fifty-three-year-old Ochoa, one of only a handful of inmates over the age of fifty, preferred to act as a loner when in prison; but bound by the prison system's method of labeling, he was finding that his group, the Southern Hispanics, were being locked down more often than not.

To keep Ochoa locked away in this super-maximum-security institution, to prevent him from committing any more acts of welfare fraud, was costing California well over twenty thousand dollars per year.[12]

In 1980, approximately 300,000 people were imprisoned in America. By the time Ochoa was sentenced that number had risen to over 1.5 million. Four years later, in the year 2000, nearly two million were behind bars—in county jails (generally for sentences of under one year), state prisons, and federal correctional centers. And, despite far lower crime levels in the year 2000 than was the case ten years previously, the number was still rising steadily.[13]

The change came about through a twofold shift in policy: first there were the initial War on Drugs laws and mandatory minimum sentences passed in the 1970s in New York and then nationally in the 1980s (the Anti-Drug Abuse Act of 1986 and the 1988 Omnibus Anti-Drug Abuse Act). These only permitted sentence reductions if those arrested for drugs cooperated with the police by naming names and then delivering the victims up to undercover agents through entrapment and sting operations. As a result, a huge system of informants grew up. After the War on Drugs had become a staple of the political landscape, in the late 1980s then-Vice President George Bush used the more general issue of crime with devastating effectiveness in his run for the presidency against Democratic candidate Michael Dukakis. Since then, politicians had latched onto the public's fear of crime as a potent electoral weapon, and had vied with each other to create ever-tougher sentencing laws. In a short burst of legislative "reform," from 1993 to 1995, several states enacted Three Strikes laws—Washington, California, Oregon, and Georgia, among others; parole was abolished in places such as Texas; truth-in-sentencing, which made prisoners serve 85 percent of their sentences before being eligible for parole, was made a part of President Bill Clinton's federal Omnibus Crime Bill; many cities moved toward zero-tolerance laws for drugs; and an increasing number began to aggressively prosecute the urban poor—vagrants, beggars, teenage troublemakers, small-time con artists.

As a result, America's vast prison network had increasingly come to serve as a dumping ground for the country's drug addicts, its deinstitutionalized mentally ill, its burgeoning homeless and urban unemployed. Men such as the prisoner in Coleman federal correctional facility, Florida, serving twenty-seven years on a marijuana dealing conviction, and the homeless man in Miami with a string of petty offenses behind him, finally sent to prison for forty years for stealing twenty-two rolls of toilet paper from a supermarket were the increasingly common, and pathetic, faces atop the uniform of the prison blues.[14]

By the year 2000, California alone, with a population of 37 million, had over 160,000 people in prison, 20,000 of whom were lifers, costing the state over four billion dollars per year; Texas, in second place, had approximately 150,000.[15] By contrast the prison population in Great Britain, a country with a population more than equal to that of California and Texas combined, is under 60,000. Partly, this is because more Americans—armed with an array of guns unavailable to most other civilian populaces the world over—commit particularly violent crimes in extraordinarily large numbers. But, to a large extent, it is due to different sentencing practices.[16]

America has long had a fascination with crime and with its concomitant, punishment. The sparsely populated and enormous landscape that the Pilgrims termed God's Own Country proved to be fertile ground not only for farming but also for crime. For pillage, piracy, and highway robbery. And also for infractions of moral and religious codes that today would be subjects for gossip rather than for the courtroom. Blasphemers in the Puritan communities were, on occasion, nailed to a pillory by their ears; others had their tongues run through with a red-hot wire. The prescribed sentence for a fornicator was thirty-nine lashes of the whip— or, if the community was in a particular uproar, execution by hanging. "Immoral women" were often tied to the back of a cart and driven through town to the jeers of the residents. Shaming and public excoriation were the favored methods of reining in those who failed to abide by the strict moral standards of the age.

And then, of course, there were the witches, women (and a few men) deemed by the Puritans to possess unnatural, devilish powers. These individuals, arguably in much the same way as drug users three hundred years later, aroused the community to such spasms of moral outrage that they brought down upon themselves the full weight of the criminal justice system of their time.

The terror of witches was a moral panic imported into the Americas from the earliest years of European colonization. For hundreds of years before the Pilgrim Fathers docked at Plymouth, Europe had become fixated on the idea of witches casting spells on unsuspecting victims, using supernatural powers gained from an unholy contract with Satan, to impose disorder and catastrophe: crop failures, plague, the death of children, fires, and floods. Thirteenth-century bishops in towns such as Ratzebourg, Lübeck, and Münster called on good Christians to exterminate these menaces, and for the next several centuries, thousands of people, the majority of them eccentric, strange-looking, outcasts, were burnt at the stake. "It was," concluded the nineteenth-century British historian Charles Mackay, "sufficient to be aged, poor, and half-crazed, to ensure death at the stake or the scaffold.[17] By 1488, the Catholic Church was so concerned by devil worshipping that Pope Innocent VIII issued a papal bull appointing Inquisitors in every Christian country, whose job it was to root out and destroy heretics wherever they might be found. Witch finders sprang up across Europe. Mackay writes that one such man, Cumanus, burned forty-one women in one province of Italy alone. In 1524, the district of Como put over a thousand witches to death. In Britain, Mackay estimates that a staggering 40,000 people were executed for witchcraft just in the 1600s.

As with America's drug wars at the tail end of the twentieth century, so the European witch hunts removed millions of individuals from their communities (dispatching them by fire rather than incarcerating them within prisons) and promoted a craze of spying upon, and informing on, one's neighbors. The inquisitors of the witch hunts thrived on cascades of rumor and mutual incrimination in much the same way as would the warriors of America's drug wars generations down the road.

But the burnings of this period proved to be a last hurrah for a mania long past its prime. By the end of the seventeenth century the hysterical war against witches was dying down in Europe. New scientific ways of looking at the world were starting to undermine the rigid superstitions that had led to half a millennium of witch-burning, and, increasingly, law courts refused to act on the local gossip and name-calling that served as foundation stones for the slaughter. In Puritan New England, however, three thousand miles from the Old World and the cultural centers that were sloughing off such medieval beliefs, the terror of witchcraft remained. In 1692, in a remote village named Salem, a group of young girls began asserting that they had been bewitched by other women of the community, most notably a slave woman named Tituba. In the weeks following, after witch finders from Boston had been called in to investigate, more than two hundred people were arrested. Nineteen of them, including a girl only five years old, were found by the courts to be witches, and put to death. "In the general atmosphere of hysteria, there was a chain reaction of accusations and confessions. It was the defiant, the hostile, the impudent who were put to death in Salem," notes the well-known historian Lawrence Friedman."[18]

Beyond the war against witchcraft, the seventeenth-century colonies played host to vicious squabbles for religious supremacy and frequently invoked the power of the courts to settle disputes. "Puritan justice," writes Friedman in *Crime and Punishment in American History*, "had a strongly *inquisitorial* flavor." The colonies "made little or no distinction between sin and crime; piety and religion especially dominated the lives of Puritan leaders and divines." In 1659, Massachusetts executed two Quakers for religious heresy. Two years later, another swung from the gallows.[19] For the men of this rigid world, the law was but an expression of God's will; and God was nothing if not a fired-up, wrathful patriarch.

The excesses of Puritanism, however, gradually gave way to the more Enlightened beliefs and laws that were pushing their way forward across the Atlantic. And, as a commercial culture replaced a theocratic one in the colonies, it was violent crime and offenses against property that truly thrived in seventeenth- and eighteenth-century America; offenses fueled in part by Britain and France's practice of deporting convicts to their overseas territories,[20] added to by the enormous economic disparities that soon emerged in the young country. Oftentimes lawbreaking and political discontent seemed to go hand in hand, with political rage and rebellion leaving a more general lawlessness and casual violence in its wake. And frequently urban riots that began with a political message ended in an orgy of looting, beatings, and even lynchings.

As early as the 1670s, the Appalachian backwoods were struck by violent political upheavals against the land-owning elite that collectively came to be known as Basin's Rebellion. The insurrection was soon squashed, but out of it emerged bands of brigands who lived deep in the wilderness and surfaced mainly to rob and to rape. Thirty years later, leading citizens of the growing commercial town of Philadelphia found themselves confronted with such large numbers of criminals that in 1703 they grouped together into a vigilante organization which they named, with not even a minimal attempt at subterfuge, The Society for the Suppression of Disorders. Soon afterwards, communal leaders in the colonies of Pennsylvania and New York prevailed upon their royal governors to introduce extraordinarily tough penal codes that provided for the execution, by hanging, of those convicted of burglary. In other parts of colonial America, the British authorities whipped thieves in public, or used hot irons to brand them with the letter "T."

Unfortunately, if newspaper reports can be used to judge popular sentiment, such codes didn't make the good townspeople and country folk of these colonies feel any safer. In the 1740s, the Philadelphia and New York papers were rife with tales of highway robbery and other acts of calumny. Robbers such as Tom Bell, embezzlers like Owen Sullivan, and the mercenary bounty hunters who tracked them down for the rewards put up by courts and victims, hogged the headlines. Already, the newspaper publishers of the age had understood an important fact about American society: a people made up of immigrants, speaking diverse languages, harking back to many different national and religious myths, needed new heroes and villains that could bind them together into a new, American, identity. The stories that the Philadelphia newspapers printed of bad guys and heroes battling it out in the streets, pubs, barns, and forests of a new world, fit this need nicely.

By the 1750s, at least in part as a result of the sensational media coverage, burglary was seen as such a serious problem in the growing cities of the north that the colonial courts had dramatically upped the ante for criminals thinking of embarking on such a career. Prior to 1750, according to the historians Frank Browning and John Garassi, in their 1980 book *The American Way of Crime*,[21] only one in ten convicted burglars was executed in New York. By contrast, in the years after 1750, more than one in five met this fate.[22]

Farther south and a half a century after the penal codes of the north had first been stiffened, Vigilance Committees emerged in North Carolina to dole out swift, often merciless, justice to the brigands who had turned much of the region into a no-man's land. And one colony to the south, in 1767, so many recently demobilized soldiers from the Cherokee Wars were marauding through the South Carolina countryside torturing, even killing, wealthy planters that estate holders found it necessary to establish the Regulator Movement to perform much the same role as their brethren in the Committees just to the north.[23]

The state of low-level, white-on-white, crime-based civil war in Appalachia continued well into the nineteenth century, into the period surrounding the Civil War. Out of these conflicts, over land and over honor, emerged levels of violence not seen in other Western countries for a couple centuries.[24] Between 1844 and 1858, writes *New York Times* criminal justice reporter Fox Butterfield in his book *All God's Children*, the county of Edgefield had 18 murders per 100,000 inhabitants. "In 1992 [at the height of the crack wars], only one state in the entire country, Louisiana, approached this figure, with a homicide rate, for whites and blacks combined, of 17.4 per 100,000." Butterfield goes on to state that "in the antebellum South, there was a fine line between heroism in the name of honor and criminality, between deeds of valor and acts of violence."

Of course, over and beyond the South's *officially* recorded crimes were the myriad acts of violence committed against slaves and the extra-judicial punishment floggings and executions that masters carried out on their human chattel. The Slave Codes that, to a degree, codified Southern treatment of Blacks, permitted an array of physical punish-ments—mainly whippings—to be meted out for the most minor of in-fractions without the court system ever stepping in. And, when the courts did get involved, it was usually to dole out the severest of punishments. Between 1706 and 1784, in Virginia alone courts sentenced 555 slaves to death. Ironically, the Slave Codes provided for the compensation of the owners when their properties were, in this rude way, so summarily removed from their employ.[25]

More generally, throughout the eighteenth and nineteenth centuries, political conflicts—over land use, water rights, wages, and racial status—periodically erupted into civil chaos and degenerated into looting. There were the Paxton Boys in late-colonial Pennsylvania, groups of impov-erished white settlers who killed dozens of Christianized Native Amer-icans and then marched on Philadelphia to demand an extermination campaign against the rest of the local Native American population. Al-though the regional authorities dispersed the thugs, the Paxton Boys left a trail of destruction behind them. Farther north, and just the other side of the War of Independence, in post-Revolutionary Massachusetts armed men led by Daniel Shays rebelled against the state's high taxes and the poverty many citizens were condemned to experience. Again, the re-bellion was suppressed, but not before many had lost their lives. Then in the nineteenth century, the young but rapidly growing cities of both the East Coast and the interior, played host to a spate of deadly riots: sixteen in 1834, thirty-seven in the year following. Philadelphia, Balti-more, New York, Cincinnati, St. Louis all saw variants on race riots and anti-Catholic pogroms. Finally, as the Civil War got underway in 1861, Irish immigrants in New York City rose up against the military draft laws—regulations that allowed the rich to buy their way out of service, while dragooning the poor into army uniforms—and dozens of people were killed over the course of a week of mayhem in what came, appropriately, to be known as the "Draft Riots." It was the apogee of urban discontent, and it provided a historical prologue for the fierce trade union battles and race riots that played so large a role in the American urban landscape of the century following.

Lawlessness was not, however, limited to the land. On the Atlantic Ocean and all the way south into the Caribbean, vast numbers of pirate vessels terrorized the shipping lanes linking the old and new worlds. By the early eighteenth century, the tiny hamlets and villages that hosted the pirates and dealt with their smuggled goods—rum, guns, slaves and gold—referred to the seafarers as "gentlemanly outlaws," or, more obliquely, the "Brethren of the Coast." According to Frank Browning and John Garassi, by 1718, at the height of this epidemic, more than two thousand pirates navigated the colonies' waters, arousing, in about equal measure, both admiration and deep loathing. Four of the most famous were Stede Bonnet, Captain Kidd, Blackbeard (whose real name was the somewhat less memorable Edward Teach) and the legendary female privateer Anne Bonney. Rumor had it that Blackbeard, at any rate, was protected by New York's governor Benjamin Fletcher, and North Carolina's governor Charles Eden. The two politicians, it was widely reported, raked in considerable fortunes through taking cuts in their protégé's business.

Perhaps because crime has always played such a prominent role in American history, so it was in the nascent United States that the institution of the prison matured into its modern incarnation. Ironically, given subsequent history, it originated out of the finest rehabilitation impulses of revolutionary America.

One hundred and sixty seven years before Judge Buckner pronounced sentence on Billy, on October 25, 1829, an eighteen-year-old Black man named Charles Williams had been escorted into the brand-new Eastern Penitentiary at Philadelphia. The young man had recently been convicted of larceny. He had, the court was told, broken into a house and stolen a silver watch, valued at twenty dollars, a gold seal worth three dollars, and a gold key with a replacement cost of two dollars. For his crimes, the court sentenced him to two years in the newly opened penitentiary. Williams's arrival marked the highpoint of another moment of reforming zeal. But, unlike the late-twentieth-century national mood swing against the coddling of criminals such as Ochoa, the mood in 1829 was far more utopian.

Built on land that until recently had served as a cherry orchard, the penitentiary was an imposing granite building, inside of which seven rows of cell blocks radiated out like spokes from a central pod. Eastern Penitentiary had been eight years in the making, and the reforming civic leaders under whose guise it was built were adamant that it be modeled on the most innovative prison architectural theories emanating out of Europe. Like the Hospice of San Michele in Rome, the beggars' prison of Ghent, Belgium, and the Liverpool Borough Gaol in England, "Cherry Hill" had been designed to ensure that its inhabitants were kept in conditions of maximum isolation, and that a regimen of austere, practically religious, solitude could most easily be enforced. Only in such conditions, according to penal theorists such as Britain's John Howard, could model citizens be molded out of the unfortunate prison inmates.

It was an idea that had been percolating for the better part of half a century. For as America expanded westward, gradually in the last decades of Britain's colonial rule, and then, after the War of Independence, with the leaps and bounds of manifest destiny, so crime loomed ever larger in the country's psyche. At times, the frontier expanded faster than the government's capacity to impose and enforce its rules. Criminal gangs preying on pioneer families on the prairie, or—farther afield and later into the nineteenth century—the mountain and desert territories of the West could raid towns or homesteads and flee back into the wilderness before the crimes were even reported to law enforcement agencies. Reining in crime thus became of vital importance as the nation headed west. Without swift retribution dealt out by local sheriffs and impromptu courts, the frontier risked descending into a gory anarchy, adrift from the laws and institutions that bound the more settled parts of the continent into a coherent political unit. Thus it was that even the roughest, newest, most isolated of western communities introduced at least a rudimentary court system. "Just as a saloon bar occasionally served as pulpit, so it also functioned as a judge's bench, transforming the thirst parlor into a courtroom," writes the historian of America's West Richard Erdoes.[26] Well into the nineteenth century saloon keepers such as "Judge" Roy Bean, from Pecos County, Texas, routinely held court in their bars, oftentimes sentencing cattle rustlers and horse thieves—two of the most unpopular forms of criminals in the west—to death by hanging. "Give him a drink and tie him to the nearest limb! Well, what'll you have, feller?" is the signature, though possibly apocryphal, statement Erdoes attributes to the makeshift Texan judge as he passed sentence in the Jersey Lilley Saloon.

It was into the chaotic colonial and early post-colonial world of expansion and angst that the prison first emerged. "Houses" should be set up, read a 1776 Philadelphia law, to punish "by hard labour [sic] those who shall be convicted of crimes not capital."[27] Paradoxically, given the prison's subsequent trajectory toward the violence of the penitentiary and the abuses of solitary confinement, it was introduced by reformers as a humane alternative to the humiliation rituals, beatings, varied forms of pain infliction, and old-fashioned lynching that dominated the seventeenth-, eighteenth-, and even nineteenth-century worlds of punishment. In many ways, it was a product of the utilitarian theories of philosophers such as England's Jeremy Bentham, and the Italian criminologist Cesare Beccaria. Lock people up, remove them from the vengeful lustings of the mob, subject them to a regular discipline, and that remarkable and malleable material known as the human mind could be remade in the most positive of manners. It was all a far remove from the fire and brimstone beliefs of the Puritans barely a century before. In place of the horned figure of Satan leading a crusade for evil, these early sociologists placed more emphasis on mundane environmental factors, on man-made ills such as slums, alcoholism, parental neglect, and violence. And to cure these ills, a new form of intervention was urgently needed.

Incarcerating people in a room behind a locked door and barred windows was nothing new. For thousands of years, political prisoners, enemies of the state, and miscellaneous other troublesome folks had been so imprisoned. Most castles and centers of power had basement or tower dungeons, places where rivals to power could be closely watched by those princes and bishops whose leadership they threatened. Indeed, some, such as the Doge's Palace in Venice, or the Bastille in Paris, could accommodate hundreds, even thousands of prisoners at any one moment. Tales of rat-infested, dank, and horrifyingly dark chambers, in which prisoners, chained to the walls, rotted away, were a dime a dozen in medieval literature and folk stories. Such places, complete with tools of torture and executioners ready to bring axes or swords down upon their victims' necks, were intended to inspire terror.[28] Those who went in rarely came out. And the idea of rehabilitation was nonexistent.

Arguably the only category of prisoner who could hope for a speedy renewal of his freedom was the debtor, imprisoned for his failure to pay moneys owed to creditors, and eligible for release upon his family or friends making good the debt. In London, in particular, large-scale debtors' prisons had grown up during the course of the eighteenth century, their purpose significantly different from the dungeons of old. For other criminals, however, corporal punishment, fines, deportation to the colonies, or execution, still remained the most common sentences.

Now, though, with America suffused with Enlightenment ideals and increasingly averse to corporal punishment, incarceration acquired a new meaning. In the 1770s, as the Revolutionary War raged, the Quaker colony of Pennsylvania had opened up the Walnut Street Prison. Its original inmates were Tories, supporters of the Crown who refused to join the fight for independence. After the fighting ended, the newly independent land found itself with a large prison built, at great expense, to contain society's enemies, but—because most criminals weren't sentenced to prison terms—with no long-term prisoners. Instead, it was filled to the rafters with vagrants, drunkards, and, more generally, those awaiting trial, men who spent their days toiling at road-building, ditch-digging, and other forms of hard labor, while they awaited for the courts to hand down their sentences. And so, an experiment—one destined to have enormous impact down the centuries—was born. In 1790, at the urgings of a reform group that referred to itself as the Philadelphia Society for Alleviating the Miseries of Public Prisons, the state legislature passed a law mandating that Walnut Street build a new cell block specifically designed to house long-term inmates.[29] If the prison was cleaned up and its staff properly trained in the caring of inmates, might not incarceration serve to *rehabilitate* criminals rather than to simply punish them? After all, oughtn't a rational, enlightened society promote order and the general good rather than some outdated, perhaps even counterproductive, notion of *vengeance*? "With the removal of the church from public authority, a new institution was needed to impose moral discipline upon the unruly lower classes: thus the penitentiary. The new Republic found no other way of dealing with its great injustice, poverty," Frank Browning and John Garassi wrote in *The American Way of Crime*. Was it not possible that a carefully thought out system of temporary removal from the broader society, and a regimen of strict discipline combined with exposure to religious literature, might actually remodel the miscreant character, molding a law-abiding, God-fearing citizen where once there had been only a rogue? Pennsylvania set to work to find out. Soon, convicted criminals were entering the new Walnut Street cells from all over the state. They worked in communal workshops, and, when they weren't working, spent much of their time in common areas, talking and eating with other inmates. Only at night, when the cell doors slammed shut and the candles were snuffed out, did silence reign.

It was out of these humble questions that America's prison system was born—the same system which more than two hundred years later would count Billy Ochoa among its two million inmates.

In 1819, New York State opened the Auburn prison, built to house both state and federal prisoners—sentenced in the federal courts created by the first Congress's passage of the Judiciary Act of 1789. In Auburn, several days' horse and coach journey north of New York City, prisoners worked all day in groups; but they were forbidden—on pain of being whipped—from so much as whispering to each other. Then, at night, they would retire to private cells, where the reign of silence continued.

Ten years after Auburn began what came to be known as the "congregate system" of incarceration, Pennsylvania opened the Eastern Penitentiary, a huge prison built, like the Walnut Street Prison, in the city of Philadelphia.

Outside the fortresslike edifice that late October day in 1829, the leaves were the golden browns and riotous reds that made an east coast autumn so spectacular. Inside, in keeping with the agreed-upon first principles, a rather grimmer order prevailed. Prison records describe the thief Charles Williams as being "a farmer, light black; black eyes; curly black hair; five feet, seven inches; foot eleven inches; flat nose, scar on bridge of nose, broad mouth, scar from dirk on thigh; can read."[30] Shortly after guards escorted Williams through the grandiose prison entrance, Williams's curly hair was shorn off, his street clothes replaced by a drab uniform of coarse cloth, and he was informed that at Eastern Penitentiary a rule of absolute silence prevailed. Then, he was escorted to what, at that point in time, was a revolutionary innovation: a private cell.

As it happened, the teenage farmer was the first prisoner to be housed in the new penitentiary. But within days, nine more inmates had joined him—horse thieves, highway robbers. One such inmate, convicted of a third offense, was to serve what must have seemed a daunting eleven years of silence.[31] Soon the prison would be home to dozens, and eventually hundreds of others. Mostly men, but also women, who were housed in a separate block from their male peers.

Unlike the inhabitants of Auburn, here in Cherry Hill, as Eastern Penitentiary soon became known owing to its being sited on land that previous boasted a cherry orchard, the prisoners remained isolated in their cells twenty-four hours a day, blanketed in the quietude. On the few occasions they were taken from these cells, guards forced them to don face masks, to prevent even eye contact from being established between the miscreants. For even the slightest interactions between criminals were enough, the wardens believed, to encourage the passions of vice to once more bubble to the surface. Talking—even hushed, hurried, whispers—were rewarded with swift lashes of the whip; prisoners who continued to ignore the rules would be stripped naked, and—even in the freezing dead of winter—buckets of ice-cold water would be poured over their bodies. On occasion, troublesome individuals would be gagged with an iron bit. Others would be tied into restraining chairs and made to sit motionless for hours as guards beat them.[32]

And so, like an austere monastery populated by reluctant converts under the watchful eye of a paternalistic abbot, a regimen of utter silence prevailed. Soon, the nation's handful of other prisons, in New Jersey, Virginia, Kentucky, and Tennessee, were also reforming their inmates through the use of either the Auburn (public but silent work spaces, combined with solitary cells for sleeping in) or Cherry Hill (inmates kept twenty-four hours a day in their cells) versions of enveloping, heavy shrouds of silence.

Always, the early wardens of Cherry Hill, and the other prisons that followed in its footsteps, would defend their guards' behavior by restating the absolute necessity—determined by the best penologists of the age—to instill discipline and a respect for silence deep in the hearts and minds of their criminal wards. "Penitentiaries attempted to eliminate the specific influences that were breeding crime in the community," the historian David J. Rothman averred, in his book on the emergence of modern penal institutions, *The Discovery of the Asylum*, "and to demonstrate the fundamentals of proper social organization. Rather than stand as places of last resort, hidden and ignored, these institutions became the pride of the nation."[33] In fact, by the 1830s, these centers of detention had become famed the world over. Men such as the French aristocrat Alexis de Tocqueville came to take their glimpses, along with thousands of curious Americans who together made the penitentiaries must-see stops on their tours of the land. "The institution would become a laboratory for social improvement," Rothman continued. "By demonstrating how regularity and discipline transformed the most corrupt persons, it would reawaken the public to these virtues. The penitentiary would promote a new respect for order and authority."[34] Soon the already renowned British author Charles Dickens would come a-house-calling. "The Falls of Niagara and your Penitentiary are two objects I might almost say I most wish to see in America," the Victorian scribe is said to have told the warden upon being received at the prison gates.[35]

The officials put on a lunch for their distinguished guest and then took him on an extended tour of the cell blocks. But, to the dismay of these penitentiary-boosters, once he had seen the prison, and, by special dispensation, talked to the normally silent inmates it contained, Dickens became less sanguine. It was, he wrote in 1842, upon his return to England, as if the men had been "buried alive; to be dug out in the slow round of years; and in the meantime dead to everything but torturing anxieties and horrible despair."[36] The elders of Philadelphia who had approved the project believed they were on the cusp of an era in which criminals, monitored within the close confines of the penitentiary, could be cured of their wayward behaviors. Dickens wasn't so sure. And, as it happened, he was right. It turned out that the silence method was suspect. Criminals rarely had the temperament or the patience of monks, and eventually, after more prisoners went mad than went straight, the states began phasing out its usage. By 1913, when Cherry Hill finally shut its doors, solitude and silence had been thoroughly discredited as tools useful for crafting better characters out of hardened lawbreakers.

Not until the latter decades of the twentieth century, when the emphasis was, once again, more on punishment than on rehabilitation, did prisons again begin widely using isolation units to control their inmates. And by then the silence wasn't given names like "the Auburn system" or "the Cherry Hill approach" — names redolent of the autumnal colors in an earlier, more pastoral, landscape — but instead was called by the rather more bureaucratic nomenclature of "Administrative Segregation." And the prison areas within which such Ad Seg cells were built were known as Secure Housing Units, or, more simply "the SHU."

In 1999, Patty Villaluazo decided to send her cousin, Billy Ochoa, a present. Something nice. Something that would be useful to him inside the barren confines of CSP-SAC. She decided upon a pair of tennis shoes. The thought of Billy running around in the yard with the new shoes that she had bought for him made Patty happy.

Patty had always had a soft spot for her incorrigible cousin, five years her elder, had even helped him get work once lifting equipment at the television station where she was employed. Of course, when some of the machinery went missing, suspicion immediately fell on her wayward cousin, and Billy had been dismissed. No matter that later on it turned out the thief was one of her boss's sons. She remembered the times her favorite aunt, Josie, would visit Patty's mother Ruth (Josie's sister); and how Josie would always worry that if she left Billy alone for too long, he'd fall asleep with a cigarette in his hand and burn the house down. He appeared so vulnerable to Patty. He had seemed so out of place in the sordid S.R.O. down by Macarthur Park where he sometimes stayed; a little man surrounded by all the slime and detritus that the large city endlessly spewed out into its streets. Even the receptionist cowered behind metal bars. How was he ever going to change, she wondered, when he was always sent "to stay in the worst part of the world"? True, she knew that Billy seemed to court disaster, that he lacked the basic ability to control his actions enough to stay out of trouble. She even harbored a suspicion that Billy, addicted to drugs and to a life of petty crime, secretly craved the regimentation and order of a prison existence. But, underneath it all, Patty genuinely believed that Billy was a loving, caring man. He'd write her with jokes from inside whatever prison he was in at the time, and he'd share with her gossip about conditions behind bars. One time, in a county jail, he'd woken up to find a large rat right next to his bed. "Oh my God!" he told Patty. "I woke up one morning and one was staring me down!"

Whenever she thought about the judge reading out the 326-year sentence, Patty had to struggle to hold her tears in check. Shoes, she thought. I bet Billy could really do with some nice, new shoes.

Of course, when Billy got his present, he was delighted for entirely different reasons. Here was an opportunity to make some real money. And since *everything* in the prison was for sale, having money meant having power. Billy had been assigned a job shortly after he arrived at the prison; he was a tier porter, basically cleaning the hallway in his cell block. But the job was not a paid one—and even if it was, that kind of prison work was only paid a few cents an hours. So, when the brand-new sneakers arrived, Billy let it be known that he'd part with them for twenty dollars.

Word went out among the younger men in B Unit, one of four huge cell complexes into which the prison was divided. Soon word came back to Billy. There was a buyer. But the buyer was only willing to part with ten dollars. Billy wasn't too pleased with this. He'd been around the prison economy long enough to know that someone was trying to rip him off. New sneakers just didn't go for ten dollars. The two men argued in the yard, cussed each other out. Billy refused to part with the shoes.

A few days later, Billy was in the yard again. He'd done his exercise for the day and was just beginning the walk back to his cell. Suddenly, he was grabbed from behind, and—faster than lightening—a shaft streaked across his throat. Billy grabbed at his throat, blood pouring from the wound. Guards rushed out. They picked Billy up; took him to the prison hospital. The wound was sewn up. And Billy lived.

But, for his pains, Billy spent the next seventy days in "Administrative Segregation," locked away from the general prison population, kept in conditions of almost pure isolation. In the olden days, the prisoners called this being put in the Hole. Nowadays, the term was "Ad-Seg." Either way, a spell there was enough to leave you craving even the most miserable of human contact.

TWO

Neither Fresno businessman Mike Reynolds nor Governor Pete Barton Wilson had ever heard of Billy Ochoa. But, along with Billy himself, these two, more than Tamia Hope, more even than Judge Buckner, were the people most responsible for his plight. Billy had got himself into trouble. But Reynolds and Wilson were the two who had pushed so strongly for the Three Strikes law.

Pete Wilson had been adrift in the early nineties. The ex-Marine (first lieutenant, rifle-platoon leader) had had the bad luck of becoming California's governor just when the state's economy had tanked. The Cold War had ended with the disintegration of the Soviet Union, and now, in the early 1990s, tens of thousands of high-paid defense industry jobs were drying up—the very jobs that had brought such prosperity to California since the days of World War II. Under President George Bush, unemployment across the United States was up; and in California it had risen more so than elsewhere. Worse still, when the national economy had begun to recover, much of California's had continued to be sluggish. The farmers of the Central Valley were hurting. The defense industry was in a nosedive. The old lumber communities of the northern counties had seen their industry wither. And the optimism that had always been such a defining feature of the huge state from the Gold Rush days on seemed to have dried up like the drought-stricken Los Angeles River. For a man with presidential ambitions—after all, his political hero, Richard Nixon, had come from California, and Ronald Reagan, like Wilson born to an Irish-American family in the Midwest, had been governor of California on his way to the White House—this was a most unhappy state of affairs.

The new governor had begun his tenure with ambitious goals and lofty rhetoric. In his inaugural address he recalled how, a quarter century previously, he had attended Governor Ronald Reagan's inauguration; and Wilson told the assembled crowd how he was "proud and grateful to return today to give my own message. And I'm eager to undertake with those on this platform what I hope will be a journey of shared values, a common pursuit of uncommonly important goals." Wilson talked about California's natural beauty, about the "spirituality of Big Sur" and the "cathedrals of Redwoods that were already old at the time of Christ." He urged earlier intervention in the lives of troubled, abused children and an end to racism. He called for better neonatal medical care and programs to help those addicted to drugs. It was a powerful speech, even a visionary one, quite possibly the high point of Governor Pete Wilson's career. "Let us demand a California of such celebrated justice and opportunity that every little boy can grow up knowing that his race or color or creed is no bar—and no ticket—to becoming chairman of the board or chief justice of the Supreme Court."[1]

Unfortunately, shortly after Wilson had been sworn in, on January 7, 1991, advisers informed their new governor that the state was facing billions of dollars in revenue shortfalls, and that the situation was going to get still worse over the coming years. The money flowing into the state treasury just wasn't keeping up with spending.[2] As it happened, things turned out even worse than these advisers had predicted. By the summer of 1993, two and a half years into Wilson's four-year term, California was short a staggering $11 billion dollars on its $52.1 billion budget.[3]

And so, instead of creating the utopia that his inaugural speech had hinted at, Wilson had spent his first two years in office doing two things politicians hate: he had been forced to raise taxes and massively slash state spending. Locked into late-night planning sessions with his director of finance, Thomas W. Hayes, deputy chief of staff Bill Hauck, and financial adviser Russ Gould, circumstances had led to the governor proposing the deepest budget cuts since the Great Depression more than a half century earlier.[4] At meetings with the Democrat and Republican leaders in the state Assembly and Senate, Wilson and his team had hammered out the unpleasant details. In December 1991, the governor had recalled legislators to Sacramento from their Christmas break, to vote on $1 billion in spending cuts, to implement an across-the-board 5 percent pay cut for state employees, and to eliminate the renters' tax credit that allowed renters to deduct a portion of their rent when working out how much state tax they owed.

As disturbing, the governor who had demanded a just and equal society had instead witnessed Los Angeles's descent into urban anarchy and rage in 1992 after the police officers accused of beating African-American motorist Rodney King were acquitted by a white suburban jury. In the country's single worst riot, thousands of buildings were burned to the ground and dozens of people were shot by the LAPD across a huge swathe of impoverished south-central L.A. Although the violence had eventually subsided into a sullen truce, the images of a desperately poor ghetto occupied by heavily armed police and national guardsmen—sent into the area by President George Bush—and, conversely, of armed suburban whites manning roadblocks and Korean shopowners toting guns on the roofs of their stores, sent an indelible message around the world: California was not the Eden its boosters liked to portray it as. And Wilson was not presiding over the unifying, inclusive, administration and community that he had pledged to create.

Now, opinion polls were showing the thirty-sixth governor of the Golden State to be the most unpopular governor in its 140-year history. In one poll, he had scored only a 15 percent approval rating.[5] As 1993 got underway, Wilson was almost sixty years old and, despite his boyish good looks and his trim figure, the sands of time were starting to run down for him. If his brilliant political career were to have a future, he had to come up with a popular, red-button issue. And quick. For opinion polls were putting Kathleen Brown, his likely Democratic challenger in the 1994 election, ahead by as much as 23 percent.[6]

Wilson had been born in the suburb of Lake Forest, Illinois, where his father was an advertising executive. His parents had sent him to a private school in St. Louis, Missouri, and as an undergraduate he had attended Yale University; but he had lived in California for most of his adult life, ever since he had attended law school at Berkeley in the 1950s, after his stint in the Marine Corps had ended. In 1963, the thirty-year-old had moved to San Diego to practice law. Since 1966, Wilson had served in one or another kind of electoral office. Politics was the man's life.

The only time Wilson had ever lost an election was in 1978, when he'd run in the Republican primaries for the gubernatorial nominee. That was the year California property owners were rebelling against rising local taxes, with an initiative on the ballot that would strictly limit the amount of property taxes that could be imposed. Known as Proposition 13, this referendum would come to have devastating consequences for California's public school system — which was largely funded by the moneys raised through local property taxes. Showing a surprising amount of principle, Pete Wilson stood up to the electorate and heartily opposed the initiative. For, as the mayor of San Diego, the state's second largest city, Wilson was all too aware of the damage this kind of populist politics could do to carefully worked out local budgets. He understood that laws such as Proposition 13, originating out of legitimate middle-class fears of a tax squeeze, could easily morph into political nightmares, constricting the freedom that elected politicians and economic experts had to establish fiscally sound revenue-raising mechanisms. His opposition cost him dearly. In a field of five Republican candidates, the forty-five-year-old placed a poor fourth.[7]

Wilson learned his lesson: in politics, especially within a democratic electoral system such as America's, it's always easier to ride a popular wave than it is to duck it.

Apart from 1978, in head-to-head face-offs with a Democratic opponent the governor had never lost at the ballot box, and he didn't intend to see that record disintegrate now. First, in the mid-1960s, he'd been elected to the State Legislature; then, in 1971, he'd won office as mayor of San Diego, where he gained renown for combining a sensitivity to environmental issues with a commitment to economic growth. Wilson was opposed to rent controls, and hostile to the city trade unions. Businessmen loved him, for under Wilson the city's economy thrived. The mayor also had been lauded by many voters for his determination to beef up the city's police department. His proud boast on this topic was threefold: first, that 75 percent of all new city hires in his term were of law enforcement personnel; second, that spending on the police rose by over 50 percent during his term as mayor; and third, that he, Pete Barton Wilson, had *doubled* the number of cops patroling the streets of San Diego.[8]

Wilson's preoccupation with criminal justice most likely had something to do with his grandfather, whom he'd never met. On January 3, 1908, when Pete's mother was still a baby, her father, Sergeant Michael Dennis Callahan, of the Chicago Police Department, had been gunned down by four young men whom he was trying to arrest. Despite a bullet in his abdomen, the thirty-year-old officer had managed to shoot back at one of his attackers, and to hold onto the dying criminal until other officers arrived. Then, staggering onto a horse-drawn patrol wagon, Callahan collapsed in a bloody heap. Two days later, lying in a bed at the Roosevelt Hospital, the police officer died. He was buried at the Calvary Cemetery, in the lush green suburb of Evanston; and his badge, number 2842, was placed in the Superintendent's Honored Star Case, along with the scores of other badges belonging to Chicago cops who had died in the line of duty.[9]

Wilson most likely grew up hearing the story of Callahan's untimely demise, and the circumstances that led up to the tragedy. Certainly, later in life he told friends and political audiences that the tough Irish cop had been the victim of brutal cocaine dealers. Whether or not this was true would remain a matter of debate. For, in 1908, cocaine had not yet been made illegal at the federal level. And even though states like New York had passed laws limiting its distribution and reformers

led by the Settlement House founder Jane Addams had convinced the
Illinois legislature to pass a law in 1907 making the sale of cocaine to
minors a criminal offense, many druggists still sold the drug over the
counter.[10] Indeed until a couple years earlier it had been a routine
ingredient in everything from Coca-Cola to quack medical "cures" such
as Birney's, Gray's, and The Crown, sold at the local drugstore.[11]

Nevertheless, by 1908 there *was* enough of a public outcry against
the sale of narcotics that many druggists had ceased to deal with cocaine;
and in their place many cities, including Chicago, had indeed seen a
fertile underground drug trade spring up, a business somewhat akin to
today's back-street sales of otherwise-legal prescription medicine. In New
York, police were breaking up "sniff parties" in the Bowery and other
infamous districts. And in Chicago, social reformers worried aloud about
the young addicts produced by the teeming slums, and about the approximately five thousand prostitutes, many of whom routinely dosed
themselves with opium, heroin, or cocaine, who were earning their live-
lihoods in the hundreds of brothels and seedy hotels that catered to the
sex trade throughout the windy city.[12] Cocaine was sold by the grain,
and four grains could be bought for somewhere in the region of twenty-
five cents.[13] These women, wrote the early twentieth-century fiction
writer William Hard, in his short story "De Kid Wot Works At Night,"
published in the January 1908 edition of *Everyman's Magazine*, employed young messenger boys to buy illicit substances for them. "All
night long these boys may be seen, slouching out of their offices, sham-
bling along the street with the peculiar foot-dragging shuffle of their
kind, passing the rows of open-faced saloons, turning down into the rows
of droop-eaved, close-curtained houses, climbing the steps of a brothel,"
Hard wrote. "From carrying messages for the women of the town they
go on to carrying cocaine and other drugs for them." Perhaps the four
men Callahan had tried to intercept were running drugs for the thriving
prostitution racket.

Whatever the exact truth of the matter, the story had impressed itself deeply in the mind of the Irish lawman's politician grandson.
And, as he climbed the ladder of power three-quarters of a century later,

Callahan's descendant focused ever more intently on California's criminal justice system.

Eight years into his mayorship, in the early fall of 1979, Wilson appointed a Crime Control Commission to explore ways of reducing crime in his sunny city. America was in a deeply unsettled mood at the time. Inflation was high; unemployment was rising; oil shortages were developing; and, every year, the country seemed plagued by more criminals, and as importantly, by more *violent* criminals. In San Diego, for example, despite the increased number of cops, and even after taking into account population increases, crime had risen more than 150 percent since 1969.[14] Increasingly, President Jimmy Carter was viewed as being a well meaning but ineffective, inconsequential head of state, a peanut farmer in charge of a ship careening aimlessly in rocky seas.

In this climate the Commission's mandate was to propose reforms of the criminal justice system and of policing strategies that would rein crime in once and for all and "increase San Diegans' feelings of personal security and safety." It was time, the mayor announced, for a full-blown "war on crime."[15]

Wilson's action was exquisitely timed to convey an aura of authority in the midst of political weakness. As the fall of 1979 spun into winter, the country's self-confidence was further shaken by the Iranian revolution, and the taking hostage of American embassy staffers in the capital city, Tehran. Gas lines worsened as the situation in the Middle East deteriorated, and Fundamentalist Islamic demonstrators a half world away chanted anti-American slogans and burnt the American flag in their streets. Backdropped by this atmosphere of gloom, Wilson's commissioners—judges, politicians, ethicists, churchmen, members of the corrections industry, even a rear admiral—went to work.

Two years later, the Commission issued its report. By now, of course, America was a very different place. The fiasco in Iran had effectively destroyed whatever chances President Carter might have had of winning reelection in 1980. And the new administration, presided over by Ronald Reagan, was committed to toughening up the criminal justice system, ballooning defense expenditures, slashing social spending, cutting taxes, and taking on trade unions. In dulcet homilies the Gipper promised to make America proud again. On September 16, Wilson dictated a letter to Edwin Meese, one of Reagan's inner circle, and at that time serving as counselor to the President. "Dear Ed, I am pleased to share with you the results of San Diego's recent effort in the fight against crime," the forty-eight-year-old mayor began. "I know you share my deep concern about increasing crime in our cities."

Inside the report that Meese received were fifty-two recommendations, premised on the tenet that "all criminal offenders — juveniles and adults alike — no matter what their offense, be subject to clear and certain consequences for their actions."[16] The commissioners advocated a combination of hard-hitting, conservative measures, and pragmatic, experimental, even progressive ones. On the one hand, they urged a clampdown on youthful offenders and the adoption of "uniform, certain and graduated penalties."[17] On the other hand, they emphasized the use of fines, community service, and work camps as alternatives to imprisonment in some instances. They called for better training of police officers, and an increased rapport between the police and community groups. They recommended that gun buyers be made to complete a gun safety course before buying weapons.

But perhaps most surprisingly, given subsequent history, the report explicitly rejected prison-building as a way to solve the crime problem. "The Commission recommends that the state forego costly, maximum security prison construction (including the proposed Otay Mesa prison)," the authors wrote. "Instead, it should expand conservation camps and community correctional centers to provide urban and rural housing in nonresidential areas for low-risk inmates. . . . The Commission recommends that the city of San Diego support and help develop an experimental community correctional-industrial center in a nonresidential area of metropolitan San Diego, to provide housing, job training, work experience and post-release job placement for up to 120 low-risk inmates."[18]

Meese wrote back to Wilson six weeks later. Not surprisingly, he focused on the conservative aspects of the report and downplayed its suspicion regarding prison building. "I noted with interest," the counselor's secretary typed, "many items that law enforcement and other groups have discussed before. It's like modifying the exclusionary rule [which ruled out-of-bounds evidence which the police had obtained illegally]; it takes repeated studies to prove the need for change."[19]

Wilson didn't make much of an effort to correct the impression that his Commission was espousing the values of the conservative revolution. It wouldn't have made a whole lot of sense, given that Wilson was now hot-on-the-trot himself to join that revolution in Washington and given that California's voters were just then beginning to revolt against the liberal social policies that had defined their state for at least the past two decades.

In 1982 Senator Sam Hayakawa announced his retirement, and the San Diego mayor decided to run for Hayakawa's seat. Ronald Reagan — the Gipper himself — flew to Los Angeles in late August to speak at a fundraiser on Wilson's behalf. In his folksy old voice, Reagan praised the younger man to the rafters. "Pete has been mayor of San Diego for eleven years," he explained, in the slow, rolling, cadenzas with which much of the electorate had fallen in love. "Much to his credit, it is considered one of the best-governed municipalities in the country. Crime is low," the Great Communicator assured the crowd, conveniently forgetting the statistics generated by Wilson's own Commission suggesting crime had more than doubled during his term as mayor, "and the quality of life is famous. His watchwords have been opportunity, jobs and progress."[20]

This time around, Wilson made sure his opinions were in tune with those of the electorate. Campaigning against California's outgoing governor, Jerry Brown, Wilson played up his support for the death penalty, and for longer sentences for violent criminals. Both stances proved deeply resonant in a state that had seen a massive rise in gang activity, gun-related crimes, and murder over the past two decades, and Wilson won by more than half a million votes. The Republican had also reversed his position on the tax-cutting Proposition 13; he now supported

the citizen's initiative, and lambasted Brown for his continuing opposition.

Two months later, Wilson was living in Washington, D.C. A few
months after that, the new senator, recently divorced from his first wife,
Betty, remarried; his new wife was Gayle Edlund. And the couple settled
down to life in the political fast lane.

There, in the nation's capital, Senator Wilson established a strong
record. On the one hand, he was known to be relatively socially progressive, a supporter of legalized abortion, gay rights, and the public
school system. On the other hand, few politicians had managed to fur-
nish themselves with as hawkish a reputation on defense, the economy,
and criminal justice policy. In 1984 the Baron Report found that he
had a more conservative voting record on economic and foreign policy
issues than 80 percent of his colleagues.[21] He voted yes on developing
the MX nuclear missiles, yes on weakening existing gun-control laws,
yes on amending the Constitution to require a balanced budget; he was
one of the most outspoken supporters of developing the Strategic Defense Initiative, more commonly known as Star Wars, as a shield against
nuclear attack; he voted to give aid to the Nicaragua Contras, and, in a
desperately close fight, he opposed an attempt to halt the production of
chemical weapons. (In the end, then-Vice President Bush had to cast a
tie-breaking vote to defeat the proposal in the Senate.) In May 1985,
Wilson had even left the hospital bed to which he had been confined
following an acute attack of appendicitis in order to cast his vote for a
major deficit-reduction plan. His action had won him a personal phone
call of thanks from President Reagan, along with Ronald and Nancy's
best wishes for a speedy recovery. But, perhaps showing he wasn't always
a knee-jerk conservative, California's new senator also voted against
school prayers, and in favor of sanctions against Apartheid South Africa.[22] He also pushed through Congress the Landmark Wilderness Bill,
preserving 1.7 million acres of undeveloped land in California, supported allocating billions of dollars to cleaning up toxic Superfund sites,
and opposed drilling for oil off the Pacific coast.[23]

It proved to be a popular combination of moderation and conservatism. And, in 1988, Wilson easily won reelection against his challenger, California Lieutenant Governor Leo McCarthy.

Three thousand miles from home, Wilson cozied up to the huge agribusiness interests of the West—successfully arguing for temporary exemptions in the 1986 Immigration Reform and Control Act, so as to allow a flow of Mexican laborers to continue to cross the border into the U.S., thus providing the farm owners with cheap, nonlegal labor. In a letter to President Reagan, Wilson told the chief executive that over half of those who could work as migrant farmworkers in the United States were being trapped in Mexico by "cumbersome and time-consuming INS and State Department procedures." He added that "Some growers have already been forced to stand by while their crops rot due to the labor shortage."[24] To make sure the workers returned south after the harvest, Wilson crafted legislation that would withhold 20 percent of their income until their return to Mexico. The legislation antagonized both immigrants-rights groups and the anti-immigration wing of Wilson's own Republican Party; but it helped solidify his reputation as a pragmatic problem solver—and it brought Wilson's political war chest much needed money from the agribusiness lobby.

Years later, with unemployment rising and the public turning against immigrants, Governor Wilson would remodel himself as one of the country's leading anti-immigrant spokespeople, supporting moves to deny illegal immigrants and their children access to schools and hospitals, and pushing for a massive expansion of the border patrols that manned the dividing line between Mexico and the U.S. Southwest. Like his reversal on Proposition 13 and his tough talk on crime, this was another wave the politician preferred to ride. But that was later on.

With the exception of his relationship to agribusiness, there was no other issue on which Wilson thrived so much as that of crime. Back when he had presided over San Diego's city government, the mayor had realized that a new political dynamic was unfolding. In an age of social change, voters were increasingly looking for representatives who could promise them stability. With the inner cities in turmoil, the hard drugs of heroin and cocaine becoming a commonplace of life in America, and crime on the rise, the country's citizens — even many of those who considered themselves touched with the liberal brush of the 1960s — wanted people who could articulate their fears and rein in the surrounding chaos.

After all, playing to public fear was a tactic that Richard Milhouse Nixon, the young Pete Wilson's mentor, the man whom Wilson had gone to work for as a campaign aide in 1962, had used to devastating effect in climbing the greasy pole to power in the 1960s, and in maintaining his hold on power in the early 1970s — until the Watergate scandal eventually sent him slithering back down that pole again. Now, in the Senate, Wilson, like Nixon a political generation earlier, sought to use the public's fear of crime to the maximum extent possible.

The politician wanted to establish himself as one of the toughest of the toughs. Although with peers like his, it wasn't always easy to stand out from the crowd; for, from the time of President Ronald Reagan's election onward, a harsher rhetoric had been dominating the discourse on crime and punishment. No longer was it fashionable, as it had been under Presidents John F. Kennedy, Lyndon Johnson, and again — after the Nixon and Ford presidencies — under Jimmy Carter, to look for complicated sociological explanations to explain poverty. Instead, everyone was rushing to attack criminals for their moral degradation, to attack the poor for their failure to thrive in the great capitalist marketplace, to demand harder penalties for those who transgressed the social code. Increasingly the fight against crime, especially that to do with drugs, was being treated as a war, to be fought on both a domestic and an international front, oftentimes using tactics — such as home invasions, warrantless searches, wiretapping, even helicopter surveillance — appropriate to those of a full-fledged military confrontation.

In 1983, Edwin Meese III, now risen to the position of U.S. attorney general, wrote that "We are not waiting on legislative action to open the battle against crime. The Executive Branch has brought the full force of Federal law enforcement agencies to bear on illegal drugs." Meese went on to say that "The battle against illegal drugs is already a war. President Reagan is correct that the war against crime demands the kind of resolve that Americans often reserve for international conflict that threatens our national security. Crime does threaten our security and deserves such priority consideration."[25] In early 1982, Florida's Republican Senator Paula Hawkins and twenty-eight other senators had joined together to form the bipartisan Senate Drug Enforcement Caucus, to push for more stringent antidrug laws, and to demand *military* aid to foreign countries needing help in eradicating their illegal drug crops. The group also called for the CIA to get involved in the fight against crime. They pushed for the assets of those accused, but not necessarily convicted, of drug crimes, to be forfeit to state law enforcement agencies, and for lengthy mandatory sentences, of up to forty years, for drug dealers. A couple years later, Vice President George Bush had presided over the creation of the South Florida Task Force, a body designed to break up the flow of cocaine coming into Florida from the Caribbean and Latin America. Customs officers, border patrols, the Coast Guard, and the military all became involved in fighting on this latest front in what Meese and Reagan had already declared to be a full-blown war.[26] Meanwhile, in Wilson's home state, the Campaign Against Marijuana Production—known to friend and foe alike as CAMP—was spraying the marijuana fields of Humboldt County with pesticide, helicopter teams were literally spying on people through their windows, and heavily armed special task forces were stampeding through homes and towns in their search for the illegal drug.

Toward the end of the 1980s, as the destruction wrought by the new drug known as crack intensified, Los Angeles police chief Darryl Gates even went so far as to tell a Senate subcommittee that "casual drug users should be taken out and shot."[27] The fury that Gates spoke to came out of the fact that even though the prevalence of burglary and many other forms of crime fell in the 1980s, violent crime, especially that related to drugs, increased. Between 1979 and 1989, for example, the number of people dying from gunshot wounds inflicted by teenagers rose more than 60 percent.[28] Indeed by 1997, writes the criminologist and onetime Yale sociology professor Elliott Currie, four out of ten Los Angelenos claimed to know people who had been seriously wounded or killed in criminal attacks.[29] New crimes such as carjackings entered the lexicon, and television reports of bloodied streets and Uzi-toting, crack-addled teenage gangsters, fueled the sense of panic, Gangs such as the Bloods and Crips proliferated, and gangster rap music, it seemed to many scared suburban parents, was glibly glamorizing casual violence. *New York Times* journalist David Anderson went so far as to argue that citizens felt the social contract itself had broken down. There they were, paying taxes and supporting a welfare system, but the state was unwilling to live up to its most basic duty—it was failing miserably in the job of protecting its populace from being preyed upon by violent addicts and gangsters.

From the time crack—the cheap, potent and easy-to-make rock cocaine drug—appeared in U.S. cities in early 1985, apocalyptic pronouncements had rained down. Crack, opined Arnold Washton, director of the 1-800-COCAINE helpline, meant "almost instantaneous addiction" for its users.[30] In place of earlier media coverage of cocaine as an elite, naughty-but-harmless, drug used by the playboy rich, articles poured forth on Black and Latino addicts, selling their bodies, even their children, for the impossible-to-resist rush that crack sent hurtling through the body to the brain. Every day, one could open the morning paper and read horror stories about crack-addicted babies, preteen drug couriers operating openly, secure in the knowledge that the courts really didn't punish youngsters, about ordinary Joes mugged, raped, or murdered on their way home from work. When people talked about car-related activities these days, they were more apt to be referring to drive-by shootings than to more innocuous automobile pastimes from decades gone such as drive-through restaurants or drive-in films. Even the music that kids were listening to blasted the worst images of urban cataclysm through the speakers and into living rooms and bedrooms, there to burrow themselves deep within the neural networks of the brain. The whole culture, it seemed, was busily soaking itself down in a drug-inspired bloodbath. Then, in 1986, a year into the epidemic, Maryland University basketball star Len Bias died of a cocaine overdose two days after signing a lucrative deal with the Boston Celtics. Suddenly, all the media seemed to care about was crack. "In the month following Bias's death," journalist Dan Baum reports in his book *Smoke and Mirrors: The War on Drugs and the Politics of Failure,* "the networks aired seventy-four evening news segments about crack and cocaine."[31] Soon *Newsweek* had run three cover stories on the deadly new narcotic threat.[32]

That year, as the public became increasingly impatient with a criminal justice system that they saw as "coddling" criminals, and with "liberal" politicians who offered up long-winded excuses about how crime was society's failure, Congress swung into action. As politicians and their aides vied with each other to outdo their colleagues, the Omnibus Drug Bill passed with not a single "no" vote cast by any member of the Senate or House. New mandatory prison sentences were written into the statute books for twenty-nine criminal offenses. The laws affected marijuana, cocaine, and heroin dealers, and set in stone a minimum five-year sentence for anybody caught with five ounces or more of crack cocaine. To make sure these sentences were carried out, the bill also eliminated parole for drug convicts sentenced in the federal courts. Over the next decade, as the mandatory minimums kicked in, and as state after state followed on from the federal example, prison spending rose by more than 160 percent, the prison population more than doubled, and the number of guards employed within the prisons also doubled.[33] Looking back on this period, David Anderson wrote that "Fearful people take comfort in the *idea* of a mandatory sentence. On paper, at least, it reinforces values."[34]

But the events of 1986 proved to be a mere prelude to the presidential election campaign of two years later.

A year after Bias's untimely death, a convicted murderer named Willie Horton was on leave from the prison he had lived in for much of his adult life. At first sight, this might have seemed strange. After all, Horton was about as serious a criminal as one could find, and a judge had sentenced him to life in prison. But Horton lived in Massachusetts, and the liberal New England state had long been at the cutting edge of experimental penal policies. Over the past few years, the department of corrections had been running something they called the "furlough program." Prisoners approaching parole or those lifers judged to no longer be a threat to society were allowed out for days at a time, some to work, others just to go on weekend visits home. They were required to check in every so often, and to return to the prison at a predetermined time. It was, the bureaucracy hoped, a sensible way to gradually reintegrate offenders back into society, or to at least hold out hope of eventual freedom to those, like Horton, whom the courts had sentenced to life behind bars.

Horton, however, had a somewhat different idea as to the purpose of furlough. One day, instead of returning to his prison, he hightailed it south to Maryland. Soon afterward, he broke into the suburban home of Angela and Cliff Barnes, tied Cliff up, beat him, and then proceeded to rape Angela. By the time he was caught, driving away in the Barneses' car, two more lives had been shattered by Horton's actions.[35]

What Horton couldn't have known was that his vicious crime — one of hundreds of thousands of sadistic acts committed in America that year — would end up at least in part determining the outcome of the 1988 election. For it so happened that Massachusetts's governor, Mike Dukakis, was the lead candidate in the Democratic primaries. As Dukakis's campaign clicked into gear, a Meals-on-Wheels coordinator named Maureen Donovan formed a group named Citizens Against Unsafe Society and began working for a ballot initiative that would end the furlough program. Dukakis and his staff refused to deal with their specific complaints. When the group's representatives met with him, the governor quoted statistics at them to prove that, overall, despite the odd mishap, his program was a success. By March 1988, however, legislatures in Massachusetts had reached other conclusions; and, at about the time Dukakis was locking up the Democratic presidential nomination, he was forced to sign a law that repealed the furlough program for lifers.

And that was where the issue might have ended — a footnote in a busy political calendar, a lesson learned by a politician on the campaign trail. But, unfortunately for Mike Dukakis, Horton's actions had already leaked into the wider world. Even during the Democratic primaries, a young candidate by the name of Al Gore had derided the governor as being out of touch with the common folk on the important issue of crime. Now, with the November election nearing, the Republican team surrounding Vice President George Bush was looking for an issue that could blow their opponent out of the water. It was at that point that Bush's hard-hitting campaign coordinator, a man in his mid-thirties by the name of Lee Atwater, remembered the Willie Horton case that Gore had brought up during the primary season.

Atwater put his researchers to work. By June, the Republican Party was running attack ads showing Willie Horton's evil-looking, and extremely Black, face leering into viewers' living rooms, while a voice-over explained that Dukakis had let this convicted murderer out of prison to rape and brutalize another innocent family. The Democrat never recovered. Unable to dig deep, to produce the emotionally resonant responses so necessary in a political climate dominated by soundbites and talk shows, Dukakis floundered. When Bush attacked him for opposing the death penalty, all the governor could do was to quote statistics. When commentators railed against the furlough program, Dukakis hardly fielded a response. Soon, Bush was hammering at the whole philosophical concept of liberalism, at the whole idea of rehabilitation, of looking for broader societal explanations for the rise in crime. Dukakis, he said scornfully, was running from "that L word."

By November, Dukakis was a defeated man. And, in the arena of crime, drugs, and punishment, the views of men like George Bush, Edwin Meese, and incoming drug czar William Bennett truly were ascendant.

In such a climate, Wilson had to struggle to be heard. But struggle he did. Soon, the California senator was calling for sanctions against Mexico and Panama because of their only half-hearted support for America's fight against the drug traffickers, and was demanding that the military get more involved in tracking down smugglers. So impressive was his rhetoric that in 1986 the Stamp Out Crime Council in San Diego voted Wilson their Legislator of the Year. He had, the announcement stated, become "a soldier in the war to stem the flow of illegal drugs." Wilson also began pushing for a law making it a federal crime to use the postal service to sell drug paraphernalia.

In 1988, the Wilson-Hunt Amendment had finally given the military an official role in the antidrug efforts. That same year, Wilson was named to a special task force to assist in writing new omnibus antidrug laws. The following year he sponsored a Drug War Bond Act, that would allow the government to sell bonds to the public to raise money for the War on Drugs. And, throughout his term in the Senate, Wilson fought to allow local police forces to take large portions of any assets seized in either state or federal drug cases, a move that essentially turned the local police into privateers against their own citizens, giving them a financial incentive to bust into houses, or stop drivers, on the flimsiest of evidence, and to then confiscate property and cash.

As the 1980s wound down, Wilson started pushing for a Crime Victims Justice Act, a largely symbolic law that would speed up criminal trials, create special penalties for crimes that involved victims being tortured, and beef up the federal death penalty. In practice, since not many crimes involved torture, and since the vast majority of death-penalty cases were tried in the state, rather than the federal, courts, the act wouldn't make that much actual difference. But, in the War on Crime, Wilson had to know that symbolic gestures often went down as well with the voters as did concrete actions. *Act tough and sound tough* was the de facto mantra of the times when it came to crime.

It also didn't hurt to *look tough*. One of Wilson's most eye-catching leaflets from his 1988 reelection campaign had shown the senator decked out in khakis, standing in between two soldiers. Inside, voters were provided with information about the senator's anticrime credentials. In other campaign literature, the conservative actor-come–National Rifle Association–spokesman Charlton Heston declared his support for the senator. And in yet another leaflet, Wilson's team boasted of their man that "One of his bills [the Comprehensive Crime Control Act of 1984] has resulted in a thirty-two percent increase in prisoners in federal custody." Raising the prison population was no longer an unfortunate side effect of necessary law-enforcement. Rather in the new equations, expanding the prison system was seen as a good in itself.

Now, with two Senate campaigns under his belt, Pete Wilson had a strong reputation as a canny political operator. As importantly for a man with his sights firmly set on even higher office, he had developed a formidable reputation as a fund-raiser. During his 1982 run, Wilson took more money from Political Action Committees than did any other Senate candidate — $962,683, according to a report in the *National Journal*.[36] It was, the *Journal* reported, the most expensive race in Senate history. And a survey conducted by the public interest group Common Cause showed him to have raised more money from the subsequently disgraced savings and loan industry than any other member of either house of Congress. California's farmers were also coughing up the dough. For big business during the Reagan years, Wilson was talking the talk, and the political contributions kept rolling in. By 1986, conservative fund-raising groups such as the recently founded Young Executives of America, could bring more than seven hundred people to fund-raisers held on Wilson's behalf. As Ronald Reagan had done in 1980, Wilson was tapping into the huge well of money controlled by conservative Southern Californian business interests.

Finally, in 1990, after having raised a $20 million campaign war chest, Wilson felt he was ready to succeed George Deukmejian — *the Duke* — as California's governor. The New York–born Deukmejian had created a political career for himself in Southern California, and had gotten elected governor in 1982, the same year Wilson went to Washington. During the election campaign, Deukmejian had pledged to cut taxes and put more criminals behind bars. He had done both, raising over $3.5 billion for prison construction through a series of bond measures passed by the voters. Over the past eight years, the governor had signed 350 bills into law that extended jail and prison sentences for a huge array of crimes.[37] He had also appointed more than one thousand judges, many of whom were committed to the governor's conservative approach to crime and punishment. As the election rolled around, California's prison population was approaching 100,000. The Department of Corrections was predicting that by 1995 it would rise to the unprecedented number of 150,000.[38] It was, Deukmejian felt, a job well done. Now, the sixty-two-year-old wanted to retire. He believed that Wilson would "continue to support tough action to fight the growing plague of crime and drug abuse."[39]

Throughout 1990, the senator was commuting between D.C. and California, honing his tough-on-crime message and perfecting the image he would present to the voters. His opponent was ex–San Francisco mayor Dianne Feinstein, whose campaign was being largely bankrolled by her financier husband, Richard Blum. The polls suggested it would be a tight race, and Wilson, along with campaign manager Otto Bros and the expensive political consultants working for the candidate, knew his best shot would be to tie himself to Deukmejian's anticrime policies, and to portray his opponent as being the kind of waffly Mike Dukakis–type liberal that America had shown such contempt for back in 1988. Wilson began to play up his support of the death penalty, which the outgoing Deukmejian had reintroduced in California. In speech after speech he mentioned his support for an expansion of the federal death penalty, and for the rate of executions to be sped up. In contrast to Michael Dukakis, who refused to abandon his long-standing opposition to capital punishment, Feinstein responded to Wilson by running commercials stressing that she, too, favored executing murderers. Wilson counterpunched by touting his support for the citizen's initiative known as the Crime Victims Justice Reform Act, a popular ballot initiative of the time that limited the scope of plea-bargains and restricted a defendant's right to bail. Feinstein came back with a proposal for a half-cent sales tax that would be used to raise money for extra police officers. Wilson declared his support for another popular ballot initiative,

Proposition 139, that would allow prisons to hire out their inmates to private industry as cheap labor. He released campaign questionnaires with questions like: "Senator Pete Wilson is a co-author of federal drug legislation which would impose the death penalty on drug kingpins. Do you support or oppose this idea?"

George Bush also weighed in with slightly more lurid language. "Pete had been an outstanding leader in the war against crime at the state and national level," the President wrote in an open letter to California's electorate. "He is co-author of federal legislation that imposes the death penalty on drug kingpins and the cop-killers they employ."

And just to make sure voters got the message, Wilson even invoked the ghost of his long-dead grandfather. "In January 1908," readers of Wilson's manifesto, *Taking Charge of California's Future*, were informed, "police sergeant Michael Callahan died in the line of duty, the shooting victim of a cocaine-related crime wave sweeping through Chicago. Seventy-five years later, in January of 1983, Callahan's grandson, Pete Wilson, was sworn into the Senate, the victor of an election highlighting his dedication to law and order."[40]

Gradually, Wilson's relentless focus on crime and punishment bore fruit. Slowly but surely, he began to pull ahead of Feinstein in the polls.

Like the Duke, who had authorized the building of twenty-five new prisons,[41] and who had presided over an increase in California's prison population from approximately 30,000 in 1982 to more than 100,000 when he left office in January 1991,[42] Wilson successfully appealed to the electorate's suspicion of welfare and fear of crime to build himself a majority in the polling booths. On election day he won 49 percent of the vote against the Democratic candidate Dianne Feinstein's 46 percent.

An election cycle later, Governor Wilson was preparing to face the voters again. And, since he knew his electorate, he knew that his strongest cards were his law-and-order credentials. In a state with nineteen million eligible voters, fewer than 60 percent were actually registered to vote.

But, within different groups the numbers varied dramatically. Among those aged eighteen to twenty-four, only a third were registered; of those over sixty years of age, over 70 percent voted. Among whites, 65 percent were registered; but among African Americans, the figure was only 58 percent, and for Latinos a mere 42 percent. Fewer than 40 percent of the state's Asian population voted.[43] Given that older whites tended to support tough law-and-order policies that tended to lead to the incarceration of more and more of the minority population, Wilson knew that the voting patterns favored politicians who advocated longer prison sentences and the construction of more prisons.

When the state's finances were melting down in the early 1990s, the governor had refused to cut spending on corrections. In fact, he had done the reverse. Welfare spending had been slashed, education spending—especially on the state's once-vaunted public universities—had contracted; but in the 1991 budget, the criminal justice budget had actually been raised by more than 13 percent, to a record $3.7 billion.[44] In that year's State of the State speech, Wilson had also pledged to pursue legislation that would curtail good-time credits for prisoners, a practice that allowed inmates who worked in prison industries to have time knocked off their sentences. The governor's office was predicting that by 1996, the corrections budget would have to rise by almost another billion dollars, to $4.6 billion.

Not surprisingly, other areas of the budget were being decimated. By 1993, after three straight years of welfare cuts, California was spending more on prisons than on Aid to Families with Dependent Children, and one in six state employees were now working for the Department of Corrections.[45] Spending per pupil in the state's schools had been frozen since 1991, and students at the state university campuses were facing yet another 10 percent hike in their fees.[46]

It was hardly a shock, therefore, when, about a year before the November 1994 election, Pete Wilson returned to one of his perennial favorites, an issue that had yet to let him down. With a vengeance, Governor Wilson began playing the crime card.

Mike Reynolds was the same age as Billy Ochoa, born in 1943. He was a bald man, slightly overweight, with just the hint of a resemblance to Danny De Vito. Reynolds made his living as a wedding photographer in the deeply conservative California Central Valley town of Fresno, taking photos at the ceremonies, and posing the couples in front of studio screens bearing images of golden arbors, antique cars, whatever fantasies the newlyweds wished to immortalize. He was basically your everyman small businessperson.

Back in the early 1960s, Mike Reynolds had joined the Young Republicans, where he had gotten to know up-and-coming local politicians such as Ed Hunt, who had gone on to become Fresno's District Attorney. The organization allowed him to develop his ideas on welfare, on racial minorities, on the family. The government, he believed, had created a destructive culture of poverty. "They literally cast the males out and keep the females in the home to get the money," he thought. "Free money becomes a narcotic. It's prevented many American families from realizing their full potential." The family just didn't seem to be as sacred as it was when he was a boy. So many kids nowadays were born out of wedlock. Blacks, in particular, he considered to be "loners," people not adequately socialized into valuing the family unit. And because of welfare, Reynolds thought, Black fathers had been driven from the home, and the male role models for young men were increasingly gangsters, hoodlums wielding guns and dealing drugs. More recently, Fresno had become home to many Vietnamese and Hmong immigrants, "little short people who look different from us." The world seemed so much more complicated than when he was growing up.[47]

In the 1964 presidential race, Reynolds had campaigned for Barry Goldwater. Two years later, he'd worked to get Ronald Reagan elected governor in California. Those were the good times, he believed, not like under Jerry Brown, who followed on from Reagan: "Governor Moonbeam," Reynolds was fond of calling him. "He was extraordinarily liberal. It was the end of the era of hippies and yippies." Under

Moonbeam, the state had been turned over to the pot-heads and the criminals. Not so under the Republicans—Deukmejian and Wilson—who had occupied the governor's mansion again in the 1980s and 1990s. Reynolds was proud of his long affiliation with the GOP.

In the living room of the large suburban house in which he and his wife, Sharon, a nurse, lived, in the house where they had raised three children, hung a framed invite to the 1969 Nixon/Agnew inauguration. Other than that, the décor was somewhat chintzy: flowery blue wallpaper; pottery rabbits hanging out on the kitchen shelves. A sparkling black 1948 Rolls-Royce dominated the garage, its huge headlights staring, eye-like, in the direction of Reynolds's darkroom. But, amongst the ordinary, middle-American ornamentation and the signs of affluence could be found hints of tragedy. In the kitchen was an angel embroidered into a beige canvas square. And on the canvas, next to the angel, were the following words about his daughter:

In memory of
Kimber Michele Reynolds
Called to Heaven July 1, 1992.
After eighteen precious years.

Kimber's photographs also stared out from the wall. A pretty young woman, blond, happy, smiling, full of life. She had intended to become a fashion designer, and had recently enrolled in a college down in Los Angeles. She had returned to Fresno in late June 1992, to attend her friend Tricia's wedding. Mike had agreed to photograph it.

Reynolds wanted to spend quality time with his daughter, his youngest child; after all, now that she lived in L.A., they didn't see each other that often. So, the day after he photographed the wedding, on June 30, he took her out to a baseball game. The game went on till fairly late; and after it was over, Mike went home. But Kimber, only in town for a few days, wanted to see her friends. So, after she'd said good-bye to her father, she met up with a guy, and the pair headed off to pick up some dessert at the Daily Planet restaurant. They ate and talked, paid the bill, and started walking back toward Kimber's car. All of a sudden two men on a motorbike, their faces obscured by helmets, roared up to them, and one of them grabbed at Kimber's purse. Perhaps not thinking clearly, perhaps just infuriated that someone would try to rob her in the middle of a crowded street, the eighteen-year-old held on. The action cost her her life.

One of the men whipped out a .357 magnum, stuck it into Kimber's ear, and without the slightest hesitation, blasted a round into her head. Then, the bikers took off. The young woman fell to the sidewalk, and shortly afterward was rushed to hospital. She lived in a coma for twenty-six hours, her parents never letting go of her hand. And then, on July 1, she died. As she was dying, Mike Reynolds made a solemn promise. *Kimber*, his inner voice declared through the frenzy of grief, *I promise you I will try to prevent this happening to other people.*

It was a bold promise: that year, Fresno County, with a population of a little over 600,000, was to witness more than 100 murders. Per capita, the county was one of the most violent in all of California, the inner city positively overflowing with drugs, vice, and violent crime.

After the funeral at Belmont Memorial Cemetery, Reynolds took to the airwaves. In an emotional speech on the Ray Appleton radio show, he appealed to listeners to phone the police with any information they might have about Kimber's murder. Within the hour, two leads had come through. The informants named the killers as Jo Davis and Douglas Walker, a couple of ex-cons who'd been in and out of trouble for as long as anyone could remember. They had, it appeared, been on a bit of a crime spree ever since their recent release from prison. Both were white, both were cranked up on methamphetamine the night they went out looking for trouble, the callers said. And, after Kimber Reynolds had gone down, they'd sped off, dumped the bike, and stolen a car. One of the callers told the police where they could find Jo Davis, the man who had actually pulled the trigger on the victim.

Fresno's police were renowned for their almost military style of operation. The city's Special Weapons and Tactics (SWAT) teams were already notorious for their recourse to heavy firepower—from the use of armored vehicles to submachine guns and low-flying helicopters. And planning was in the works to create a Violent Crime Suppression Unit, with more aggressive tactics than any other police department in the country, that would take on the gangs of impoverished south-side Fresno with what the author Christian Parenti terms "the equivalent of search and destroy missions."[48] In a situation like this, with a brutal killer holed up in an apartment building, there was no reason for them to change their tactics. As they approached Davis's hideout, the SWAT team readied their shotguns and their service automatics. On the other side of the door, Davis was preparing his own weaponry. When he saw he was surrounded, the murderer came out shooting.

An officer went down, wounded, with a bullet in his chest. A moment later, Davis's body was ripped by twenty-one rounds from the automatics and thirty-one pellets from the shotguns. His bloodied, punctured body lay splayed at the bottom of the stairs.

"I was happy to see that," Reynolds's friend, District Attorney Ed Hunt, recalled several years later, sitting in his friend Mike's living room while waiting to film a political commercial with him. "It reduced my caseload."

Two weeks later, Douglas Walker was caught. Unlike his friend, Walker survived the arrest. Because Davis had done the shooting, Walker was able to plea-bargain on an accessory-to-murder charge. He was sentenced to nine years, making him eligible for parole after only four and a half.

Walker went off to begin doing time in Calipatria Prison. Mike Reynolds set about realizing his deathbed promise to Kimber.

A month after his daughter's death, Reynolds organized a meeting in his verdant backyard. The garden consisted of a stone patio, out of which a tall Monterrey pine tree grew, a lawn, and an ample veranda, covered over by a sloping wooden roof, under which was a wooden table and a basic outdoor kitchen. Squirrels, made tame by Kimber having put food out for them over the years, scampered over the boughs of the Monterrey. (Carrying on the tradition, Mike and Sharon often left nuts for the squirrels near their daughter's grave.) At this meeting, local police officers, lawyers, and crime victims began looking at why cons such as Davis and Walker kept cycling in and out of prison. *They should be locked away for life*, the voice of rage inside Reynolds's heart kept shouting. *They had already shown their criminal faces. It's not fair that they got out and killed my daughter.*

Sitting under the pine tree, the participants identified three major problems with the criminal justice system: first, through abiding by the rules inside prison, and by taking on work assignments, prisoners could get themselves released after serving only half their sentences—that was why Walker stood a good chance of becoming a free man sometime in 1997. Second, because the courts were always overworked, prosecutors frequently offered defendants plea bargains. Agree to plead guilty to a lesser crime than the one you actually committed, these agreements went, and instead of nailing you on a more serious charge in a jury trial we'll take this to a judge and recommend a lighter sentence. Finally, Reynolds and his guests determined that too many judges were spineless liberals, always willing to give criminals the benefit of the doubt. Judicial discretion, they believed, was allowing violent criminals back onto the streets. Eliminate these three problems and animals like Davis and Walker would soon find that America was no soft touch.

In quick succession, two more garden meetings followed. Among the guests who attended these sessions were three local judges and Ed Hunt. After the third meeting, Reynolds and his colleagues decided they would draft a bill that they would present to the state legislature, in the hope that the politicians in Sacramento would decide to eliminate the three flaws which they had identified in the system. In the fall of 1992, Ed Hunt called Attorney General Dan Lungren's office and arranged for Reynolds to head north to Sacramento to meet Lungren. The attorney general was a friend of Hunt's, and Ed felt sure he'd agree to the meeting.

Lungren had made his name a decade before, while serving as a United States Congressman from the port town of Long Beach, California, as a no-nonsense crusader in the two wars that were shaping up: the War on Drugs and the War on Crime. The young lawyer was a part of the brigade of antidrug warriors that had tried to prevent those accused—but not yet convicted—of drug-related crimes from using their own money to hire a defense attorney, and, like many within the Justice Department under President Reagan, he had favored reining in defense attorneys who did accept drug money through charging them under broad drug-conspiracy laws. He had also been instrumental in calling for the creation of a Sentencing Commission that would examine the sorts of sentences judges were handing out across the country, and that would recommend a series of guidelines designed to standardize these sentences. In 1984, Lungren was one of the leading voices in support of the Comprehensive Crime Control Act. When its passage had looked doubtful, Lungren had forced the House to vote for it by attaching the measure to the year's major appropriation bill. It was a nifty bit of politics, for had the Democrat-controlled House voted against it, all federal government spending would have been frozen—and that was something nobody wanted to see. The Act increased the prison terms of those convicted of dealing drugs, allowed prosecutors to appeal "lenient" sentences, and ended the practice whereby young, first-time drug offenders could have the crime expunged from their criminal records upon completion of their sentences. It also allowed police forces to keep the profits that they accrued through seizing the assets of those suspected of being involved with drugs. As Lungren put it, somewhat understating the case, "We took the Federal system and toughened it up quite a bit."[49]

Dan Lungren believed that in the 1960s and 1970s a governing elite had imposed a philosophy on America "in which punishment became passé and rehabilitation became the name of the game." Incarceration rates had fallen at the exact same time that crime was going up. It was, people like Doris Tate, the mother of one of Charles Manson's victims, were telling him, a suicidal state of affairs. By contrast, Lungren supported the prison-building plans of both George Deukmejian and Pete

Wilson. "We believe in deterrent," he explained. Toughen up the laws, imprison more and more people, and inevitably, eventually, crime would begin to fall. It was, in Lungren's mind, a simple equation.

In 1988, then-Governor George Deukmejian had attempted to appoint him as State Treasurer, to fill in the post left vacant by the death of then-Treasurer Jesse Unruh. Democrats in the state legislature had successfully fought the appointment, citing his opposition to the Clean Water and Clean Air Acts, and his congressional vote against the creation of a Martin Luther King Jr. holiday as evidence that he was too conservative for the position. In 1990, Lungren had run for the state attorney general's office, and in the November election he had beaten Democrat Arlo Smith by the smallest of margins: a mere 0.4 percent of the vote. An unpretentious man, Lungren and his wife had decided to keep their modest family home in the suburb of Roseville; the attorney general would drive the twenty miles to work each morning and return home often late into the night.

During the campaign, Lungren had told supporters that he wasn't "running for attorney general because of the civil side. I'm concerned about crime, gangs and public integrity."[50] Now that he was actually in a position to do something, Lungren wanted everybody to know that he was going to tackle the mean streets of California, that he was going to restore law and order and make the good people feel safe again. He and Wilson were making a good team together. And the attorney general had hopes that one day, when the boss moved on, he himself might step into the governor's shoes.

When Reynolds went to Sacramento, he was accompanied by his friend Sam Federico, who ran a local beauty college, and Judge Buck Lewis. Lungren had already heard about what Reynolds was trying to do from a sympathetic assemblyman named Bill Jones; and himself being the father of young daughters he could only imagine what Reynolds must be going through in the wake of his daughter Kimber's murder. It soon became clear that Lungren was interested in what they had to say. He fixed his steely blue-gray eyes on his visitors and started taking notes. He brought in two aides, Deci and Kennedy. These two would go to future meetings in the Reynoldses' back garden and help draft what became known as the Three Strikes and You're Out law. It was a catchy phrase, homey, almost comforting in its associations. Everybody who'd ever thrown a baseball, or even just watched a game on TV, knew what it meant. Now, Reynolds was proposing a law that embraced the most elemental of ballgame rules: *get convicted of three felonies*, Reynolds argued, *and you're outta here*. No ifs, ands or buts. *Three strikes and you get sent down for life.*

Lungren and Governor Wilson had both been looking to tighten up California's criminal code, and in Mike Reynolds's fury, the righteous fury of a grieving father, the attorney general saw a way to turn the tables on the liberal politicians and judges who had stood in the way of an all-out war on crime. Here was an opportunity to generate a "firestorm" of public outrage that would dramatically alter the political debate in California.[51] Soon, Lungren was sharing speaker platforms with Mike Reynolds, as the two men stumped for Three Strikes across the state.

Reynolds's strategy was twofold: first, convince members of the California Assembly to sponsor a Three Strikes bill in the legislature. Second, to generate such a groundswell of popular support that even if the politicians up in Sacramento refused to act, the citizens of California could vote it into law through a popular ballot initiative. They hired a signature-gathering company, American Petition, to start bringing in the hundreds of thousands of signatures that were needed to qualify an initiative for the ballot in 1994, and they began to solicit donations.

The trouble was, nobody seemed that interested in Mike Reynolds's crusade. When people like California Assembly Speaker Willie Brown heard his story they felt deeply sorry for him; in the same way as they felt sorry for all the victims who had gradually been coalescing into "victims rights" organizations over the past few years. But that didn't mean they were about to embrace Three Strikes. California had too many other problems to worry about. Earthquakes. Cataclysmic wildfires. The 1992 Los Angeles riots. The last thing it needed was a law that would ratchet up the prison population even higher than it already was. After all, it cost well over $20,000 per year to house a single inmate, and money was tight these days.

But that was all about to change. In the late summer of 1993, a diagnosed psychopath by the name of Richard Allen Davis left the half-way house he was living in in Daley City to visit his sister in the sleepy northern California town of Petaluma. He took a Greyhound bus, and got off at the Petaluma terminal, across the street from a little park in which the local winos hung out. Davis immediately gravitated to this ramshackle crowd; he'd leave his sister's house and head back to the park, where people would offer him cheap liquor and drugs. Davis decided Petaluma was a town worth staying in for a while.

The thirty-nine-year-old Davis had recently been released from prison after serving eight years for kidnapping, whipping, and robbing a woman. By all accounts, prison had singularly failed to rehabilitate him.

While in Petaluma, Davis spotted a little girl on the streets. Something about her appealed to the ex-con, and—investigators later hypothesized—he began stalking her. Witnesses later came forward to say he had been prowling about the neighborhood, where the child, Polly Klaas, lived, for the better part of six weeks. Some recalled his extremely gruff manner, his dead eyes, the smell of alcohol on his breath.[52]

At ten-thirty in the morning, on October 1, Polly Klaas and some of her friends were playing inside the Klaases' house. Davis crept up on the back of the building and began trying to find a way in. Soon, he found that one of the doors was unlocked, and he slipped inside the house. The girls were playing alone. Davis tied up Polly's friends, and then he picked the little girl up and sped off out of the house. "Please don't hurt my mother and sisters," Polly is said to have screamed as the large man grabbed at her.[53] And then they were gone.

The Polly Klaas case attracted international attention. Here was a beautiful, intelligent, young girl in the sanctity of her own home, abducted in broad daylight by a lunatic. This was every parent's ultimate nightmare. And if it could happen in a town like Petaluma, a little place not known for its violent underside, it could happen anywhere. *What was America coming to when an innocent little child could be taken in such a manner?* Like the kidnapping and murder of aviation hero Charles Lindbergh's infant son Charles August Jr., sixty-one years earlier,[54] this was an event capable of engrossing, of emotionally drawing in, tens of millions of people. So appalling was it, that it was also an event capable of turning your average couch-sitting, television-watching, citizen into a latter-day supporter of lynch-mob justice. With criminals such as Richard Allen Davis, and crimes such as the abduction of Polly Klaas, intruding into every home on every evening news show, surely it was time the country cracked down on the evil lurking within.

For nine agonizing weeks, the police combed the country. Time seemed to move in slow motion. Polly Klaas and Richard Davis had vanished. The Klaases waited, numbed with dread, knowing, but not wanting to acknowledge, that they would probably never find their daughter alive. Polly's image was beamed around the world as television news crews latched onto the horrible story. Within a few weeks, America had whipped itself up into a frenzy of fear and rage. On November 15, Governor Wilson addressed the California Peace Officers Association at their annual convention in the Hyatt Regency Hotel in La Jolla. "There is such a thing as a career criminal," Wilson thundered. "I say, let's give 'em a new line of work. Let's make 'em career inmates." He paused for full dramatic effect. Then, for the first time, Wilson embraced the proposal that Mike Reynolds had been stumping up and down the state for well over a year. "Three strikes and you're out!"[55]

In early December, the inevitable happened. After a series of witnesses came forward to report the presence of a suspicious vehicle and individual fifteen miles north of Petaluma the night of the little girl's disappearance, on November 30 the police arrested Richard Davis. Five days later, as forensic evidence linking the ex-con to the kidnapping mounted, Davis confessed to the crime and told his interrogators that he had murdered the little girl and dumped her body in a field near a deserted sawmill in the vicinity of the small town of Cloverdale. A few hours later, searchers found Polly Klaas's body. The twelve-year-old had been raped and then strangled.

Within minutes, the news was being broadcast around the world. And, in America, the country gave itself over to an outpouring of national grief.

Pete Wilson, now cranking up his reelection efforts, lost no time in harnessing his fortunes to this tragedy. At the enormous memorial service in Petaluma held for the murdered child on December 9, the governor spoke at length. "For sixty-five days we held our breath, hoping against hope. It sometimes seemed as though the outpouring of love and support for Polly alone could bring her home. We now know that God had already called Polly home. While we waited on this earth, Polly waited with the angels." Then, as the cameras whirred, Wilson hammered home his tough-on-crime message. "We must join Marc [Klaas] and take action by supporting the 'three strikes, you're out' initiative, the work of another California father driven by grief and anger over the wanton murder of his beautiful daughter."

Two days later, on his weekly radio address, Wilson again dwelt on the Polly Klaas case and further committed himself to Three Strikes. "Polly's father is joining with another grieving father, Mike Reynolds, whose daughter Kimber was brutally murdered by a career criminal trying to steal her purse in June of 1992," Wilson reported. "These two grieving fathers are supporting an initiative known as 'three strikes, you're out' . . . I endorse this initiative, and I hope you'll join me in supporting it. It's time to make these career criminals career inmates."

No matter that, within a few weeks, Marc Klaas himself disowned the Three Strikes movement and came out as one of its most vocal opponents: the emotions surrounding his daughter's killing, were, Marc had concluded, leading to some terrible public policy, lumping small-time crooks such as Billy Ochoa in the same boat with psychopathic killers like Richard Davis. Klaas believed men like Davis deserved no mercy, but, as a political liberal, the bereaved father also wasn't comfortable with a Three Strikes law that he feared would lead to thousands of minor offenders from the inner cities being dumped in prison for the rest of their lives.[56] By then, however, Klaas's voice was a whisper in the wilderness. The emotions surrounding his daughter's killing had taken on a life of their own. And the murder had become the latest high-profile crime to stoke the fires of America's rage.

Money began pouring in to Mike Reynolds's Three Strikes campaign: $40,000 from the National Rifle Association; $80,000 from the California Correctional Peace Officers Association (the prison guards' trade union); close to $200,000 from the eccentric millionaire Michael Huffington, then in the midst of a quixotic, expensive, and ultimately futile, run for the U.S. Senate. And bundle upon bundle of signatures flowed in from every corner of the state. Soon, over 800,000 people had signed up for their support of the Three Strikes ballot. And the governor began phoning Mike Reynolds to discuss the progress of this citizens' crusade.[57]

In much the same way as George Bush's 1988 campaign team used the image of Willie Horton—the murderer who had escaped from a work-release program in Massachusetts and gone on to rape a young woman and terrorize her husband—to destroy the presidential candidacy of Massachusetts governor Michael Dukakis, so Wilson's people now put images of the Klaas murder to work on their candidate's behalf. Here was a golden opportunity to shift the focus onto the tough law-and-order terrain that Pete Wilson was so comfortable atop. No matter that crime rates in 1993 were actually lower than they were in 1980,[58] here was a murder that could really whip up some public hysteria about criminal degenerates and their liberal judicial and political defenders. And who better to reap this harvest than Wilson himself?

THREE

Nearly five years before Billy Ochoa was sentenced to 326 years, on the other side of America a twenty-three-year-old man named Anthony Williams was given twenty-five-to-life for selling crack cocaine.

When Anthony was a youngster, living in an impoverished neighborhood of Queens, in New York City, he'd been attracted to the vigilante Guardian Angels organization, to their berets and red uniforms and to their tough, no-nonsense attitudes. But then, like so many other teenagers in his part of town, he'd gotten himself convicted on a marijuana charge and had been sent upstate to Camp Gabriel. In Anthony's case, his first encounter with the law occurred when his own mother turned him in to the cops after she'd rifled through his pockets and discovered a small amount of grass. Now, for the past four years he had been a Black Muslim, and, in addition to the handful of business courses that he had taken after high school, he was teaching himself Arabic. By the time he was in his early twenties he had two infant sons and was living with the mother of his youngest child, in a small apartment in Rego Park. For relaxation, Anthony liked to cook and to dance.

In the autumn of 1991, the young African American journeyed north to the state capitol of Albany, ostensibly to check out a college in the city. He stayed for a while, phoning to tell his mother, Nazimova Varick, that he was working, and that he was thinking about enrolling in college up in Albany.[1] Perhaps he was, perhaps he wasn't. Either way, it never happened. One night, Anthony—a large man, weighing in at more than two hundred pounds—came out of a store and found himself confronted by undercover police. They suspected he was a drug dealer who had been operating out of a local motel, and ordered him to stop; instead he ran into a building where the officers chased him down, cornered him, and placed him under arrest. Williams would later claim that the men beat him savagely inside the building.

When the police offered him a deal — one to three years in exchange for becoming a "confidential informant" — Williams refused the terms. He claimed he was innocent, wanted nothing to do with snitching on, and wearing wiretaps around, his friends, and told his legal aid attorney to prepare for trial. It was quite possibly the biggest mistake of his young life. When the jury came back with a guilty verdict, the judge invoked the state's draconian eighteen-year-old antidrug legislation known as the Rockefeller laws, and sentenced Williams, who by any estimates was only a minor dealer, to a mandatory sentence of twenty-five years to life behind bars. Given the terms of the law that then–Governor Nelson Rockefeller had pushed through the legislature in 1973, the trial judge really hadn't had much choice. Soon Anthony Williams had been processed through the prison-admissions system and was getting used to his cell inside the maximum-security prison of Greenhaven.

Nine years later, his health undermined by chronic headaches, stomach pains, and weight loss, Williams remained in prison. Meanwhile, his mother, a pastor at God's Divine Church, had become an outspoken activist in a statewide campaign to repeal the Rockefeller laws under which her son had been taken from her. Whenever family and friends of Rockefeller prisoners gathered to protest, Nazimova Varick would be there, waving her placards and, frequently, speaking into the microphones to urge political action. Staying active, the fifty-five-year-old cancer survivor found, was the only way to keep her sanity. "I'm a Pastor," Varick explained, "and I sometimes ask that question: 'God, have you forsaken me? Where are you when I'm going through this? I'm serving the time *with* my son. He's been stolen from me and I've been stolen from him, by way of the judicial system."

Every year, the fathers, mothers, brothers, sisters, and children of drug-law prisoners would gather on the north lawn of the vast neogothic stone Capitol Building, across from the Justice Department, at the foot of one of the imposing staircases that led up to the Capitol's austere entrance. The building looked like an over-the-top hybrid of a European cathedral and a Victorian London railway station. At these events, ex-prisoners, such as Elaine Bartlett, would tell the crowds how they had been given twenty-year sentences for a low-level first-time drug offense. A mother told of her son, crippled by muscular dystrophy, wasting away in prison after being convicted on a drug charge. A wife told of a husband in prison for life after being convicted of possessing four ounces of cocaine. Even celebrities such as ex–New York City vice squad police officer Frank Serpico and the aged actor Al Lewis, better known as Grandpa Munster, would turn up to show their support for reform.

The demonstrators at these emotional gatherings would hold up photographs of their imprisoned loved ones alongside of which they wrote out brief life histories. At the May 2000 demonstration, Varick, wearing a bright yellow blouse, tight tan jeans, a brown straw hat, and flamboyantly large tinted sunglasses to hide the crows' feet surrounding her tired eyes, held up her photograph of Anthony. "A victim of racial profiling and 'racial targeting,'" the sign held in between her long, curling, sparkling blue fingernails stated in small, felt-tipped letters, "Williams was handed a sentence befitting a mass murderer by [a] lock-em-up-throw-away-the-key-if-they're-black [judge] who never met a perjuring narcotics agent he didn't like."

After nine years of unsuccessful lobbying, Varick was frustrated, as willing to blame a judge who was just doing his job as the politicians who had crafted the Rockefeller laws in the first place. The prison system, she now believed, was providing too many jobs upstate for any politician to want to tackle. "The farms upstate," the embittered mother declared, "go out of business. So they need a new industry, and we become the new vegetables."

If Pete Wilson was the man responsible for the extraordinary length of Billy Ochoa's sentence, Nelson D. Rockefeller was the chief nemesis of

Nazimova Varick's son. In early January 1973, the wealthy governor, who had been running New York since 1959, gave a powerful State of the State address. For ten years now, heroin use had been widespread enough to constitute a devastating plague for the inner cities. Recently, however, New York City crime rates had fallen a dramatic 21 percent in the first half of 1972[2] following on from the federal government's establishment of a national methadone-maintenance program for heroin addicts. But in 1973, the moderate Rockefeller was beginning to seriously consider a run for the presidency in 1976 and he urgently needed to throw a sop to the Republican Party's right wing. It seemed the perfect time to make a play for their law-and-order vote. Ignoring the falling crime rates, Rockefeller declared that "The crime, the muggings, the robberies, the murders associated with addiction continue to spread a reign of terror. Whole neighborhoods have been as effectively destroyed by addicts as by an invading army. This has to stop. This is going to stop."[3]

To tackle this menace, fueled by images of a subversive, drug-ingesting counterculture and warnings that 10 to 15 percent of Vietnam veterans were returning to America as dangerous heroin addicts,[4] the governor proposed something truly extraordinary: for anyone caught selling any amount, no matter how small, of heroin, methadone, LSD, amphetamines, and even hashish, Rockefeller demanded a mandatory life sentence with no possibility of parole. It was a suggestion, he knew, that would instantly garner vast amounts of national attention for its author, as a similar idea had for the Louisiana Congressman Hale Boggs back in the early 1950s, when Boggs—running for the governorship of Louisiana—had proposed, and succeeded in passing, a raft of federal mandatory sentences for drug dealers. These laws had stayed on the books until only a few years previously.

Nelson Rockefeller didn't quite get a life-without-parole bill, but, with polls showing a majority of New Yorkers supporting his zero-tolerance ideas, he *did* manage to push the state legislature to adopt some of the toughest antidrug sentences in the country. Soon, dealers in New York found to possess over one ounce of marijuana were facing fifteen-year prison terms, while those in possession of an ounce or more of heroin did indeed become eligible for a lifetime behind bars. And, with plea bargaining strictly limited, the only sure legal way around the Rockefeller Drug Laws was to start snitching on clients and other dealers in exchange for a shorter sentence.

Despite their draconian nature, and the judiciary's reluctance to impose such sentences, the Rockefeller Laws proved such a hit with the public that that summer, as the Watergate scandal swirled all around, President Nixon also tried to divert the electorate by proposing mandatory sentences for dealers that would range from five years to life depending on the severity of the crime. (The proposals didn't succeed in quite their original form, but some mandatory sentences *were* introduced.)

But the Chief Executive's reinvigorated Drug Wars didn't prevent Congress moving toward his impeachment. And a year afterward, after President Richard Nixon had resigned in disgrace, the country's new leader, Gerald Ford, rewarded Rockefeller's actions, and his decades-long service to the Republican Party, by appointing him vice president of the United States. The irony was that, with several states passing laws to decriminalize marijuana, in the mid-1970s Gerald Ford's own advisers were urging the president to fundamentally reconsider the nation's approach at least to the softer drug of pot.

Of course, those laws weren't overhauled, either at a federal level when it came to interstate trafficking, or on the state level, and now, a generation later, with a majority of inmates in New York's desperately overcrowded prisons serving sentences for drug crimes, Rockefeller's legacy remained intact. Tens of thousands of young men and women, the vast majority of them from desperately poor inner-city neighborhoods of the Big Apple, were serving sentences for relatively minor drug crimes that would keep them behind bars well into their old age.

Rockefeller's actions hadn't come out of nowhere. Periodic moral panics and mass hysterias have been a part of the American landscape since the Puritans first landed at Plymouth Rock. And, in one manifestation or another, the terrifying image of a supposed crime wave is a beast that has romped throughout American history, all too often whipped up by the prevailing media of the day.

In Philadelphia, in the 1740s, newspapers routinely played up crime stories. Nineteenth-century New York was rife with tales of mayhem and murder. "Reefer Madness" hysteria about juvenile, often Black, marijuana users terrorizing local communities surfaced as early as the 1920s and 1930s, as an underside of the radio-era Jazz Age. The National Criminal Justice Commission's report *The Real War on Crime* mentions a mythical "crime wave" against elderly people in New York in 1976 that radically changed New Yorkers' attitudes to crime at a time when, in reality, crime rates against the elderly were actually falling. In the wake of this communal panic, New York's juvenile justice laws were dramatically toughened up and the NYPD swept the streets of supposed hoodlums. Yet, the commission found, "murder of the elderly dropped 19 percent during the course of the so-called crime wave—despite the fact that the crime wave began with media reports of several gruesome murders of elderly people."[5] The most recent hysteria, and the one fueling a continuous growth in America's prison population through the last decade of the twentieth century, throughout a period when crime rates were in fact falling on a yearly basis, is but the latest in this series.

Ex–crime reporter David Krajicek, in his book *Scooped*, wrote that the current frenzy has several very identifiable jumping-off points: the launching of Fox TV's sensationalist *A Current Affair* in 1986, which put a premium on gory, fear-inducing footage; the Polly Klaas murder in northern California, a spate of tourist killings in Florida, and the Long Island Railroad massacre, all of which took place in 1993. "About four months before the Klaas killing," Krajicek argued, "an ABC News/ *Washington Post* poll found just 5 percent of respondents named crime as America's most important problem." But by January 1994, "31 percent of respondents named crime as the nation's top problem. All this reporting about carnage had an unmentioned catch: national statistics showed that crime had declined during 1993." Similarly, the Center for Media and Public Affairs found that news programs on ABC, CBS, and

NBC ran 571 crime-related stories in 1991, and 1,632 in 1993. Again, this during a period when crime was actually on the decrease.[6]

In the last twenty years, the incidence of robbery has decreased by 17 percent from its high point in the late 1970s and rape by 30 percent. Murder rates, after soaring during the height of the crack epidemic, have also fallen. Yet the public perception of ever-escalating crime rates remains stubbornly high.

None of which is to downplay the seriousness of the crack wars, the rise of seemingly random and devastating gun violence during the 1980s and early 1990s, and the legacy of fear and heartbreaking loss that this has left on the American landscape. Crack did indeed create legions of addicts, spawned child and spousal abuse in its wake, led many users into lives of crime to fund their habits, and spawned some of the nastiest gang wars America has ever seen. And certainly terrible acts *have* been performed by criminals in recent years. But terrible acts have been carried out by thugs, smugglers, and murderers throughout history. What makes the crimes of today *seem* so much more pervasive is at least in part to do with the saturation coverage that the television and tabloid media has accorded these acts in recent years. But, had the thirteen colonies had Fox TV, the inhabitants of that time and place too, terrorized by pirates, brigands, roaming gangs, and murderous feuding clans, might have been equally horrified of the scenes of carnage that they presented to themselves and equally inclined to view their travails as unique in human history.

In fact, from the earliest days of the English colonies on the continent's eastern seaboard, crime and punishment have captivated the American public's imagination. Law breaking appalled the young country but at the same time it fascinated her populace. Sometimes criminals were eulogized as heroes, at other times they were damned as worthless parasites. For some, gangsters such as Jesse James or pirates such as Blackbeard were the Robin Hoods of the American frontier, while for others they represented a bloodthirsty challenge to the social order.

Hundreds of years after Blackbeard's and James's heydays, crime still played, still plays, a pivotal role in defining America. Hollywood movies and the morning papers have made Mafiosi household names, and the genre of westerns created legends out of frontier gangsters. Film noire captivated audiences with portraits of the fast-talking, hard-drinking detectives and criminals living just below the urban radar. On television, cop shows have mythologized the streetwise, crime-busting law enforcement officer. Even the practitioners of bounty hunting, one of the lesser-known legal leftovers from colonial America, have found their professional exploits avidly followed by millions of television viewers. The vicarious joy felt by the crowds in a movie theater during a particularly gripping good guy–bad guy gunfight is perhaps matched only by the extraordinary fear felt by so many millions of ordinary citizens that they will become the victims of some strung-out, crazy thug going after some quick cash or bloodthirsty thrills.

It was this gut fear, this terror of coming face to face with something, or someone, truly awful, that politicians such as Pete Wilson were responding to so vocally.

But the question Wilson, or indeed Rockefeller, never answered was this: Were the people being locked up for years, even decades at a stretch, really the stuff of which so many nightmares were made?

And the answer, all too often, was "no." Perhaps the saddest thing about Billy Ochoa's case was how pitifully common this kind of thing had become. Not since centuries before when England had deported thousands of petty offenders to distant colonies such as Australia — or for that matter, America — and hanging judges had been as quick to mandate death for thieves as for mass murderers, had notions of "justice" been so vindictive in a democratic nation. In the few years since the passage of Three Strikes, California had struck out over 5,000 people — and for the majority of these, their third felonies were nonviolent. From 1994 until January 2000, 5,887 Californians had "struck out," less than 2,400 for violent crimes.[7] One hundred and eighty were car thieves, 26 were marijuana pushers, and just over 1,000 were in for either possessing, intending to sell, selling, or manufacturing other controlled substances.[8] As a result of the law changes, people like Ochoa, and others of life's mess-ups such as Steven White, were facing life behind bars for crimes which a few years earlier would hardly have even warranted time in the county jail. Many were resorting to extreme measures to avoid these sentences.

A year and a half before Judge Buckner handed down Ochoa's sentence, Steven White was holed up in a run-down Las Vegas motel room, from the window of which he had spent the past three and a half hours firing rounds of ammunition off at the local police. The gunman was out on $10,000 bail, posted by his father, from jail in San Diego, and he had used his temporary freedom to drive across the hot, scrubby Mojave desert to Vegas. He was trying, without success, to provoke the police into killing him. It was April 6, 1995, and White had decided that it was time to die. The alternative, according to the three suicide notes that he hurriedly scrawled during lulls in the shooting, was too awful to contemplate; life in prison following certain conviction for the crime of walking into an electronics store with an old VCR receipt and walking out with a new video player, worth $146, that he hadn't paid for. When he'd shown the receipt to the security guard the man had immediately called the police. Now, one year after California had passed Three Strikes, throwing away the key on thousands of repeat offenders, White was about to become a statistic.

The thirty-two-year-old White had been a drug addict for years, since he was a teenager, hooked on coke and methamphetamine. In the early 1980s he'd picked up two felony convictions for burglary. He had no history of violence. He did, however, have HIV. White didn't want to slide into his grave deep within the Californian penal system.

Now, on the shabby outskirts of the great gambling mecca, as the police lobbed tear gas canisters into his room, the video thief picked up his shotgun and emptied a load into himself. When the cops entered the room, they found his bloodied body. "Sorry I did this," the note addressed to the police said. "It was because of three strikes."[9]

So, in a way, White had gotten his wish: he didn't end up a sick and withered prisoner destined to die inside a prison. Ochoa, however, preferred to take his chances on the inside. One of nearly two million prisoners serving time in the largest prison system on earth.

Leaving the judge with no discretion as to sentencing, Three Strikes trials in California are, says Peter Liss, the then–deputy public defender who represented Steven White, "like show trials. They're slam dunks. There's nothing you can do." If a prosecutor decides to go after a non-violent offender with a "Third Strike" charge, that person is a goner. Mostly their pasts are, like White's and Ochoa's, generally tapestries of despair, often stupidity, and missed chances.

Many committed truly awful crimes while in their teenage years, renounced violence, put their lives back together and then struck out on the most pathetic of offenses decades later. Russell Benson, for ex-ample, had dabbled with drugs since he was a teenager. Strung out when he was eighteen, he attempted to rob and murder a friend of his. It was, Benson knew, about as heinous an act, as terrible a betrayal, as one could possibly perform.

For a crime such as this, Benson deserved to spend a long time in prison. One could argue that the five and a half years in prison he served for the two felony convictions he picked up for this act were nowhere near enough; but that was how his sentence worked. In prison, Benson got his drug habit under control. He was paroled and made a career for himself as a tow truck driver. For ten years he drove trucks and stayed out of trouble. Then in 1994, while living in Palmdale, fifty miles east of Los Angeles, with his girlfriend and her three children, Benson was laid off from his job. Now thirty-eight, he wrote from the California Men's Colony prison, near the college town of San Luis Obispo, in a childish scrawl, on yellow legal paper, that "The day I was arrested I was not out to steal. I needed to get back to San Fernando Valley [an hour west] for an opportunity at a good job. The ride I had set up for fell through and I couldn't get a hold of anyone who could make a 100-mile round trip to come and get me. The little money I had left wasn't enough to pay for a train ride. I was on the phone which was inside a Target Store and walked out of the store with a carton of cigarettes."

A security guard saw the frustrated trucker walking out of the store with the unpaid-for box, and he hurried over to tackle the thief to the ground. Benson struggled. When the police arrived, they told him he would be charged with shoplifting. It was a misdemeanor offense and would, almost certainly, have not resulted in a prison sentence. But when the officers did a background check and found out that Benson was a Two Striker, they jacked up the charge to robbery. Because he was convicted under California's catch-all Three Strikes law, Benson is now serving twenty-five years to life in a state prison for his ill-timed crime of frustration, a situation that even one senior prison official says "doesn't make a lot of sense. It doesn't really serve society."

There is a prevalent image in America of a violent lumpen underclass, what the Victorian journalist Thomas Wright, describing nineteenth-century London's slum-dwellers, termed "The Great Unwashed," controllable only by punishment. It is an image that influential conservative criminologists such as James Q. Wilson, urging a far more expansive recourse to imprisonment, pandered to back in the 1970s and 1980s, when the groundwork for today's massive prison system was laid. And, to a degree it's true: The country *does have* a phenomenal number of murders and murderers, gangsters, mercenary drug pushers, kidnappers, rapists, and armed robbers. Arguably, since the very birth of the nation — complete with the roving gangs of brigands in Appalachia and privateers off the Atlantic seaboard — it always has. And, like all things American, violence here, whether it be the gang violence associated with illegal drugs, or the urban upheavals of the rioting poor, happens on an epic scale. At the height of the crack wars of the 1980s, more than 25,000 people were being killed annually. Parts of inner-city Los Angeles, Washington, Detroit, New Orleans, New York, Chicago, and several other cities, *are* indeed virtual war zones. No two ways about it, but there are an awful lot of angry, brutal, and trigger-happy men in America. And there are an awful lot of weapons available to these people to carve out their twisted realities on the American landscape.

Super-maximum-security prisons such as the notorious Pelican Bay—nestled in the coastal Redwood forests of California's northernmost county, surrounded by two high razor-wire fences and a lethal electronic barrier and more escape proof than the island of Alcatraz in the San Francisco Bay—house thousands of men, many of them mass murderers, rapists, kidnappers, and other seriously disturbed individuals.

But no matter the hysteria, there aren't nearly enough American psychopaths, enough real-life Hannibal Lecters, to justify a prison population that now hovers in the two-million range, incarcerated in hundreds of facilities across the fifty states.

In fact, for the first time in history, most U.S. prisoners—*over a million people*—have been convicted of nonviolent, often victimless crimes: offenses, such as marijuana possession, that hurt nobody, and immediately affect nobody but the person arrested. Hundreds of thousands are now serving ten-, fifteen-, and twenty-year terms for crimes that in Europe or Canada would generally result in noncustodial sentences and commitment into drug-rehab programs. And so, in addition to housing the violent menaces which they were intended to incarcerate, maximum-security prisons such as CSP-SAC have seen an increasing number of inmates such as Billy Ochoa pass through their phenomenally secure gates. Meanwhile, in many cases, the big-time criminals go free: trading information, snitching on subordinates, hiring million-dollar attorneys who will do anything possible to limit the years their clients spend in jail. The land of the free has become a place where rural backwaters—catapulted into economic collapse by deindustrialization and the oft-vaunted global market—now bid for the privilege of building new high-tech prisons to incarcerate the urban unemployed, and the urban addicted. People like Ochoa—or, to take another convict, Lillie Blevins.[10]

Blevins is a diabetic in her mid-fifties. She has chronic high blood pressure, back problems, knee problems. A couple years ago her appendix ruptured. She is scheduled to spend the rest of her life in Carswell Federal Medical Center, inside the Fort Worth army base, just outside Dallas, Texas.

Lillie's crime was conspiracy to sell crack cocaine, allegedly head of a family operation involving three of her sons and her brother. The evidence against her: the word of a snitch who was friends with her drug-dealing sons, along with three grams of crack cocaine found in her Mobile, Alabama, house by federal agents. Her status is a nonviolent, minimum-security federal inmate, no prior time served in prison, no money, and hence no lawyer working on her case; at the time of her sentencing, her husband was in jail on an unrelated charge.

An African American woman born in the Deep South, in the town of Selma, Alabama, Blevins was pulled out of school in the third grade to look after her seven brothers and sisters. Her father had just died. Her mother, Pearlie, was in the fields all day, picking cotton. Lillie had her first child, a boy, when she was fourteen, and moved south to Mobile, on the hot, sultry Gulf Coast, shortly after. Over the next decade and a half, six more sons followed. Lillie was an active member of the Shallow Baptist Church. But in a world of grinding poverty and limited horizons, no amount of religion could prevent some of her boys, and at times herself, from being tempted by drugs. In the early eighties, the police arrested her for growing what she terms a "reefer bush" in her garden. Later on, she was hauled in for possession of crack. Neither arrest resulted in prison time. Then, in 1990, three of the Blevins boys, now living in an apartment away from Lillie, were caught up in a federal drug sweep, turned in by a friend who bartered twenty-eight names to federal agents in exchange for probation. For good measure, the friend, who had once lived down the road from Lillie, added her name to the list. One morning, when Lillie was at home, the agents knocked on her front door. She opened it, and they stormed into her house. They found three grams of crack—she claimed they planted it, they said it was already in the house—and carted the forty-two-year-old woman off to jail. The snitch said she was in charge of the family operation. Her sons denied she had any knowledge of their actions. Their denials counted for little: Blevins was sentenced to life imprisonment in a federal prison.

As of the summer of the year 2000, 144,750 people were serving time in federal prisons—convicted in the federal courts for crimes ranging from the murder of a federal employee to drug trafficking across state lines to simple drug dealing in a place where the state police passed the arrest onto federal agents. The latter had become common practice, because federal law—the very laws championed by then–Senator Pete Wilson—allowed for the *local* police to keep a high percentage of any moneys or assets confiscated from drug suspects in *federal* busts. As long as the courts judged a law enforcement officer's suspicions to be justifiable, you didn't even have to gain a criminal conviction in order to seize a person's car or cash or even, on occasion, their property and bank accounts. And as a result agencies had fallen over themselves trying to take advantage of this easy new source of revenue. Asset forfeiture was proving such a bonanza that even the Bureau of Land Management had set up their own antidrug SWAT team.[11] Six in ten of these inmates were serving sentences for drug crimes. Fully 56,238 were African American.

The sentences handed down by the federal courts are staggering: 33,168 have bought five-to-ten; 21,439 are serving ten-to-fifteen; 10,057 are doing fifteen-to-twenty; and 10,731 are locked up for over twenty years. According to the Rand Drug Policy Research Center, these sentences "reduce cocaine consumption less per million taxpayer dollars spent than spending the same amount on enforcement under the previous sentencing regime. And either enforcement approach reduces drug consumption less than putting heavy users through treatment programs."[12]

And while it might be tempting to shrug one's shoulders and utter those poetic words of resignation *qué sera sera*, in reality it hasn't always been this way. In fact, like the state penitentiaries at Cherry Hill and Auburn, the federal prison system began its life as a child of reform.

In the hundred years following the birth of the nation, America's prisons grew, and, gradually, a state and federal bureaucracy emerged to administer them. From the Jacksonian age of the 1820s onward, state after state built grandiose granite cell blocks to contain their criminal classes, and "doing time," either in the local jail or the state penitentiary, entered the American lexicon. In 1849, the federal government joined in. That year, the Department of the Interior was made responsible for the construction of a series of federal prisons that would be used exclusively to house felons convicted in the federal courts of criminal acts that occurred across state boundaries, that affected the well-being of the federal government, or that involved attacks on federal employees or institutions. The going was slow, however, and by the time the Civil War broke out twelve years later, the prisons still had not been built. Not surprisingly, the four years of fierce fighting put all these plans on hold. Abraham Lincoln had more pressing matters at hand than pushing the staff of the Interior to build edifices in which to house common criminals, and with manpower desperately needed by the warring armies the idea of putting thousands of able-bodied men into prison was a luxury nobody could afford.

But once the battles ceased, prisons began anew to vie for national attention. Five years after the Yankee victory, war-hero and now-President Ulysses S. Grant brought into being the Department of Justice, and once again the idea of creating a network of federal prisons came to the fore. By now, more than three-quarters of a century after the Quakers of Philadelphia had opened the new wing at Walnut Street, the prison system had spread across the country. By 1880, forty-five prisons were being operated in thirty-eight states, and the country's prison population had swelled to more than 20,000. Another 8,000 men and women were serving short sentences in district jails. On top of this, on any given night, perhaps as many as 15,000 more could be found drying out or sleeping off a particularly heavy binge in the country's 2,000 county jails.[13] Now, however, where once the penitentiary had itself been seen as a symbol of reform, as the crown jewel atop this multi-tiered system of incarceration, many critics saw the institution itself as a petri dish of social disorder. As the last third of the nineteenth century passed, so a growing prison reform movement flourished. And one of the main demands of this movement was for the federal government to build its own prisons in which those sentenced in federal courts could serve out their time.

State after state had constructed their own penitentiaries in the eighty years since Independence. Now, in the ruins of the old South, a particularly vicious new form of imprisonment had arisen in the years immediately following the Confederate's defeat. The system was known as "prisoner-leasing," and, since the institution of slavery had been abolished, it was intended to provide almost-free, mainly Black, labor to the states' landholders, mine operators, and railroad developers. Instead of Blacks being ruled by the Slave Codes and being largely outside the criminal justice institutions of the prewar South, they now became subject to a court system that was bending over backward to accommodate the needs of the recently defeated white slave-owning elite.

With the hatreds of war still boiling during these years of Reconstruction, and with hundreds of years of race-based power on the line, the South began arresting thousands of newly freed Blacks. Vagrancy, petty theft, drunkenness, all became excuses by which to entangle the ex-slaves within the legal system. Once there, juries were quick to convict and judges were only too pleased to impose extraordinarily harsh sentences. It wasn't uncommon, wrote the journalist George Washington Cable, himself the scion of a slave-owning family, for Blacks to receive sentences of "twelve, fifteen, twenty, and in one case forty years," for the minor crime of larceny.[14] By the 1880s, Black prisoners in South Carolina outnumbered whites by more than sixteen to one; in neighboring Georgia the ratio was almost eleven to one.[15] And once in the Southern penitentiaries, convicts swiftly learned the limits of emancipation. For, after being decked out in bug-ridden prison garb and fitted for shackles, the prisoners were then leased out by their wardens to local business interests who would usually work their laborers quite literally to death.

Soon, throughout the ex-Confederacy, chained, semistarving prisoners could be seen working coal mines, building roads and railways, turnpikes and levees. In Tennessee, the prison population in 1882 stood at

1,336. Of these, 685 worked on chain gangs inside the penitentiary; 28 were laboring to build a railway tunnel; 123 had been leased out to farms; and 495 were toiling in the local mines.[16] In North Carolina, 800 prisoners were leased out to the railways and wagon roads. They "returned to the prison with shattered constitutions and their physical strength entirely gone," wrote the warden. In the years 1879 and 1880 alone, fully 178 of these prisoners died. Not surprisingly, prison reformers such as Cable had come to believe that a prison term in the South was tantamount to a death sentence. In Louisiana, the infuriated journalist told his startled readers, after plowing through reams of prison data, 14 percent of the state's inmates died in 1881 alone, an attrition rate roughly comparable to the penal labor camps of the Soviet Gulag during Stalin's rule a half century later.[17]

Cable described convicts "in filthy rags, with vile odors and the clanking of shackles and chains," being transported by train to work in the coal mines of the South. "Which shows the greater maliciousness," Cable mused. "For one man to be guilty of hog-stealing or for twelve jurors to send him to the coal mines for twenty years for doing it?"[18]

By the 1890s, the situation had gotten desperate. The Civil War might have preserved, at least on paper, the idea of a unified nation, but a generation after the cessation of hostilities on so many issues the country was evolving in two diametrically opposed directions. And, at the root of these differences lay the South's absolute aversion to even the vaguest forms of racial equality. Despite the brief flurry of Black civic and political inclusion during the Reconstruction decade, once the occupying Yankees had returned north again, a ferocious web of laws—the notorious Jim Crow code—was rapidly put in place to intimidate Blacks back into a position of subcitizenship.

The prisoner-leasing system had proven a pillar of this new order. But in addition to this, there was one other area in which the segregationist politicians of the South were able to use the criminal justice system to further their goal of removing Blacks from the political process. And that area was the introduction of "felony disenfranchisement laws" that prevented those convicted of a felony from ever again voting, from the time of their sentencing right through till they died and were buried in the local cemetery.

In the last decades of the nineteenth century, state after southern state began amending their constitutions. Poll taxes were introduced, and those wanting to register to vote were subjected to literacy tests. Both measures were intended to severely limit Black citizens' access to the ballot box, and hence to the governing mechanisms of political power. The third part of an unholy trinity of disenfranchisement laws was made up of the rules that barred those convicted of felonies from political participation, and that dramatically expanded the definition of a felony to include everything from the use of vulgar language to the stealing of pigs and cattle through to preaching the Gospel without a license.

There was nothing new about barring those currently doing time for felonies from voting. Virtually every state in the Union had such a statute. After all, the argument ran, if somebody had committed a crime serious enough to warrant imprisonment in a penitentiary, then it made sense to think they had forfeited their right to full political participation while incarcerated. But the permanent disenfranchisement laws were on a whole different order: go to prison, do your time, rehabilitate yourself, come out of prison and start working, and, these laws decreed, you would still never be able to take part in choosing those people who governed in your name. Because none of these rules explicitly mentioned Blacks—and because some impoverished whites also fell within their mantel—the recently secessionist region felt that in these laws was a method for preserving white supremacy without overtly abandoning the constitutional framework of the United States of which they were reluctantly still a part. "What is it we want to do?" John Knox, the president of Alabama's 1901 Constitutional Convention asked his delegates. "Why it is, within the limits imposed by the Federal Constitution, to establish white supremacy in this state."[19]

Now, faced with such a welter of evidence as to the South's misuse of the prison system, Congress came under enormous pressure to at least prevent federal prisoners from ending up in the infamous southern state penitentiaries. In 1891, seven years after the publication of Cable's shocking exposé *The Silent South*, the politicians of Washington finally passed the Three Prison Act, providing for the construction of three large federal prisons: at Leavenworth, Atlanta, and McNeil Island.

From the get-go, these national prisons satisfied some of the populace's most voyeuristic impulses. In the 1830s, Philadelphia's Eastern Penitentiary had been one of the great tourist destinations of the age. Now, sixty years later, the three federal prisons raised this macabre pleasure to an entirely new height. Middle-class sight-seers and social reformers just couldn't gawk enough at the inmates. At one point, in the early years of the twentieth century, William Moyer, warden of the federal prison at Atlanta, reported an astonishing three thousand tourists per day visiting his prison,[20] meaning that oftentimes these fortresses were hosting more visitors than inmates. Some returned so often that, to avoid the long lines for tickets, they purchased a year-long pass. They came to stare, secure in the knowledge that guards would protect them from the uniformed villains, but also, perhaps, nurturing secret admiration for the desperadoes who populated the cell blocks before them. "The sagas of the outlaw and the gangster, the rebel and the mob, the crusader and the horde, are played back again and again in counterpoint to the dominant themes of unbridled progress and prosperity," Frank Browning and John Garassi theorized.[21] In the hundred years of the penitentiary's existence, America had developed a startling romance both with the prison itself, and also, in a love-hate kind of way, with the rogues who ended up inside. It was a relationship that a later age would maintain toward Alcatraz, the crown jewel in the federal prison system during the mid–twentieth century; and that would continue with the mythologizing of prisons such as Marion after Alcatraz closed down.

One hundred years after the first three federal penitentiaries opened for business, the federal prison system has itself become a behemoth. And, like the transformation of the southern state penitentiaries into citadels of oppression in the years following the civil war, so today's metamorphosis has roots in broader political changes. The number of people incarcerated in federal prisons at the outset of the twenty-first century is a reflection of very deliberate changes in criminal justice policy. In 1970 the total federal prison population was a mere 21,266, and only 3,384 were in for drugs. As late as 1982, only 5,518 were serving federal prison time for drugs. And then, as President's Reagan's social policy took root, the numbers began to soar.

Throughout the 1980s, taxes on the wealthy were slashed, and government spending on social programs for the poor and inner-city economic aid declined. Columbia University professor Manning Marable reports that in the single year of 1988 alone, despite rising numbers of inner-city residents suffering from asthma, tuberculosis, and AIDS, more than eighty community hospitals, serving the poorest of the poor, shut their doors.[22] The administration's policy was exacerbated by changes in international markets: as the world's economy globalized and corporations moved their production sites into Third World countries that could offer cheaper labor, more and more American jobs disappeared. In Los Angeles alone, 80,000 low-skilled industrial jobs vanished.[23] And, again, this chronic urban unemployment was made worse by the Reagan Administration's decision to abandon the more than three-billion-dollar Comprehensive Employment and Training Act program, followed by its cutting off of more than 400,000 families from federal and state welfare rolls.

By the end of Reagan's first year in office, according to Marable, the number of poor Americans had risen by well over two million, and the real median income of Black families had fallen by more than 5 percent.[24] By 1985, the Field Foundation released a study indicating that across the nation half of all Black men between the ages of sixteen and sixty-five were chronically unemployed. In many parts of inner-city America, the only signs of economic vitality by the end of the 1980s were the open-air drug bazaars — purveyors of crack and heroin — that flourished along street blocks and in overgrown lots from Harlem to South Side Chicago to Watts.

Not surprisingly, as inner-city economies nosedived, crime flourished.

Throughout the 1980s, murder was the fourth leading cause of death for Black men of all ages in the United States.[25] And by 1994, the homicide rate for American men of all colors aged fifteen to twenty-four was 37 per 100,000 — compared to a rate of only 1 per 100,000 across the Atlantic Ocean in Britain. Among Black men in this age group, it was a truly astonishing 167; and for Black men in New York the number was an even more incredible 247.[26] And as the brutal gang-dominated underground economy came to employ more and more youngsters, so the broader public demanded tougher policing and longer prison sentences to deal with what many people were coming to see as a state of full-blown urban warfare. Political figures such as Texas Senator Phil Gramm — whose subsequent run for the Republican presidential nomination was based around his tough-on-crime credentials — demanded stringent legislation to counter what Gramm evocatively termed "a tidal wave of crime."[27] By the time the crime rates stabilized in the mid-1990s, and then began falling back to the levels common generations previously, an entirely new social equilibrium, based around unprecedented levels of incarceration, had been created.

The majority of prisoners, in both state and federal prisons, are poor and either Black or Latino — although a sizable minority of those serving time in federal prisons on drug charges are middle-class, often college graduates, men and women snared in the seemingly unstoppable War on Drugs. Between 1986 and 1991 the number of African American women in state prisons on drug-related charges rose 826 percent; *and by the end of 1999 over one million Black men, not far short of 10 percent of the African American adult male population*, were behind bars. One in four Black men in their twenties are either in prison, on parole or probation, or awaiting trial. Estimates are that by 2020, about one in three Black men of all ages will have had some prison experience. Since 1980, according to Human Rights Watch, a staggering 250,000 to 300,000 people have served time in New York State's burgeoning prison system. Nearly half of new admissions in New York in recent years have been for drug crimes. The vast majority of prisoners are from New York City. Ninety-four percent of inmates sentenced for drugs in New York are

Black and Latino, although surveys indicate a similar percentage of whites as Blacks are involved with narcotics.[28]

Up until she was sentenced, Lillie Blevins didn't believe it could happen to her. "My lawyer said they were talking about a life sentence. But he said I wasn't going to get it. He said there wasn't enough evidence to get me no time," Lillie remembers. "My lawyer didn't represent me good. We paid him about $6,000. My husband gave it to me, and my sister and my mother. Everybody was trying to help out, to give me what they have. I sold my black Trans-Am car for $3,000 and gave him that." None of the money helped. The lawyer put in a cursory defense, and Lillie Blevins suddenly found herself with a life sentence. Prisoner number 04204-003. "I'd never been out of Alabama before I went to prison," she says, speaking by telephone from her place of incarceration. "I was sent to a prison in Kentucky, then I got transferred to Texas." Another lawyer put in an appeal. "But I losed it. I losed that about a year after I been in prison. Since then I haven't had anything else. Nobody else been working on it." Now, the diabetic prisoner spends her days dressed in a khaki green uniform, sometimes working as a cleaner in the prison for five to ten dollars per month, sometimes just sitting in her small three-person cell. "I still pray," she avers. "Read my bible. Go up to the chapel. It's the only thing I can depend on. The only help I got. I pray to get out and see my mother alive. I pray God to get me out of here alive because I don't want to die in prison. I pray God to see the fourteen grandkids I've never seen. I don't know if I'll get out. I'm just prayin."

Close to a thousand miles east of Carswell, Texas, lies the small, rural town of Springville, in northern Alabama. It is a run-down, cracked-paint-and-trailers community, home to two little meat-and-potatoes restaurants, a gas station, a couple groceries, a high school sponsored by Coca-Cola, and several Fundamentalist churches. It is only three miles, through the woods, from the maximum-security prison of St. Clair.

As of 1999, St. Clair had the dubious honor of housing five middle-aged men who have been sentenced to life without parole for marijuana crimes: William Steve Bonner, Vernon McElroy, Rex David Norris, and two others. Bonner and Norris were nabbed after "confidential informants" brought large quantities of drugs, from state stashes, to them; McElroy was arrested for possession of a bag of wild hemp, which he claimed didn't contain enough THC to produce a high. Whether he was right or wrong isn't known, because the state failed to conduct the necessary tests.

Bonner was arrested under a highly dubious "anticipatory warrant." Agents didn't tell the magistrate who issued it that they suspected drugs were already in Bonner's possession; instead they asked for the warrant on the understanding drugs would be present at Bonner's house at the time of the search—brought into his house by the informant at a pre-arranged time. Previously convicted of motorcycle theft and marijuana possession, and frequently in trouble as a teenager with the cops in the small town of Tuscaloosa, where he grew up, Bonner was sentenced, as a habitual offender, to life in prison without parole. He went from being a well-paid, tax-paying heavy-machinery operator with a three-bedroom house in Tuscaloosa, three children, a wife and hopes for the future, to being prisoner number 112711X in a maximum-security facility. "When I heard the sentence," Bonner's sixty-six-year-old mother, Helen, recalls, "I died. I could not believe it. Steve is my first-born. It's the hardest thing to visit him and then leave him locked up in an iron cage. It's horrible." A Fundamentalist Christian, Helen calls down fire and damnation, plagues and car accidents on those who are responsible for her son's sentence. "When you send a man to prison, you send his family as well," she explains in self-justification. "The sentence isn't just to the one being tried. It's to the whole family as well. We all feel the pain, the torment."[29]

In Mobile, Alabama, Thomas Haas, a long-serving criminal defense attorney, says that he knows "at least fifteen or twenty people who have got life without parole down here in the last year or two—including one juvenile." Bordering on despair, the sardonic old lawyer says he will no longer represent drug cases such as Blevins or Bonner. "I can't help them," he explains. "So I can't take their money. They're doomed. The ones who are getting out are the ones who are snitching on their mothers, fathers, friends, cousins, anybody they can. It's a terrible condemnation of this country and the people who live in it."[30]

Warehousing millions of people for petty crimes has become America's number one Public Works program, what the radical sociologist Mike Davis calls "carceral Keynesianism."[31] The reference is to the economist John Maynard Keynes, who urged governments to spend their way out of the Great Depression, through throwing vast sums of money into public works programs that could employ the unemployed and provide them with enough spending money to rejuvenate depressed local economies. Now, Davis argues, instead of dams, roads, and grand public buildings, instead of rural electrification programs and hospitals, the public works of our age are the sprawling concrete prisons. And nowhere more so than in Davis's state of California.

Half a continent away from St. Clair, across the prairies, over the Rocky Mountains, across the sprawling western deserts, California's incarceration industry is big business. Super-hi-tech prisons such as the one now housing Billy Ochoa are sprouting up across the state, no money spared. Take a drive down any rural highway in the state, whether it be in the mountains of the Sierra Madre, the spectacular coastal route of Highway 1, or the concrete roads through the inland desert, and you will pass a new prison. Local newspapers advertise job fairs at which these institutions seek out the local talent and local politicians trumpet their achievements in bringing such employment into the district. Each prison costs hundreds of millions of dollars to build, and guards, represented by the politically powerful California Correctional Peace Officers Association, are attracted to the industry by the relatively high salaries. Says Bruce Gomez, the community resource manager at the 1.7 million-square-foot super–maximum security Corcoran prison (home to, among others, Charles Manson, and Bobby Kennedy's assassin, Sirhan B. Sirhan), "a correctional officer, with a high school education's starting salary is $2,500 a month. Their counterparts

round here [in a remote agricultural region in the Central Valley] make
$1,200 to $1,600 a month outside. So it's a real sought-after job."[32]

Behind the razor-wire fences, the deadly electronic barrier (covered
with netting to stop the birds from flying into a nasty surprise), the
computer-operated gates, and the watchtowers, a vast complex is laid
out, low-lying under the immense blue California sky; concrete blocks
each one housing hundreds of prisoners, each either confined to a private cell or double-bunked with another inmate, lead onto large exercise
yards, watched over by gunners ready at the first hint of trouble to set
the red alarms off. Deep inside the complex, a series of "pods" contain
the Secure Housing Unit inmates—men, like Charles Manson, who are
segregated from the general population and kept in conditions of near
isolation. Even deeper inside are the workshops—a dairy, a metal-
working unit, a furniture shop. There is a medical facility and a mental
unit, convenience stores, and a gym—currently being used to house
overflow prisoners. In a real sense this is a town, albeit a highly auto-
cratic, violent sort of town, unto itself.

California's Department of Corrections estimated in the late 1990s
that the state's prison numbers might hit 300,000 in the not-too-distant
future; although recently the state's prison population has given some
signs of stabilizing, and possibly even declining slightly.[33] Since it costs
over $20,000 per year to incarcerate one person, $35,000 to incarcerate
them in solitary confinement, and over $60,000 to incarcerate and pro-
vide medical care to elderly inmates, the RAND corporation and other
researchers have concluded that over the next twenty years, California's
investment in its once-vaunted public universities will dramatically
wither away as the state struggles to find money to pay for new prisons
and to staff existing ones.[34] Already the state's elementary school system
is in such disarray, partly as a result of two decades of spending cuts,
that its fourth graders scored second to bottom in the country in a recent
study of reading ability.[35]

Over the past two decades, California's Department of Corrections,
along with those of Texas, Illinois, Pennsylvania, a handful of other
states and the federal prison system's facility at Florence, Colorado,

have perfected the panopticon, a control mechanism dreamt up by eighteenth-century English philosopher Jeremy Bentham. The panopticon was a space in which a person in a central room could see into every nook and cranny of the institution, thus denying inmates even the barest modicum of privacy. California's computerized prisons, built as a series of bleak concrete cell "pods" radiating out from central control rooms, watched over by gunners, surrounded by razon-wire fences and lethal electric barriers, offer up as little chance of escape as a Nazi concentration camp. New "level four" institutions at Corcoran, Pelican Bay, and High Desert—a prison deep within the mountainous landscape north of the preternaturally blue Lake Tahoe—have been built specifically to house the worst of the worst, according to Pelican Bay's Deputy Warden Joe McGrath; to isolate predatory, dangerous prisoners, people who "preyed upon other prisoners and were assaultive." Since the new prisons were created ten years ago, violence within the prison system as a whole *has* indeed declined.

In Pelican Bay, like Cororan a huge camp, this one in the rainy north, just south of the Oregon border, on ground that used to be lumber land, 40 percent of the 3,242 inmates are lifers. At any one time, between 1,300 and 1,500—those deemed a threat to other inmates, those with known gang affiliations—are housed in a Secure Housing Unit. There, behind perforated orange metal doors, they remain isolated in their cells, eight feet by ten feet, approximately twenty-three hours per day. When they receive visits—which is rare, since Los Angeles, where most of the prisoners are from, is a sixteen-hour drive to the south—they visit through a bulletproof glass window. Anybody from the outside admitted onto the SHU has to don a bulletproof vest to guard against sharpened debris being launched through the perforated doors. Most are there for an "indeterminate sentence," often for years on end. They eat and they shit in their cells. They exercise, alone, in barren concrete yards ten by twenty feet. In some SHUs in America, even the showers are built inside the tiny cells. This is, says Lieutenant Ben Grundy, an African American and himself an ex-marine, "no picnic. We don't want to make this a fun place for them."[36]

Although the prison now has an extensive mental health program — a safety valve that is noticeably missing in Texas's enormous super-max prisons such as Huntsville — senior psychologist Dr. David Archambault says that at least one person a month has some sort of psychotic collapse inside the SHU. When the mental health unit first opened, more than one hundred prisoners were removed from the SHU with severe mental disturbances. Many isolated prisoners routinely self-mutilate as an expression of impotent rage at their confinement, slashing at veins and arteries until the spurting blood has covered the walls of their cells in a spectacular mosaic of deep red slime. Oftentimes, inmates "gas" guards through their doors with a pungent mixture of urine and feces. Violence feeds on violence here, and the guards themselves have been known to abuse inmates in return. In Corcoran in the mid-1990s, guards routinely organized "gladiatorial" combats between rival gang members in the small triangular exercise yards. The guards would then proceed to shoot the antagonists apart. First round, wooden bullets. Second round, for those who didn't stop fast enough, high-impact explosive bullets. Seven inmates were killed and numerous others injured over the years before the practice was eventually exposed, and the prison's administration was overhauled. Yet, despite grainy black-and-white videotapes of the incidents that were captured by the security cameras, juries in California refused to find any of the officers responsible for the deaths of these inmates.

In Pelican Bay, a full day's drive north of Corcoran, an African American inmate who had gone mad in isolation and had covered his body in shit, was dropped by guards into a tub of scalding water, and held down in it until the skin boiled off his legs. "Nigger, we're going to scrub you until you're white," the guards were quoted as telling their victim.

Few Californians know about Pelican Bay and, according to Mc-Grath, even if they did, hard time stories generally wouldn't concern them. "The average person out there in society isn't very concerned about the criminal," he asserts. "They just want to be able to conduct their life without becoming a victim." Somewhat pensively for a prison official, McGrath goes on to say that "the things, like family, that have held us together as a society are breaking down, and we now expect prisons to socialize people. There're a lot of things we need to be working on as a society and a culture to treat the illness rather than just the symptoms." But, twenty-first century America is showing no signs of a new War on Poverty. And so the prison numbers continue to rise. How many prisoners is too many in a supposedly free society? "I guess I'd have to ask the question: What is the alternative?" McGrath answers slowly. "I'm somewhat of a utilitarian on this. I'd weigh the cost and I'd weigh the benefit. I'm a civil servant and I'm here to serve the state. If that's what the people want, I'm here to implement that."

FOUR

Sometimes it seemed as if Billy Ochoa's whole life had been nothing but a prelude to a finale behind bars.

The first time Billy took heroin he was sporting a fancy brown leather belt and a pair of expensive cordovan shoes. He also had a wispy thin pencil mustache hovering above his upper lip. He was nineteen, had just come out of detention in the California Youth Authority camp in Ontario, and he had some catching up to do with one of his older cousins, Jamie. [Author's note: "Jamie" is a pseudonym used in place of his relative's real name.]

Since Billy was fourteen and his cousin sixteen, the pair had been in and out of trouble, in and out of California Youth Authority camps. Camp Jo Scott. Camp Oak Grove, up in the picturesque San Gabriel Mountains. They were young toughs, out for a good time and not afraid to break the law in pursuit of it. Mostly, they'd steal cars, just for kicks. The big, bulky pastel-colored autos that Detroit was producing in record numbers throughout the 1950s. They'd go joy-riding, perhaps end up at a party somewhere on the East Side, get drunk on cheap satin wine, maybe smoke some grass. Oftentimes, they'd get caught, hauled off before judges, and sent away for a few months of reformatory time in one of the rural camps the CYA had been setting up around the state.

Josie Ochoa, always the doting mother, would pack her other children onto buses, and, despite the painful swelling of her legs, despite all the bodily failings that her untreated diabetes was inflicting on her at an age when healthier, richer women could still consider themselves young and beautiful, off they'd go to visit the wayward eldest son. She'd even take snapshots of her son and nephew standing together at Camp, in the slightly awkward pose of teenagers still uncomfortable with their bodies. Mementoes from her trips to the country to visit her boy.

Jamie and Billy were Trouble: but, then again, many of the kids in their part of town were just as much of a handful. It seemed to come with the territory. The children of the Mexican immigrants in the barrio called it *la vida loca*, the crazy life.

As far back as the 1930s, Mexican-American prisoners, ex-cons, and local toughs, *pachucos*, had arranged themselves into "clubs," *clicas* — with members identified through tattoos, secret hand signs, and graffiti tags scrawled onto the walls of local buildings.[1] It was a way for them to find a protective space in a city whose powerful white elites were deeply suspicious of the Mexican poor living within their midst. It was a means of asserting oneself in a society which either ignored the aspirations of Mexican Americans, or set its aggressive police force to work harassing, beating, sometimes even killing, the peoples of the barrios. Oftentimes, the groups, complete with their own jackets, colors, and membership cards, served as both social clubs and self-protection organizations. "We were invisible people in a city which thrived on glitter, big screens and big names," one-time gang member-turned-author Luis Rodriguez wrote. "This glamour contained none of our names, none of our faces."[2] The gang, Rodriguez explained, was "how we wove something out of the threads of nothing."[3] Two of the largest groupings, Las Lomas and Sangra, had been feuding for literally generations.

Several years before he'd ever encountered heroin, at Hollenbeck Junior High Billy had joined one of these mushrooming gangs, the Midget Dukes; and, after considerable pleading, he had prevailed upon his father to buy him the requisite black leather jacket that would mark him out as one of the cool kids, one of the *vatos* of the gang. Despite his short stature, Billy had taken part in the initiation ceremony — a hazing that consisted of the new recruit fighting four or five bigger guys, all pumped full of adrenalin and wearing steel-tipped shoes to increase the pain, to prove his mettle. And, since then, he'd hung out with the

Midget Duke pack: going to dances; attending rumbles in which teen-agers fought for honor with fists, knives, chains, occasionally even guns; driving round L.A. in the large, tail-finned cars of the day, music blaring from the car radio, looking for nothing more than a few kicks and a girl. Billy's car, which he'd bought off his father when he was sixteen, was a 1950s Fleetwood Ford. Billy was working a summer job and pay-ing his Dad twenty-five dollars a week toward the vehicle. He painted it green, put a "tuck 'n' roll" leather sofa in the back, and set off on a tear around town. One time he was driving so fast, his father remembers, with perhaps just a touch of hyperbole, that the cops pulled him over and gave him a five-hundred-dollar ticket.

It was the age of Elvis Presley. And it was a decade when teenage gang members had models like the scowling, motorbike riding, leather jacket-wearing Marlon Brando in *The Wild Ones* to emulate. Or even James Dean, in *Rebel Without A Cause*. For the teenagers of East L.A., the music of Ritchie Valens—whose original name was Richard Val-enzuela, and who had grown up in the barrio of Pacoima[4]—represented the decade at its very best. "La Bamba"; "Donna"; "Come On, Let's Go." These were songs to dance to and to make love to. Or to low-ride to in a souped-up, personalized, car. Personally, Billy liked nothing bet-ter than turning up the car radio and, as the rock 'n' roll pulsated around him and his Midget Duke friends, cruising for girls, or, at times for trouble, down a palm tree–studded boulevard. Or even the less mani-cured streets of Boyle Heights.

In East L.A. the poverty of "the hills"—many of the backroads of which, in areas of the San Gabriel Valley, were still dirt, with chickens, pigs, and wild dogs sharing the streets with the local people—was a perfect breeding ground for gang culture. Repeatedly discriminated against by the wider, whiter culture, here was an opportunity for frus-trated young men to demand "respect," to show who was in charge. Here was a way, albeit a particularly twisted, violent one, to demonstrate one's worth.

Ultimately, in the years after Ochoa had grown into a man, the thug-gish, though generally nonlethal, *clicas* of the 1940s and 1950s would evolve into the murderous, feuding street warfare that claimed tens of thousands of lives from the 1960s onward. *"De donde eres?"* rival gang members would challenge each other. "Where you from?" Frequently followed by the drawing of weaponry. And as gang activity in cities such as L.A. intensified, so eventually the general populace's attitudes toward crime and—more to the point—punishment would harden to a degree scarcely imaginable back in the days when Ochoa was cruising the streets in his stickshift Ford, decked out in the paraphernalia of his schoolboy gang, the Midget Dukes. Eventually, many juvenile offenders such as Ochoa had been, would start drawing stiff penalties in the country's adult institutions, and adults such as Ochoa had become—local nuisances and screw-ups—would be sentenced to serve the kind of long sentences previously reserved for the very worst of the *pachucos* in generations now old or dead.

In the early 1960s, the cousins' delinquency had taken a turn for the worse. Jamie had been convicted of assault, and Billy, who had taken to using the moniker of "Goldie," had been confined to a CYA camp for his and Pinky's kidnapping of the girl from the party. One of his friends was stabbed to death in a gang fight. Another time, Billy and some friends were driving around in his car when a gun that one of the backseat passengers was carrying went off accidentally. The bullet ripped through the fabric of the driver's seat and went straight through Billy's arm. It was probably just as well for Billy that he'd been sent to Ontario before he'd had time to really hurt somebody. Or to be himself hurt really badly. It gave him a chance to calm down—not much, but just enough to put the brakes on his violence. Quite possibly Billy learnt more in CYA classes than he ever did in the overcrowded local schools. He hadn't finished high school, but at the CYA camp in Ontario he did manage to graduate with a General Equivalency Diploma (GED). Decades later, Billy gained the only real professional certification he would ever receive: as an X-ray technician. Again, he achieved the vocational qualification while serving time in prison.

———

Jamie had been introduced to heroin a couple years earlier, back when you could buy a Number Five capsule, good for two highs, for two dollars. It was a cheap thrill, Jamie figured, "a dollar and you're loaded for twelve hours," and he'd begun indulging every weekend. Heroin, which had entered America in 1898, during the age of patent medicines and quack miracle cures, as the latest in a long line of opium derivates, as a medical curative mainly indulged in by the middle classes, was becoming *the* drug of choice in the barrios and ghettos of the large American cities. Most Chicano gang members in Los Angeles had tried the drug by the early 1960s, according to the sociologist Joan Moore.[5] And if you had the right friends you could *always* find an easy drug connection. He'd buy a capsule off of some friends, break it open, put it on a spoon, and cook it up. After a while, even the smell, an odor like burnt hair, ceased to bother him. Then he'd use a baby pacifier to suck up the mixture and drip it into a hypodermic needle. He'd nurse one of his veins to the surface and plunge the needle in. Pow! There was no feeling like it. Jamie couldn't imagine feeling any better than he felt the moment the drug reached his brain. He'd even go to funerals loaded. It just felt so extraordinarily good.

So when Billy came back to L.A., midway through John F. Kennedy's presidency, it was only natural for Jamie to want to share the good news with him. Plus, somehow—more than likely through none-too-legal means—the younger man had managed to squirrel away some cash while at the camp, and Jamie was hoping he could use twenty dollars of it to invest in a gram of heroin for the pair of them.

They drove over to a friend's house in the Estrada Housing Projects, and Jamie got Billy to take his belt off. He tied it around Billy's left arm, pulled it until the veins popped out, and then injected the heroin into his young cousin's bloodstream. After a few weeks of hanging around with his relative, Billy was addicted, the money that he'd managed to save up blown on the drugs. Even tap water tasted better to Billy when he had heroin in his system.

It was a fate far too many barrio youngsters were encountering. "The sensation [of heroin] began like a pinhole glow at the inner pit of my stomach," Luis Rodriguez wrote. "And then spread throughout my body. There was nothing like it, this rush. And here I was on the edges of a new fraternity which crossed barrio and sex lines, the fellowship of *la carga*, so integral to *la vida loca*."[6] All over town were smack houses populated by tired-looking addicts with collapsed veins and hollow eyes looking toward the bags of powder on the tables, testament to the destruction wrought by the opiate.

From then on Billy was at the mercy of his high. "Drugs was really my weakness," he wrote from New Folsom prison nearly four decades later. Even as the boy matured into the man, and his adolescent appetite for violence dissipated, still there was always the need for money to appease the cravings etched into his mind and body by addiction. "The only crime I did was to get drugs. My cousin and myself thought along the same lines, because we both used drugs." In another letter, Billy writes, "I don't blame anyone for my criminal history. I just happen [sic] to go down the wrong road. I guess drugs was my great downfall. It came a time when I became a little depressed that I would use Heroin to make me feel good; and I liked the way Heroin made me feel. So the only people I associated with was people that used drugs. Heroin. Because it was easy to talk to these kind of people and we had drugs in common."

Billy Ochoa was born in the spring of 1943, in White Memorial Hospital on the corner of First and Fickett streets, just east of Downtown Los Angeles. It was a small building, a two-storied cream-colored edifice, surrounded by a garden sprinkled with palms, as good a place as any to make an entrance onto the grand stage of life.

A year previously, Billy's parents, William Senior and Josephine Cata, had gotten married. They were young, she seventeen (everyone called her "Josie"), he nineteen. William had just come off a stint working as a cleaner for the Pacific Railroad Company.

Like thousands of other Mexicans, the Ochoa family had worked their way northward and then westward at the tail end of the nineteenth century. At the time, Mexico was being stifled under the dictatorship of Porforio Diaz, and wages for Mexican peasants during these years were pitifully low—sometimes under ten cents a day. Meanwhile, across the border, employers were paying more than ten times that amount. Railway lines had recently been constructed linking the Mexican interior to Texas, Arizona, New Mexico, and California; and labor recruiters were working the land in the central and northern states of Mexico, luring workers north with the promise of high wages. For the United States, fulfilling what was popularly perceived as its Manifest Destiny, was busily taming a continent, and needed all the extra work-hands it could get. Sometime during that period, William Ochoa Senior's grandparents had joined the migration. William's father had been born in the bustling border town of El Paso, Texas, in 1884, and had hopped trains westward to Los Angeles at the age of thirteen. There, in the first decade of the new century, he had met Victoria St. Onge, and they had gotten married.

By 1920, at the end of ten years of political turmoil and revolution in Mexico, more than 100,000 *Mexicanos*—as they called themselves— were living in the City of Angels. A decade later, that number had almost doubled again. Mainly working as unskilled laborers in the packing houses, stockyards, rubber and auto factories, most lived near the old Plaza—the focal point of the Spanish pueblo that dated back to 1781; back to the days when Alta California was a northern province in the vast empire of the Spanish New World; back to a lost world of ranches, imposing Catholic Missions around which dispossessed Indians congregated, and the 141 pueblo settlers who made up the first Angeleno census in 1790. This was an America that had evolved independently of the thirteen British colonies of the eastern seaboard, that had played no part in the War of Independence, that had only become a part of the United States in 1848 at the conclusion of the two-year-long Mexican-American war. Geographically and historically, California was tied to its southern neighbor.

Through the 1880s, Los Angeles had been a small town—really nothing more than a glorified market, in which were traded livestock and agricultural produce. Then, as migrants from the eastern and midwestern states began descending on California, and as the pace of immigration from Europe picked up, L.A. started to expand. Buoyed by ambitious water projects that provided the dry landscape with copious amounts of water from the Colorado River and the lusher northern parts of the state, and by flamboyant voices of boosterism such as that of *Los Angeles Times* owner General Harrison Gray Otis, the city grew and grew. The warm climate, gorgeous sandy beaches, and soaring mountains attracted the movie industry, and the movie industry attracted more migrants, and so the city expanded—like a green caterpillar endlessly eating away at the hills and desert around it. And as it ballooned, so a network of electric trolley cars and railways developed to bring workers into the center of the city from the outlying districts. By the mid-1920s, according to the historian Ricardo Romo, the "Red Cars" were carrying over 100 million passengers a year. The Los Angeles Pacific Electric Railway had recently expanded its service to areas east of Downtown, to communities such as Brooklyn Heights, Boyle Heights, and Ramona. To these areas, tens of thousands of poorer immigrants began to move.

Over 20,000 Jews were living in the hills and "Flats" of Boyle Heights by 1930, up from a mere three households in 1908. They shared the terrain with Italians, 7,000 members of a religious sect from Russia known as the Molokans, Poles, and an increasing number of Mexicans. Then, as many white immigrants climbed up the economic ladder, bought cars, and moved to suburbia, areas such as Boyle Heights became increasingly Mexican. Kept from the good jobs by discriminatory hiring practices and inadequate access to the segregated school system of Los Angeles, prevented from moving to the suburbs by a thick web of covenants and restricted housing codes, the Mexicanos increasingly concentrated in East Los Angeles. "In contrast to the overall population of Los Angeles," University of Texas historian Ricardo Romo wrote in *History of a Barrio: East Los Angeles*, "which lived in a fragmented metropolis par excellence, the Mexican community emerged by 1930 as a group tightly clustered residentially and socially." Thirty-five thousand Mexicans were living in Belvedere; and in the slightly more upscale areas of Boyle, Brooklyn, and Lincoln Heights, the still racially mixed neighborhoods were starting to give way to a more exclusively Mexicano population.

There, families struggled to survive in a city that identified itself as a mainly white, mainly Protestant, mainly conservative heartland kind of town. Despite the immigrants from southern and eastern Europe, most of the whites that lived here were Anglos, many of them internal migrants from the farmbelt of the Midwest, conservative types who had fled the Dust Bowl during the 1930s, often with nothing more than the broken-down bundles they had strapped to the roofs of their cars. Long-time Californians sometimes referred to them derogatorily as "Okies." They were unfamiliar with the language and the culture of their Mex-icano neighbors; and their unfamiliarity often bred contempt and fear. Many restaurants and businesses barred Mexicans from their premises; schools in Mexican areas were overcrowded, underfunded, and often staffed by teachers of the worst caliber—who would sometimes take it upon themselves to hit students of theirs who persisted in speaking Span-ish during class time; realtors generally refused to sell houses in "white" neighborhoods to those with darker skin tones; and factories often straight out refused to hire anyone of Mexican descent.[7] Those with political and economic clout were, it seemed, doing everything they could to keep their Mexican neighbors out of the American party.

Worse still, the police and the press seemed to agree that Mexicanos were biologically predisposed to commit as much crime as possible, in as bloodthirsty a manner as any human could conceive, and that they were also a lazy people incapable of bettering their impoverished lot. As early as 1910, local newspapers were giving overly sensational cov-erage to supposed Mexican attacks against merchants and shoppers in the Downtown business district. And the LAPD had made it virtually official policy to arrest as many Mexicano youth as possible. "Police regularly arrested whole groups of Mexican American juveniles who congregated on street corners or on someone's front lawn and charged them with vagrancy, curfew violation, or suspicion of some other crime," the Chicano historian Edward J. Escobar writes. "The police held them for seventy-two hours and, if the suspicions were unfounded, let them

go. In this manner, Mexican American youths began compiling extensive arrest records from a very early age." And since, in those years, the
police estimated crime rates in given areas based on extrapolations from
their arrest statistics, by arresting such large numbers of young men it
was a cinch to then denounce the Mexican community for its depraved
criminal tendencies. The racial prejudice of both ordinary white citizens
and institutions of power were coming together to criminalize entire
communities and to shape public policy, especially toward the urban
poor and citizens of color, around that criminalization.

"The myth of Mexican American criminality," Edward Escobar con-
cludes, "became a self-fulfilling prophecy." It was a destructive circle
that, with variants, had been and would continue to be played out from
the earliest days of the American Republic. The twin pillars of fear of
racial minorities—especially African Americans and Latinos—and fear
of crime would, over the decades, come to prop up the vast prison
system that Ochoa found himself a part of at the tail end of the twentieth
century.

By 1939, Mexicano youth made up 38 percent of the juveniles in
L.A. arrested for violent felonies. A mere five years later, that number
had risen to a staggering 63 percent, and police captain Edward Duran
Ayres was writing in an official report that there was a "biological basis"
for Mexican crime, and that Mexicans as a race lusted after human
blood.[8] Young Black men were also arrested in huge numbers, although
at the time they made up only a small minority of the population in
Los Angeles. This despite the fact that the police's own statistics showed
crime in the city was actually falling during those years.[9] The mass
arrests were supported by the ostensibly reformist Republican Mayor
Fletcher Bowron.

Nevertheless, despite the brutality and the poverty, more and more
migrants journeyed north, seeking what every other immigrant group of
the time was dreaming after. A land of liberty crisscrossed by streets
paved with gold. By the time World War II broke out, even though tens
of thousands of unemployed Mexicans had been pressured to return to
Mexico during the Depression years—many of them given train tickets

to leave by the Southern Pacific Railway and the Los Angeles Citizen Committee on Coordination of Unemployment Relief—hundreds of thousands of Mexicanos were calling the City of Angeles home. Indeed, so large had this Mexican community become that Los Angeles had recently supplanted San Antonio, Texas, as the city with the largest Mexican American population in the United States.

When Billy entered the world, the family was living with William's parents, Cruz William and Victoria St. Onge, in the community of Lincoln Heights. Their house was in a manufacturing area, near an old paint shop and the large San Antonio winery. Railtracks ran alongside their dwelling. It was a wooden frame house, complete with three bedrooms, a small bathroom, and a living area. The two pillars of the front porch presented at least a façade of gentility to anyone looking in that direction. Not a large house, but at least a place they could call home. And it was certainly better than many of the ramshackle tenements being constructed at the time by giddy contractors. On one spot, Romo, wrote, "developers constructed twenty-two one-story habitations on a lot occupying a space of 44 by 171 feet. . . . On each side of the lot stood eleven houses, all of them two-room dwellings, 15 feet wide and 12 feet deep." These "houses" were lived in by families of eight or more people.

William wasn't particularly religious and he usually avoided going to church; but Josie was still attached to the old Catholic faith. And so, at the church of La Placeta, on the site of the old Los Angeles Mission, Billy was baptized. William also hung a painting of Jesus Christ on the wall above his son's bed. After all, given the indifference of the rest of the city to the poverty of East L.A., it couldn't hurt to have God on his infant's side.

Later on, Josie would take her children—first Billy, and then the three who followed—to St. Mary's Church, one of the more than dozen old adobe churches of their neighborhood. Still later, their ailing mother would stay at home and pack the kids off to church on their own; as often as not, the children would pretend to go and would instead walk right past the house of worship and on to the local park.

America had entered World War II a little over a year previously, but William had been classified 4-F. Short, and with chronically flat feet, Ochoa was not regarded as good soldier material. So, while the City of Angels boomed around him—the movie business now supplemented by the wartime aircraft industry—William took work at the Wilson Packing House on Vignes Street, a short walk from Olvera Street, the famed and lively old center of Mexican L.A. There he worked from morning to night cutting up meat and packing it, to be sent off to the boys in uniform. All over town, in Mexican households as much as in Anglo households, front windows boasted flags, a testament to the fact that a family member was off fighting against the Nazis or the Japanese. William hardly had time to see his family. But at least some cash was coming his way.

Two months after Billy was born, in the early part of June, the city was ripped by what soon became known as the Zoot Suit Riots. Mobs of Anglo sailors—many of them barracked in and around East L.A.—along with civilians and even some police officers roamed the streets attacking young Mexicanos, in one of the country's worst race riots since gangs of whites in Chicago had killed dozen of Black men, women, and children in 1919.

Over the past few years, a radical style of clothing, the zoot suit, had found its way into the barrio from urban Black neighborhoods such as New York's Harlem. The suits were flashy and colorful, with long-legged pants—William was struck by the way the cloth flared out, by as much as twenty inches, at the knee—and extremely narrow arm cuffs. The coats had wide lapels and hefty shoulder pads, and oftentimes they extended down to the knees.[10] Accoutrements included a wide-rimmed "pancake" hat and thick-soled shoes. And many of the men also wore their hair long and combed into a ducktail. Of course, like the long hair and tie-dyed shirts of the hippie generation a quarter century later, the appearance of the zoot suiters was intended to convey something beyond a sense of style: here was a Mexican American appearance meant to demonstrate a lack of respect for white authority, an in-your-face, I'm-here-and-what-are-you-going-to-do-about-it slap at the mores of the mighty. Large numbers of the zoot suiters spoke a derivative of an ancient Iberian gypsy dialect—indecipherable to the outside world and, noted Edward Escobar, also "to their Spanish-speaking elders"—called Caló;[11] and a small minority of them adopted the full-blown bad-boy criminal image of the *pachucos*.

By the early 1940s, more than two-thirds of young Mexican American men in L.A. were wearing all, or some part of, the zoot suit uniform.[12] William and his relatives, however, wanted nothing to do with the craze. It was, William later recalled, "a bunch of baloney," a fad adhered to by "a different breed of people. I didn't want nothing to do with them." Like so many of the *pachucos'* critics, William, putting in up to eighteen hours a day at the packing factory, was offended by the fact that most of them didn't work. As a newly married man, he felt he had too many responsibilities to get mixed up in that world of crime, tattoos, street fights, and confrontation.

Now, with the country at war, and with the government urging austerity and abstinence in the name of victory, the flamboyant zoot suits worn by many hipsters in the barrio, especially those who made up the *pachuco* gangs, served as red flags to a bull. At a time when millions of young men were putting on uniforms, and when clothing manufacturers were being pressured to design more cloth-efficient styles, the colorful, ostentatiously excessive, cloth-heavy zoot suits flew in the face of the prevailing war ethos. Fueled by ever more sensational newspaper headlines that had manufactured a largely mythical Mexican juvenile crime wave over the previous years, the white citizenry of the region had fused their fear of crime with their intense dislike of the young zoot suit culture into the explosive fury of the mob. "Zoot Suit Revolution" the *Los Angeles Times* proclaimed. "Zoot Suiters Blamed in New Killing," blared another paper.[13]

After a series of scuffles between groups of sailors, out on the town, and zoot suit–wearing Mexicanos, the papers warned sailors that their antagonists were out for blood. Perhaps not surprisingly, the sailors, many of them bored and looking for adventure, took the bait. They were, William thought, jealous of the zoot suiters, most of whom had 4-F exemptions from the army, and who seemed to be living the high life while others went off to fight in Europe and in Asia. From June 3 until June 10, in a quintessentially Los Angeles upheaval, hundreds of sailors cruised through the barrios in fleets of hired taxis, stopping the cabs whenever they saw boys and men in zoot suits, and getting out to beat their victims senseless. "Zoot Suiters Learn Lesson in Fight with Servicemen," the *Times* crowed on June 4.[14] Over the coming days, hundreds, then thousands, had their offending apparel ripped from their body, to be left naked and injured in the streets. Citizens joined in. And, it soon became apparent, the police were content to either let the sailors go about their business, or—if the zoot suiters tried to defend themselves—to step in and themselves throw their fists and billy clubs around before arresting the young Mexicano men.

By June 7, the *pachucos* had begun to organize the barrios in resistance. That day bands of young men met the sailors with fists, bottles, and knives; and the streets of Downtown L.A. eastward became a bloody, sprawling free-for-all. The next day, military authorities finally declared the area out-of-bounds to the servicemen.

But it wasn't until June 10, a full week after the rioting had begun, that the epic pogrom subsided. By then, more than six hundred Mexicanos had been arrested, and thousands had been injured. It was, wrote the author and lawyer Carey McWilliams, a miracle that nobody had been killed in the days of violence.[15] By then, too, the *pachucos*, previously shunned by most as hoodlums, had acquired a potent reputation as desperadoes; as street-fighting heroes who had refused to sit back and let the mob rampage through their homes and neighborhoods. Even William felt that the soldiers and sailors had exaggerated the zoot suiters' misdeeds as an excuse for a good old-fashioned street brawl. The media frenzy, and the police prejudice, had created the riots. And the riots had, paradoxically, enhanced the reputation of the very gangs that had provoked such fear in the first place. Down the road, boys like the teenage Ochoa would be initiated into these burgeoning organizations; and still further down that road, when the voting public's next spasms of anticrime fear—also fueled by banner headlines—resulted in the metaphorical rampage of the Tough-on-Crime and Three Strikes movements, the descendants of the zoot suiters, both African American and Latino, would again bear the brunt of the popular fury. By the mid-1990s, in Ochoa's home state of California, just over one-third of prisoners would be Hispanic and just under one-third African American.[16] And nationally, by the year 2000, groups such as the D.C.-based Sentencing Project and sociologists such as Jeff Manza, at Northwestern University, and Christopher Uggen, of the University of Minnesota, were estimating that close to one in three Black men born in the 1990s in America would spend time in prison at some point during their lives, and in many states upward of one-third of Black men would end up losing their right to vote because of felon disenfranchisement laws.[17]

After the war ended, William's older brother Rudy, who had served as an infantry sergeant and a cook in the armies that had liberated France, Belgium, and Holland, returned to civilian life. The two brothers decided to go into business together. Somewhere along the way, William had bought a flatbed truck for himself—a red 1938 International Tractor, the kind that drivers used to call a "bobtail." It was, the brothers figured, a perfect sort of vehicle for selling vegetables and fruit from.

Rudy—twelve years older than his kid brother—and William got the necessary permits and started to work. Every morning, at five o'clock, they'd get up, drive to the wholesale market at Seventh and Central down by City Hall, and stock up on lettuce, tomatoes, chili, apples, watermelons, and whatever else was on sale that day. They'd pile the food into the back of the bobtail and start driving around East L.A.— like the ice-cream men today. William didn't speak much Spanish; he was an English-speaking child of immigrants, speaking a tongue that the *pachucos* derogatorily called *gabacho*. But he taught himself enough of the mother language to get by in the business. Rudy usually brought a little flask of whiskey, which he'd slurp from at breakfast; and, as the hours went by, the older man would get progressively drunker. After all, it was hard work but not complicated work, and you could hawk the produce just as well hammered as stone-cold sober. His younger brother preferred a couple bottles of the local beer. Balboas, 102s. Rudy and William could sell a small watermelon for thirty-five cents; a large one for as much as a dollar. Most days, the brothers would work late into the night. If the Ochoa boys were lucky, they could each clear as much as ten dollars a day. Rudy would go out and find young women to spend his money on. William would arrive home exhausted, sleep for a few hours, and then begin the whole process again the next morning. It didn't make for the happiest home environment—William and Josie were spending much of their time shouting at each other these days— but there didn't seem to be any easier way of making money.

Now, William felt that he could afford to move his family into their own house. He and Josie had had a second son, Kenneth, in 1945, and the old house by the railway tracks was beginning to feel a little too crowded. So, in 1946, using a $1,000 gift from Josie's mother as a down payment, William bought the family a little grayish-blue wooden bungalow house on Matthews Street, in Boyle Heights, a couple miles south of his parents' abode. The previous owner, Mrs. Smitters, sold it to the Ochoas for $4,500. And their mortgage payments came to forty dollars a month. The house was tiny, a shabby construction barely bigger than the garages attached to the larger houses in the more affluent parts of the city. "It was," William was fond of saying, "the kind of house where you walk in the front door, take a step, and you're out the back door." But, the way he and Josie looked at it, with so many demobilized soldiers returning, starting families and looking to buy property, and with the housing market as tight as it was, they were lucky to have found anything. People they knew were sleeping in living rooms, in the backrooms of stores, in cars even, sleeping anywhere while they waited for housing to become available. William bought some wood, got out his hammer and nails, and partitioned the already minuscule living room. Behind the wall, he created an extra bedroom. Sleeping in bunk beds, the boys shared this room. William painted the wooden walls of the house beige. And the Ochoas settled down as best they could in their new abode.

Josie set up her wringer, to wash the family's clothes, on the minuscule back porch.

Photos of Billy from this period show him on the sidewalk outside the house, across the street from the sprawling buildings of Roosevelt High School, a smiling child in a buttoned-up jacket, a white sailor's cap perched on his small-boy head.

Things certainly weren't perfect for the Ochoa family, but, as the postwar boom spread wealth throughout California, even people as far down the social scale as William and Josie were managing to save up some money and buy a house and a car and, later on, a television for the children.

In these years, with defense industry money pouring into Los Angeles and tens of thousands of ex-soldiers choosing to relocate their families in the eternally sunny state, entire tracts of farmland, orchards, and desert were being eaten up by tract-housing developments, and the city was soon spilling over its traditional boundaries in all directions. With its allure of easy sex, drugs, fame and fortune, the city was, depending on how one looked at it, either an embodiment of heaven or of hell. Quite possibly of both. It was rapidly becoming a city of cities; a sprawling megalopolis of dozens of practically autonomous towns, strung along necklaces of glittering, neon-lit freeways, each with their own malls and cinema complexes, drive-ins, restaurants, parks and—in many cases— police departments. While the older cities of the East and Midwest boasted suburbs built around a core epicenter at the heart of the city, in L.A. the center only seemed to retain its meaning by the grace of the periphery. Take away the *idea* of Los Angeles, the seductive dream of "Hollywood", and there was very little to prevent each minicity from going its own way. Unlike New York, where neighborhoods crowded upon each other so intensely that residents couldn't help but intermingle, share dreams and fears, and swap and mix parts of their cultures, L.A. was maturing into a vast conglomeration of divisions and lines, of areas physically separated one from the other by freeways, and of populations ever more divided by distance and mutual suspicions.

The Ochoas almost could be said to live in two places. On the one hand, they were Los Angelenos, as affected by the broader political trends of Southern California as wealthy professionals living in the condominiums of beachfront Santa Monica. On the other hand, their daily lives were molded by the events and experiences of the neighborhood in which they resided.

Boyle Heights in the postwar years was a quiet working-class neighborhood, still populated mainly by Armenians, Italians, some Japanese who had trickled back after their internment during the war, but now with a smattering of Chicanos. Some whites, attracted by the burgeoning suburbs, the allure of what was back then a painless car commute along the new multilane freeways that were being developed, and the easy availability of cheap mortgages thanks to the G. I. Bill, had already begun moving out; but the neighborhood was still a potpourri of different colors, languages, and cultures. Near the house was a little barber's shop and a storefront beauty salon. There was a Japanese market and a hole-in-the-wall Chinese restaurant. On the corner of Fourth and Soto, Big Jim's hamburgers doled out its patties. Not far away, on Brooklyn Avenue — later renamed Cesar Chavez Avenue — hundreds of Jewish families still lived. It was a vibrant home to non-white, non-Protestant families who often found nothing but hatred and housing covenants whenever they looked toward the affluent suburbs of which so much was being written about.

When Billy turned five, William and Josie enrolled him at St. Mary's Elementary School. It was a small Catholic school on a hill, a brick building with a shiny metal cross raised above the name plaque, and a basketball court adjacent to it. The teachers were nuns. If the children misbehaved, these nuns would make them come in weekends and work in their yards. To get to it, the boy would walk to the end of Matthews Street, turn left on fourth, pass Chicago Street, and make a left on St. Louis. It was only five minutes from the house.

Billy seemed to like school. He was a happy child, somewhat on the chubby side, alert and full of life. Though perhaps a little on the quiet side. His hair was jet black, parted slightly on the right side, and he had a gentle-looking smile. He wore stiff khaki pants to school, pants lovingly ironed by his mother. "Just an ordinary kid," his aunt Dal recalls.

While he was attending St. Mary's, Josie gave birth to two daughters: first, when Billy was seven, to Virginia. Then, three years later, to Gloria. Now there were four children. Into the living room, went two bunk beds. Now, six people were living in the bungalow on Matthews Street. It was as tight as steerage on an ocean liner.

On the rare occasion he could spare a day from the vegetable business, William would load the family into the truck and take them to the Pacific Ocean Park fairground in Long Beach. Occasionally, they'd journey west to the beach at Santa Monica. William would buy his young children hot dogs and take them on the rides on the Santa Monica pier. One time, he put a sombrero atop Billy's head and took him on a pony ride. Not too long after that, Billy began raising pigeons in the family's backyard. He was, his family agreed, a smart child. If Billy misbehaved, William would try to spank him; but usually Josie intervened. She was not going to let anyone hurt her baby boy. She was, Billy believed, his "best friend." Even later on, when as a teenager he'd come home drunk, or would phone his parents after having gotten himself into a car wreck, Josie would force her husband to stop screaming at their eldest child.

Time passed. Billy began to grow up. He spent more time in the garden with his pigeons. He took on the protective role of older brother, stepping in to stop kids from bullying Ken in the schoolyard. The brothers would go to school ball games together. Afterwards, at night, they'd lie in their bunk beds, listening to the small radio that their parents had bought for their bedroom.

When Billy was eight, his father, William, got a job as a machinist at the Price Pfichter factory in nearby Lincoln Heights. The company made faucets, and, since it was a union job and the postwar economy was booming, William now began bringing home fairly decent money. Plus, in the evenings, he'd still sometimes join Rudy on his rounds with the vegetable truck. For the first time in his life, thirty-year-old William could afford to buy little luxuries for the family. A new car. Toys for the kids. One Christmas, he even surprised Billy with a brand-new guitar. Billy taught himself how to strum simple tunes. He sat outside and played. "Spanish songs. Any songs he could," William recalls.

In 1955, Billy finished St. Mary's and his parents sent him around the corner, to Hollenbeck Junior High. He wasn't the most academic kid in the world, but he seemed to be interested in engineering, in woodshop, and in auto parts. Billy liked to tinker, to take things apart and try to put them back together again.

He also liked to play sports. Especially basketball and football. The young teenager might not have been as tall, or as bulky, as some of his classmates, but he made up in quixotic spirit what he lacked in height. One day, when he was playing football, Billy tried to tackle a bigger guy, missed him and careened straight into a tree shoulder-first. Two teammates had to practically carry the wounded hero back to his house on Matthews Street.

But by that time, it wasn't such a happy house. William and Josie were fighting more and more. And suspicions were swirling about whether the husband was seeing other women. When they weren't fighting, William was out working, or drinking beers in bars with his friends. Soon Billy began stealing cars. Perhaps he was just a punk out for thrills. Or maybe the teenager was crying out for attention as his parents' marriage crumbled.

FIVE

Barely a month after Polly Klaas was buried at the end of 1993, the popular television news program *20/20* aired a glowing report on Mike Reynolds and the Three Strikes movement. As footage of Kimber Reynolds's funeral rolled, reporter Tom Casriel intoned that "a funeral for an eighteen-year-old California girl two years ago has inspired a movement to combat crime." The camera cut to Governor Wilson, dapper in a dark blue suit, a white shirt, and red-and-white-striped tie. "Let's double the penalty for two-time felons," Wilson declared. "And put three-time losers behind bars for life." Then, while showing grainy black-and-white photos of murderer Jo Davis's body lying in the stairwell of the apartment complex where he had been shot by the police, the report cut to a voiceover by Mike Reynolds. "Unfortunately these people have given up their dues cards in the human race," Reynolds told his audience. "They're little more than animals. They look like people, but they're not. And the unfortunate thing is they're preying on us. And we have to get them out so the rest of us can go on living our lives."

With the media playing up sensational crimes and playing down the fact that overall crime rates were actually falling, it shouldn't have surprised anybody that public opinion was swinging ever farther from the old, liberal concepts of justice, and ever more in favor of quick-fix, tough-on-crime actions.

This was Wilson's turf, and the governor knew it. After all, the prison population in California had gone up 300 percent over the past decade, and each year the Department of Corrections budget had soared by an

average of 15 percent.¹ Here was a golden opportunity to drive the unemployment stats, the budget cuts, and the tax hikes out of voters' minds,
and to reverse the 23 percent lead that some polls were showing his
likely opponent, Kathleen Brown, to hold over him.² Already, in the fall,
the Republican had started focusing on "the plague of crime that is
turning our state into a slaughterhouse."³ He had signed a raft of laws
against violent criminals, gang members, drug dealers, and sexual predators, creating longer prison sentences for such offenders and pushing
for a reduction in the "good time credits" they could receive to reduce
their sentences once in prison. He had already declared war against
carjackers and drive-by shooters, letting it be known he would seek legislation to make the death penalty apply in such cases. And his speech-
makers, invoking the opening of new prisons at Wasco, Calipatria, North
Kern, Lancaster, and Centinela, as well as plans for the building of still
more prisons to house an additional 6,400 inmates, were sprinkling his
speeches with optimistic but forceful references to "a great California
comeback against crime."⁴

As far back as August, Wilson's team had been planning how to get
maximum publicity for the governor when he signed bills in September
stiffening the penalties for drive-by killers. Michael Carrington, Wilson's
Deputy Director of Planning and Policy Development, had even sent a
detailed memo on this subject to Cabinet Secretary Joe Rodota. The
idea was to have their man surrounded by police officers and members
of crime victims' organizations as he signed the bill. It was, as with so
many carefully scripted political events, to be a moment of pure theater.

Two of the women who would attend this event would be Bobbi
Murphy, from Sacramento, and Charlotte Austin, from Los Angeles.
Both women had lost children to drive-by shooters and both had gotten
involved in campaigns to toughen up the state's criminal code. Then,
wrote Carrington, "The governor would use two pens for the signing
process; one for his first name, and one for his last name. Before actually
signing the bill, he would look into the cameras and say: 'Throughout
the long battle to get this bill passed, we have been fortunate to have
the hard work and support of two courageous and caring women whose

children died at the hands of drive-by assassins. As I sign this bill, I am signing it Charlotte (turning toward her) for your daughter, Jamee; and for all of the other victims who did not have the protection which we all hope this bill will help provide.' " Carrington's notes do not indicate what Wilson was to say to Bobbi, but presumably the governor was also supposed to mention her lost child too.

And then would come the kicker, the emotional catharsis that Carrington knew would play so well in front of the cameras. "After the bill is signed," he wrote to his colleague, "the governor would get up from his chair and take the pens. He would walk over to Bobbi and hand her one of the pens. Knowing Bobbi, at that point in time she would probably begin to cry, she would thank the governor for sponsoring the bill, and would probably hug the governor's neck. The same process would be repeated with Charlotte with the same results."[5]

But, even with the distressed women and the governor's manly hugs, these types of events focused on easy targets and garnered relatively small political pickings. After all, who in their right mind would stand up before the electorate and *oppose* a law that added several years in prison to the sentences of carjackers who used guns in the hijacking of the vehicles? Almost everyone was for this kind of symbolic get-tough measure, certainly almost any Democrat likely to run against Wilson in the upcoming gubernatorial race, and so its use as a campaign weapon was limited. So the governor stepped up the rhetoric a notch and, wrapping himself in the cloak of populism, began appealing to "the people" to take on the liberals in Sacramento preventing real "reform" of the criminal justice system. On September 18, he told a cheering audience of Republicans at the Anaheim Hilton Hotel, not too far from the Disneyland theme park, that he was going to bring this fight home. "If we can't get enough Democratic votes to pass the death penalty for drive-by shooters," he threatened, "we may again have to go to the people and change the law ourselves, as we've done before. You only have to look at the carnage reported on the evening news day after day to see that our laws aren't tough enough to deal with the thugs on our streets."[6]

Now, in the waning moments of 1993, the public was *really* enraged.

After Polly Klaas's kidnapping and especially after the discovery that she had been murdered, people wanted revenge against the criminals preying on their young; and they weren't spending too much time sorting out the murderers from the petty nuisances. Here was a perfect chance for Wilson to not only identify himself as being tough on crime, but also to label anyone who *did* bother to look at the implications of waging war on *all* classes of criminals as being "soft."

A month after Polly disappeared, Wilson had gone on the offensive in much the same way as had Governor Nelson Rockefeller in New York and President Nixon in Washington in the early 1970s. Invoking scenes of chaos and images of societal emergency, the governor had called a press conference at the Granada Hills Recreation Center. There, surrounded by the parents of murdered children, many of whom were part of a group called Mad About Rising Crime (MARC), he announced the convening of a Crime Summit for the third week in January of the following year.[7] It would be held at the First Presbyterian Church Community Center right in the heart of Hollywood. In the rooms of the First Presbyterian, in front of the cameras, surrounded by the glitz of L.A., community activists, police officials, crime victims, and politicians would gather to discuss crime and propose solutions. Many of these "solutions" would involve the tough legislation that Wilson had been bandying about for years. It would, for example, discuss the idea of life in prison for repeat arsonists—a harsh sentence, but one that Wilson's advisers knew would go down well with voters in the wake of the recent devastating fires that had ripped through the beachfront community of Malibu.[8]

The next day, November 11, Wilson spoke to the Hispanic American Law Enforcement Officers Association in Los Angeles. Then he flew north to the beautiful alpine scenery of Lake Tahoe. In the afternoon, he was back on the campaign trail, this time scoring points before the California Narcotics Officers Association. He reminded them of his support for the asset-seizure laws that permitted local police forces to keep most of the assets seized in raids on suspected drug criminals. And he again called for his anticrime proposals to be voted into law.[9] Four days later he was down south once more, at the Hyatt Regency Hotel in La Jolla, giving the early-morning keynote speech at the California Peace Officers Association annual meeting, once again demanding passage of Three Strikes. No great surprise, the peace officers lapped it up.

The governor took a break from his domestic agenda for two weeks in late November, and went on a tour of Asia's tiger economies. He visited Taiwan, Japan, and Hong Kong, and met with business associations and investment groups that might prove useful to California's Pacific trade connections.

But when he returned, he picked up right where he had left off. Meeting after meeting, radio address after radio address, the governor hammered home his point. Stiffer sentences for graffiti vandals. Truth-in-sentencing to put criminals in prison for longer terms. Enhanced sentences for gun-carrying hoodlums. Laws allowing schools to forbid their students from wearing gang colors to class. He railed against "cowardly assassins,"[10] and he demanded more use of the death penalty. By the time Polly Klaas's body was found, Wilson had tuned his rhetoric perfectly to match the pitch of the general public's disgust. "I promise that California will do everything possible to make sure her killer receives the penalty he deserves," he told the state on December 6. "And I will demand legislation that will lock repeat offenders—like the chief suspect in Polly Klaas's kidnapping and murder—in prison for life without the possibility of parole, so they can never terrorize our children again."

As the year wound down, things began moving quickly. For a whirlwind of anger was roaring through the country and the political capital to be gained from waging war on criminals was huge. On December 10 the governor called for an immediate end to the conjugal visits allowed violent inmates.[11] The next day he devoted most of his weekly radio address to Three Strikes, and to his support of the wide-ranging version that would affect *all* Third Strike felons. He called for violent teenagers to be tried as adults. He reiterated his demand for a One Strike law for rapists and child molesters, and announced his belief that career criminals caught with a deadly weapon should receive an automatic life sentence. He called for a repeal of the Inmates Bill of Rights—a 1975 law signed onto the books by Kathleen Brown's brother, Governor Jerry Brown, granting basic legal protections to prisoners, and acknowledged by friend and foe alike to be one of the high-water marks of liberalism in California. It was this bill that allowed inmates to sue prisons that denied them the right to receive pornographic magazines in the mail, that mandated certain basic standards for prison living conditions. It was, said its critics, responsible for the prison-as-country-club image that the public was so hostile to these days.

Then, on December 29, Wilson performed the coup de grace. In perhaps the most brilliant tactical move of his career, the governor essentially transformed the business of state politics into a single-issue affair: that of waging war on crime, with the ex-marine leading the charge. It was so brilliant that his political opponents could only look on in silence. That morning, Wilson called a press conference at the beautiful Capitol Building to announce to the world that he was convening a special legislative session, to begin the following week, devoted entirely to tackling crime in California and to getting the politicians of Sacramento to bend to the popular will on criminal justice "reform." "There can be no more excuses for inaction on toughening criminal penalties," the reinvigorated sixty-year-old declaimed furiously. "I'm anxious to get these bills on my desk so I can sign them into laws, which will make it easier to get the unwanted criminal element off the streets and into prison where, in many cases, these degenerates belong for life."

Wilson had pointed the weapon of public wrath at Sacramento and had ushered into being a Crime and Punishment legislature devoted, almost to the exclusion of all else, to toughening up California's criminal justice system. It was a political spectacle unprecedented in American history.

Three major, and related, ideological rivers were coursing through the landscape of American politics in the mid-1990s. First, all across the country, politicians from both major political parties were running on stunningly tough anticrime platforms. Second, antipoverty programs such as Aid to Families with Dependent Children were coming under attack for producing a "dependency culture" that bred both continued poverty and also contempt for the social mores of America—and that ultimately led to a degenerate underclass culture hemmed in by crime, drug addiction, and teenage pregnancy. For the first time, Democrats as well as Republicans were seriously talking about dismantling, or "reforming," many of the welfare props instituted during Roosevelt's New Deal and expanded during the Great Society years of Lyndon Johnson's presidency. Thirdly, as the number of immigrants and refugees rose in the years after the end of the Cold War, many politicians had jumped aboard an anti-immigrant bandwagon, associating immigrants with poverty, unemployment and crime, and calling for these new arrivals, both legal and otherwise, to be denied access to government programs such as Medicaid and public housing. In all three cases, wrote *The New York Times* columnist Anthony Lewis, the voting public's mood favored drawing "a line between Us and Them."[12] Between the prosperous, law-abiding, native majority and the impoverished, criminal, foreign Other.

Born out of fear—of crime, of drug addiction, of economic change, of jobs being downsized—and out of uncertainty in the only recently post–Cold War world, a tide of conservatism was sweeping inland. It was somewhat paradoxical, given liberalism's hopes only a couple years earlier, at the onset of Bill Clinton's presidency. But it was hard to deny. Being "liberal" on the above three issues was seen to be auguring political death as the 1994 election season rolled around.

In California—the most populous state in the union, and one that had been setting national political trends for decades—Wilson had fused the three rivers into a single torrent. He was a governor running for reelection as a man who had already slashed his state's welfare rolls, and who was pledged to fight "the tidal wave of illegal immigrants,"[13] to chase the children of such immigrants out of the California school and hospital systems and to support English-only legislation for the public schools. And, like a gung-ho nineteenth-century sheriff, he was the ex-marine-turned-politician who was finally going to kick the backsides of the West's criminal hordes. Several important citizens' initiatives were wending their way toward ballot status, and Wilson wanted to garner the benefits of these movements, to take on the mantle of a populist leader opening up a cumbersome political bureaucracy to the will of the people. He was going to support what became known as Proposition 187, an initiative that denied the families of illegal immigrants access to education and even health care, and he was certainly going to go all out for Proposition 184, Mike Reynolds's Three Strikes initiative.

Pete Wilson's ability to hone in on crime—and the slightly lesser issues of welfare and immigration—to the exclusion of virtually all else might have been uniquely potent; but in the mid-1990s, as the national populace's angst had risen, the basics of this anticrime, welfare, and immigration template had become commonplace for Republicans and Democrats countrywide.

Determined not to appear as weak on crime as Michael Dukakis in 1988, the Democratic governor of Arkansas, Bill Clinton, had proven his mettle during the 1992 presidential race, when he had returned to his home state to sign the death warrant for Ricky Ray Rector, a severely brain-damaged man sentenced to die for the murder of a state patrolman more than a decade previously. Both as candidate and later on as president, Clinton had promised to fund an additional 100,000 police officers. "The Clinton–Gore national crime strategy will use the powers of the White House to prevent and punish crime," the pair's quickly written political credo *Putting People First* had promised voters. "We need to put more police on the streets and more criminals behind bars.[14] By 1994, President Clinton's administration was urging states to introduce Truth-in-Sentencing statutes, which would eliminate parole for large numbers of offenders. And despite early hopes that a Democratic regime staffed by socially progressive Baby Boomers would end, or at least modify, the War on Drugs, if anything this war was intensifying. Each month, the numbers in prison and jail were soaring. Just about 1.29 million in January 1993, when Clinton had been inaugurated; 1.365 million a year later; close to 1.5 million by the end of 1994.[15]

It was a trend that would continue throughout the 1990s, with the prison population growing by an average of 6.5 percent each year, until, by the end of Clinton's tenure, one out of every 137 Americans, or just under two million people, would be living behind bars.[16] If there was one thing Bill Clinton was adamant about, it was that nobody, *but nobody*, was going to be able to attack his administration for waffling on public safety issues. No matter how good his other policies might be, he knew that they would count for naught if the public, fired up as it was on the issue, felt that crime was still spiraling out of control.

As 1994 got under way, the Justice Department was doing what justice departments under Presidents Nixon, Reagan, and Bush had done. It was busily centralizing the traditionally local functions of law enforcement. This time around, its policy wonks were starting to work on an Anti-Violent Crime Strategy (AVCS) that would lead to ever closer cooperation between federal prosecutors and local police departments; and the president was preparing to order the FBI and other agencies "to wage a coordinated war on gangs that involve juveniles in violent crime."[17] Clinton was also calling on states that wanted to qualify for federal prison-building moneys to introduce truth-in-sentencing rules that would mimic new rules in the federal prison system and severely limit parole for inmates. The result could not be anything *but* an increase in the size of the nation's prison population.

Now, with the midterm elections less than a year away, the Clinton administration in early 1994 was pushing Democrats in Congress to get a running start on their tough-talking Grand Old Party foes by passing a mammoth bit of legislation known as the Violent Crime Control and Law Enforcement Act. This was intended to earmark $30 billion in federal funds for local and state law enforcement efforts, $8.7 billion of which would be specifically funneled into state prison construction. The bill would also create a federal Three Strikes law and would expand the federal death penalty to include crimes such as terrorism, murders committed by federal prisoners or by escaped prisoners, and the murder of witnesses scheduled to testify in federal trials. Although largely symbolic — most potential capital punishment cases get tried at a state level and nobody had been executed or, until Oklahoma City bomber Timothy McVeigh's execution in June 2001, would be by the federal government since the kidnapper Victor Feguer had swung from a hangman's noose at the Iowa State Penitentiary in Fort Madison on March 15, 1963 — these provisions were clearly intended to show that the Democrats on Capitol Hill were as capable as their Republican opponents of working out which way the popular winds were blowing and of legislating accordingly. It was a trick Bill Clinton was proving himself a master of, not just on issues of crime, but on matters ranging across the spectrum from the national debt to the state of the military.

Eight and a half months into the year, on September 13, when President Clinton signed the act into law, he boldly declared, "Today the bickering stops. The era of excuses is over; the law-abiding citizens of our country have made their voices heard. Never again should Washington put politics and party above law and order."[18] Here the Democrat was, surrounded by mayors and police officers, basking in the knowledge that he — the man opponents denounced as a countercultural, pot-smoking, draft-dodging, ultraliberal — had just signed some of the toughest anticrime legislation ever. Two years later, all of Clinton's hard work in this area would pay off when the Fraternal Order of the Police endorsed him in his reelection campaign and the Order's president Gil Gallego told America that "rank-and-file police officers have never had a better friend in the White House than Bill Clinton."[19]

The problem was, with both parties playing, this was a game with no end: the tougher one politician got, the tougher his or her opponent had to appear in order to score "out-toughing" points with a scared electorate. And then, the next time the local television news carried a grisly report of some bloody crime (which, given the salacious nature of television news, the low costs involved in sending out reporters and camera crews to local crime scenes, and the ever-fiercer competition for ratings, was fairly likely to be the next day), the public would receive a bracing fresh jolt of terror and demand even tougher laws to tackle this "epidemic." The Polly Klaas killing, Colin Ferguson's mad gun rampage on the Long Island Railroad, Susan Smith driving her car into a lake in South Carolina and drowning her two young children, all added fuel to this fire. Now, with the midterm congressional and gubernatorial elections approaching, even the slightest chinks in the anticrime armor were being soldered shut. Twenty-three states were considering legislation to increase the prison penalties for repeat offenders, despite the fact that because of the War on Drugs the majority of the country's prison population was now serving time for *nonviolent* crimes, despite the fact that by 1994 all the signs were that crime rates were falling throughout America.

Perhaps most indicative of the changing approach to crime were the death penalty numbers. In 1982, the year Pete Wilson was elected to the Senate, two prisoners were executed, one in Virginia, another in Texas. Four years later, with the active support of Senator Wilson, conservative voters in California successfully mobilized to recall the state's chief justice, the liberal judge Rose Bird. Bird, who had been appointed by Governor Brown in 1977, was a lifelong opponent of capital punishment and had voted to overturn every death penalty case that came before her for review. In 1987, the year following the California chief justice's ousting, twenty-five people were put to death nationwide. Then, the numbers declined again, to eleven in 1988, rose to sixteen the following year and twenty-three in 1990, before once more dropping off, to fourteen in 1991. But, that was the last year the numbers would be that low.[20]

In 1992, with over 2,500 people residing on Death Rows throughout the country, 31 people were executed—and for the first time since the Supreme Court again allowed capital punishment in 1976, the death penalty began being used in states outside the old South. That year, California executed, by lethal injection, Robert Alton Harris—the first execution to be carried out in the state in a quarter century. A year later, California began using its gas chamber again. "The number one cause of death for Death Row inmates should not be old age," the governor repeated solemnly whenever he was asked about the resumption of capital punishment. That same year, 1993, with politicians such as Wilson and Texas gubernatorial hopeful George W. Bush Jr. calling for a speeding up of the death penalty process, thirty-eight executions were carried out, and for the first time the numbers on California's Death Row surpassed Texas's. (Jumping forward a few years, by 1997, the number of executions would have almost doubled again, and California alone would have almost half as many people on Death Row as the *national* Death Row total in 1982.[21]) In New York, then–Governor Mario Cuomo, a lifelong liberal who had resisted the reintroduction of capital punishment throughout his residency in Albany, was being battered in his bid for reelection by Republican candidate George Pataki's attack ads on his opposition to the death penalty.

It was the same with welfare. Polls showed the public thought— mistakenly—that hundreds of billions of dollars per year were being spent on AFDC, more than the nation was spending on defense; and they didn't like it. In fact, the real expenditure, while far higher than it had been during the initial, early years of the program, was only a fraction of this, at a little under $25 billion. [22] Now, with perceptions and realities merging in the electorates' minds, politicians promising to "end welfare as we know it" and to put welfare recipients into workfare programs were reaping their rewards at the altar of public opinion.

In New York City, ex–federal prosecutor Rudolph Giuliani was elected mayor in November 1993, defeating the incumbent Democrat, David Dinkins, on the back of pledges to both move hundreds of thousands of welfare recipients into workfare, and also to curb the Big Apple's notorious crime problem. In Wisconsin, two-term governor Tommy Thompson had slashed welfare by 30 percent in six years and had gone further than any other governor in instituting workfare: largely as a result of this, he was ahead by 40 percent in his reelection race.[23] "If, as Mr. Thompson insists, Wisconsin holds the clue to the future," wrote journalist Jason DeParle, in *The New York Times*, "the welfare debate may increasingly resemble a game of chicken," with each party egging its opponents to go ever further in dismantling the country's social safety net.[24]

Meanwhile, at the national level, the radically conservative fifty-one-year-old Congressman Newt Gingrich was busily positioning himself at the forefront of a newly ideological Republican Party; one harking back to the golden days of Ronald Reagan's presidency and determined to take control of both houses of Congress come the November elections.

Gingrich's team was crafting a conservative manifesto, based around policies focus group studies had shown to be particularly popular, that would soon be known as the Contract with America. It would, Gingrich declared with typical bombast, "renew American civilization" and "re-direct the fate of the human race."

Along with the now-standard calls for tax cuts and a balanced budget, Newt Gingrich's hard-hitting manifesto, signed with much fanfare by over three hundred House of Representatives' candidates, included the promise of catchy laws such as The American Dream Restoration Act, which pledged a five-hundred-dollar per child tax credit and elimination of the "marriage penalty"; and The Personal Responsibility Act, which would eliminate extra welfare payments given to women who had more children while on AFDC, would "cut spending for welfare programs, and enact a tough two-years-and-out provision with work requirements to promote individual responsibility." For the first time since the crea-tion of a national welfare system, the Republicans were separating out the need for welfare payments from the supply, positing strict limits on the amount of money available, no matter how many people might be unemployed, or homeless, at any given time. The party was also com-mitting itself to legislation that would deny cash welfare payments to unmarried teen mothers, and that would prevent even *legal* non-citizen immigrants from applying for public housing, AFDC, and Medicaid. Anyone who opposed these policies, was, Gingrich declared, an "enemy of normal Americans."[25]

On crime, the Republicans swore to introduce a series of laws that, in total, they chose to name the Taking Back Our Streets Act. *If you're sick and tired of heinous crimes such as the much-publicized Susan Smith saga*—the tale of the South Carolinian mother who had driven her car into a lake and callously drowned her two young children—*then vote Republican*, Gingrich told the electorate.[26] The promised legislation, the writers of the contract opined, would toughen up truth-in-sentencing laws; allow evidence that the police had seized illegally to be used in court against defendants; expand the death penalty and limit the right of appeal for those sentenced to death; cut "social spending" on nonprison anticrime programs; increase the federal funds available for prison building; and release money to states and cities for the employment of more police. If the November elections resulted in a Republican congressional majority, these fundamental legislative changes would, Gingrich, the self-styled revolutionary, promised, be rushed through the 104th Congress in the first hundred days of its existence.

Back in California, as the new year of 1994 dawned, former lieutenant Wilson was clinging to crime with almost monomaniacal tenacity. He was like a pitbull terrier locked onto a hunk of raw meat, his teeth sunk into the bloody scrap. With opinion polls showing almost eight out of ten voters supporting capital punishment, he began regularly calling for the death penalty for carjackers, drive-by shooters, and hostage-takers. His campaign literature called for immediate expulsion from school for any students caught bringing weapons or drugs to school, and called for teenagers as young as fourteen years old to be tried as adults if charged with violent crimes.[27] Other leaflets trumpeted the fact that Wilson "was the first governor in decades to carry out the death penalty."

State assemblymen and senators allied to the governor rushed to add their voices in the special legislative session. In the first days of January, Republican Senator Bill Leonard, from Upland, introduced SB20X, a bill that would institutionalize truth-in-sentencing. Republican Assemblyman Dan Andal, from Stockton, introduced AB20X, repealing the inmates' bill of rights. Leonard popped up again with SB23X, allowing for fourteen-year-olds to be tried as adults. His colleague Larry Bowler introduced AB26X, defining burglary of an inhabited dwelling as a serious felony—a law that would later come back to haunt the convicted burglar Billy Ochoa, as his Three Strikes welfare fraud trial got underway. Others crafted legislation toughening the penalties for child abusers, arsonists, and wife beaters.

Now legislators who had previously scorned Three Strikes, who had denounced Mike Reynolds's proposal as a recipe for financial chaos and as a destructive intrusion on judicial discretion, stampeded to introduce their own Three Strikes legislation. After all, it was an election year and polls showed that Reynolds's initiative, now backed by the National Rifle Association and millionaire Republican senate-hopeful Michael Huffington, and infused with fifty thousand dollars donated in late November by the California Correctional Peace Officers Association, had overwhelming popular support.[28]

Some, like Republican Assemblyman Richard Rainey, tried to introduce laws similar to that recently passed in Oregon, which only applied to people convicted of three *violent* felonies. But others wanted it to be more of a catch-all law. The most punitive bill was AB971, originally proposed by Assemblymen Bill Jones and Jim Costa in March 1993.[29]

Jones was a Fresno Republican, and at the time was minority leader in the State Assembly. Costa, also from Fresno, was a Democrat. When the duo had first met with Reynolds to begin crafting their legislation, they knew that most of their colleagues would oppose them. Less than a year later, however, the world had changed. As 1994 got underway, so more and more assemblymen and senators clambered aboard this speeding juggernaut. Better to sit up in the driver's seat than to be crushed underneath the speeding wheels.

While the legislators were debating, and voting on, these anticrime laws, the crime summit, intended to maintain citizen pressure on the Sacramento politicians, approached. It was to be the perfect bridge between the special legislative session and the next stage in Wilson's blossoming campaign for reelection.

Sometimes, though, even the best-scripted of events are intruded upon by the blind forces of chance. And such was the case with the January summit. For on January 17, in the early predawn hours, the San Andreas fault ruptured underneath the suburbs of the San Fernando Valley and the region shook with a devastatingly powerful earthquake. As highways buckled under the quake—which measured 6.7 on the Richter scale—hundreds of thousands of apartment buildings and houses collapsed or were otherwise significantly damaged and fires raged, much of the Los Angeles area, especially around the epicenter of Northridge, took on the appearance of a war-devastated apocalypse.[30] In the chaos, seventy-two people died, crushed under concrete and steel, and hundreds more were injured. And the financial losses were almost incomprehensible: eventually, the Office of Emergency Services would calculate them at $42 billion[31] — nearly equivalent to the entire California state budget for the year. Faced with disaster on such an epic scale, there was no choice: despite all the carefully prepared hype, Wilson had to postpone his Crime Summit and instead declare a state of emergency in the region.

But, as the wreckage clearers and highway repair teams set to work putting L.A. back on its feet and the insurance claims adjustors stumbled through the sun-baked rubble, the postponement was only brief. This was too hot an issue to put on the backburner for long; in the wake of Polly Klaas's murder the public was too stirred up to accept such an anticlimax; and it was soon decided that, despite the incredible amount of damage and destruction wrought throughout the L.A. area, the summit would convene on February 7.

The night before, the governor flew into Los Angeles and attended a Sunday-evening dinner at the Simon Wiesenthal Center's Museum of Tolerance. The dinner was being put on to support anti–hate crime legislation, and it seemed an auspicious, noncontroversial start to the event. Early Monday morning, with the cameras clicking, the governor placed a photograph of a slain Manhattan Beach police officer, Martin Ganz, onto a Wall of Remembrance at the Wylie Chapel. And then his entourage sped off through the start-of-the-week rush hour, through streets pockmarked by the scars of the recent quake, to Hollywood, to the First Presbyterian Church, where Wilson was to give the opening speech. As the governor's minders had expected, everybody who was anybody in state politics was packed into the church, summoned forth to hear this two-day progress report, this sermon, on the War on Crime. Attorney General Dan Lungren. Democrat majority leader Willie Brown. Numerous members of the state legislature. Every prominent leader from the Victims' Rights movement. Conservative crime scholars such as James Q. Wilson. Police chiefs. Prison guards. And, best of all, an army of television and newspaper journalists from practically every media outlet in the state.

As the participants walked in, they were handed a little blue program, on the front of which was a sheriff's star, emblazoned with the logo: "California Crime Summit 1994." This was, after all, Hollywood, the town that had imprinted Sheriff Wyatt Earp and the other law enforcers of the Wild West onto the world's imagination, and theatrics never went amiss. Why *not* make crime fighting sexy, make a meeting about criminal justice reverberate with the glitter and glam of the Oscars?

Governor Wilson gave a brief opening speech. He said nothing he hadn't already said numerous times in the past months, merely using the platform to reiterate all his standard calls for tough anticrime legislation. And then, after the plenary session, it was onto the panels for more of the same. Pete Wilson speaking about zero tolerance for gun-carrying students, in the panel on school violence. Wilson demanding that "the worst juvenile criminals" be tried as adults, in the panel on juvenile crime and gangs. Wilson calling for citizens and police to work together "to enforce zero tolerance for crime," in the panel on Taking Back Our Streets. Tuesday morning, the press response was dramatic. "Crime Summit Opens with Call for Tougher Penalties," the *Los Angeles Times* front page headline blared. "Wilson Talks Tough at Crime Summit," stated the *San Francisco Chronicle*. From the *Sacramento Bee*, "Crime Summit's Message: Enough." Across the state, in towns and in villages, citizens opened their morning papers to find crime splashed across the front pages.

After two days of panels, the governor was ready to close the summit with yet another speech. As the soft, velvety dusk spread over the hills of L.A., the traditional smog having been temporarily banished by the cool nights of winter, the politician once again rose to the podium. Having heard the specially convened voices of the people, Wilson knew what needed to be done. Three Strikes must, he declared, be enacted *immediately*. Sexual predators should face a One-Strike-You're-Out law. And, above all, it was time to institute an effective, and *swift*, death penalty. To make sure that the public's voice continued to be heard, he, Governor Wilson, would travel around the state, holding a series of local town hall meetings on the fertile topic of crime.

The very next day, the governor was up north again, in Monterrey, the old adobe capital of Mexican California, and, more recently, the fishing town made famous by John Steinbeck's book *Cannery Row*. There, with the February waters of the Pacific Ocean slapping against the nearby shore, Wilson addressed the California Peace Officers Association's annual meeting. "Even in these tough budget times," he announced with grit in his voice, "I intend to make the tough choices that give public safety priority—even at the expense of other programs." The Crime Summit had been a glorious success, and now, as promised, Wilson was taking the message on the road.

He remained on the campaign trail throughout the month. Finally, on February 26, Wilson wound up this tour at the California Republican Party convention. *Where*, he asked, *had Kathleen Brown, Tom Hayden, and John Garimendi, the three Democrats duking it out for the gubernatorial nomination, been when he had fought for a Victims' Bill of Rights, for more cops on the streets, and for the expanded death penalty?* "To lead the war on crime you've at least got to be on the battlefield! You've got to be present. And in the war on crime, Kathleen, John, and Tom have been AWOL."

The following week, the inevitable happened. Bill AB971, the severe Costa/Jones version of Three Strikes, which had already been voted on by the Assembly, was passed overwhelmingly by the Senate. In the end, the votes were sixty-three to nine in the Assembly and twenty-nine to seven in the Senate. Many politicians who had initially opposed the bill ending up voting in favor out of a fear that otherwise they would suffer the next time they were up for reelection. "I will vote for these turkeys because that's what our constituents want," stated one distraught Democratic Senator, Leroy Greene. "But they are wrong."[32] That Monday, March 7, Wilson and the trailing journalists made their way to the

Hollywood Division of the LAPD. And there, exuding sheer delight, Pete Wilson got out his trusty pens again and, with a flourish of blue ink, signed his name to the most muscular Three Strikes law in the land. "It's the toughest, most sweeping crime bill in California history," he crowed. "And it sends a clear message to repeat criminals: find a new line of work, because we're going to start turning career criminals into career inmates."

PART 2

PLAYING TO THE CROWD

I have found great audience response to this [law and order]
  theme in all parts of the country.
Including areas like New Hampshire where there is virtually
  no race problem and relatively little crime.
—PRESIDENTIAL CANDIDATE RICHARD MILHOUSE NIXON,
  WRITING TO DWIGHT D. EISENHOWER ABOUT WINNING
  VOTES THROUGH TALKING TOUGH ON CRIME.
  EARLY 1968.*

*As quoted in Dan Baum, Smoke and Mirrors, page 11

SIX

Billy Ochoa didn't know it yet, but at that moment, with the public, the press, and the political leadership of California in full battle cry, his fate was sealed. For despite his innocuous appearance and gentle sense of humor, Ochoa was, quite clearly, a career criminal.

By the mid-1960s, William senior and Josie had split up. William was now working at the Price Pfichter Company—in a union factory that paid decent wages to members of Local 387 of the Mechanics Union; nevertheless, to supplement his income, he spent his weekends working for a local tortilla shop named El Sol, delivering corn and flour tortillas, freshly made by the Spanish-speaking Mexican immigrants employed by the company, to supermarkets throughout East L.A. After all the years working the vegetable route, hard work and long hours were second nature to William. He'd done all he could, he believed, to keep his family together; he'd raised the four children, and now they were old enough to get by on their own. William had moved in with another woman and Josie had stayed in the old bungalow, the paint flaking off the wood below. Kenneth and the two girls, Virginia and Gloria, were teenagers, with their own lives and needs, and, despite William senior's absence, the tiny house felt more crowded than ever.

Somehow, Billy just hadn't ever managed to put his life in order. After he'd been released from the juvenile camp at Ontario, he had gotten himself repeatedly arrested for drug and drug paraphernalia possession. In early 1964, his parole was revoked after officers pulled his car over and found Seconal, a hypodermic needle, an eyedropper, spoon, and matchbook on him, and Billy returned to the juvenile authority. By August, he was out on the streets again. Two months later, the young adult went to county jail. He made parole in March of 1965, just shy of his twenty-second birthday, and almost immediately ended up behind bars again for possession of a hypodermic kit. "Probation file indicates defendant was apprehended in a vehicle with another person as both were apparently about to fix heroin," a later probation officer's report dryly comments. In June, the LAPD arrested Billy again, this time for providing a fourteen-year-old girl with ten yellow barbiturate pills.[1]

Within a few years, Ochoa's rap sheet was several pages long. In quantity, if not quality, Billy's criminal career had taken off.

His parents had hoped he would leave his delinquent behavior behind him, an embarrassing memory of teenage angst and braggadocio. But that hadn't happened. Neither William's shouted threats nor Josie's endless cajoling and sympathy had steered their eldest son back toward the straight and narrow. Instead, the older Billy grew, the more his life was defined by law breaking. After he left Roosevelt High, it was the dope that finally turned the boy into a pretty much full-time bona fide adult outlaw. Not exactly a Jesse James or a John Dillinger, but an eighteen-karat nuisance nevertheless. A pest, hovering on the margins, always looking for a fast buck and an easy fix.

As the Ochoa household imploded, Billy moved out. For several years he had tried to hide his addiction from the family. A sort of don't-ask-don't-tell arrangement prevailed. The family knew what was going on, but by unspoken mutual agreement they turned a blind eye. "He was smart," Gloria says. "He'd inject into his feet instead of his arms, to hide the needle marks." He even held down a job for a year working as a machine operator cutting pipe parts at the Great American Pipe Nipple Company. The company specialized in making interlocking pipes—and the long threaded ones that fitted snugly inside other, larger pipes, had somehow been christened as "nipples." Great American's owner was a friend of William's and had offered to hire his son as a favor. But perhaps inevitably, eventually the drugs overtook Billy again and the job dried up.

Now he no longer cared enough to make the effort to hide his addiction. Heroin—bought off a childhood friend, who, rumor had it, had killed somebody in a fight[2]—was the focal point of the young man's existence. Seconal and downers also made their way into Billy's narcotic diet.[3] In 1966, with drugs eating up most of his money, Billy Ochoa overdosed on heroin and had to be rushed to Morningside Hospital for emergency treatment.[4]

His mother and sisters hardly saw him. When he did show up, he'd often be in a heroin haze, sitting glassy-eyed in front of the television and drifting in and out of sleep. Josie worried that he'd leave a lit cigarette in his mouth while he dozed and she'd come back to find their little building burned to the ground. Oftentimes, she'd hurry home from visits to her sister or her friends, panic-stricken lest she'd arrive too late to stop the inferno.

Virginia and Gloria found their elder brother increasingly difficult to deal with. He'd shoot up in their bathroom, leaving a nauseating odor somewhat akin to burning hair wafting through their living space—the kind of smell that sears itself into the mind and a generation on still leaves one shuddering with disgust at all the associated sadness and tears. When he wasn't at the house, Billy hung out with other addicts. Occasionally he'd show up at his paternal grandfather's, Cruz William Ochoa's, house on the corner of Bird and Cornwell streets. "They were pals. They got along," Billy's father remembers. The old man, already well into his eighties, didn't bother his grandson about his lifestyle, and the place was as good as any other to relax and watch the world go by.[5] Other nights, Billy would end up crashing at his uncle Rudy's house. No longer drunkenly working the vegetable truck, Rudy was partying as hard as ever. He'd start drinking early morning and stop late at night. He'd bring home twenty-year-old girls. The World War II veteran was a fun-loving, fast-living character; people got on with Rudy, he joked with them, made them feel comfortable. But he wasn't exactly the uncle most likely to get a wayward nephew to change his destructive ways.

Billy had started burglarizing houses to fund his habit. Stealing televisions, jewelry, whatever he could get his hands on. He'd cruise a neighborhood looking for empty houses, force the lock on one of the doors, and sneak into living rooms and bedrooms. Then he'd go to work, quickly appraising what was stealable, rifling though drawers, throwing valuables into bags. Within a few minutes he was done, and speedily leaving the scene of his crime.

Sometimes he'd store the loot at his mother's house until he could arrange to sell it to a fence. At times, the family would even buy some of it off of him. Josie knew that Billy was stealing, but, as her diabetes worsened and her life grew more painful, she could never quite bring herself to confront her firstborn child. Even when she used the house as security for Billy's bail one time and he failed to appear in court for his hearing, Josie defended him. It was just lucky for the family that the police caught up with Billy before they lost their home.

Billy turned up at his aunt Victoria's house with other people's jewelry. He tried to give some of it to her as a present. Victoria refused her nephew's gift. Another time, Gloria discovered that her big brother had taken somebody else's high school ring. It wasn't worth much, but the teenage girl was horrified that Billy could be so uncaring, that he could take something so personal away from a stranger. More than thirty years later, Gloria still remembered the incident. "I felt so bad for that person," she recalled. But Billy was unremorseful. "When you're stealing in somebody's home," he scolded his sister, "you don't stop to sort through the jewelry to leave the personal stuff." After a while, the sisters lost all patience with Billy. They even stopped buying the TVs that he offered to them at special discounts. "We realized," Virginia reflected, "this could be my stuff somebody had stolen. You get older." Both the sisters were enrolled in Catholic school, where they made their Confirmation. And although they had flirted with joining a girl gang in the neighborhood, neither had taken to *la vida loca* with the zest of their elder brother.

The problem was that while Virginia and Gloria were maturing, Billy didn't seem capable of growing up. His cousin Pat came to think that his inability to protect himself from danger and risk was almost pathological. Fairly soon, he had fallen so far outside the mainstream that it was almost as if *he* were the younger brother, causing endless anxiety and heartache to his more responsible siblings. Gloria would come home from her after-school job, and Billy would be lying on the sofa with one girl or another, drugged to the eyeballs and idly listening to rock music. They didn't have much to talk about. Billy was secretive and defensive, unwilling to discuss his drugs or how he raised money to buy them. Only once, when Gloria was writing a high school project on drug addiction, did Billy uncoil emotionally and discuss his habit. "On heroin," Gloria recalls him explaining, "everything tastes better. Even glasses of water." It was hardly satisfactory, but it was the only explanation Billy ever offered.

Even without talking about it, though, heroin continually intruded into the family's life. One day, the cops were banging on the door, and Billy hurriedly handed Virginia his little balloons of dope to hide. Josie snatched them out of her daughter's hands and flushed them down the toilet just before Billy opened the door to the police. Another time, Billy was so desperate for heroin that he crept into his sisters' bedroom and stole the sixty dollars that Gloria had painstakingly saved over the past year to buy a prom dress. That was when the girls tried to get Josie to ban him from their house.

Opiates had been widely used in the United States since the middle of the nineteenth century. Indeed poppies, from which opium was culled, were legally cultivated in the Arizona territory, California, Connecticut, Florida, Georgia, Louisiana, South Carolina, Tennessee, Vermont, and Virginia.[6] During the Civil War, field doctors had given morphine to thousands of wounded combatants as a painkiller. And by the 1880s, the drug constituted a prime ingredient of dozens of miracle-cure medications peddled to the sick, the tired, and the aching from coast to coast.[7] In addition to the opiates, cocaine had also become an everyday part of the American medical cabinet. "Salesmen sold cocaine door-to-door," the historian of addiction Clarence Lusane wrote in *Pipe Dream Blues*. "It was distributed free by employers to their workers to give them a productivity boost. The American Hay Fever Association made cocaine its official remedy due to the product's ability to drain the sinuses."[8] So many people were taking morphine or cocaine as an everyday tonic that by 1895 perhaps as many as 4 percent of the adult population found themselves addicted to the drugs.[9] By the end of the nineteenth century, sociologist Troy Duster writes, addiction was "probably eight times more prevalent" than was the case in 1970.[10] It was, however, primarily a vice of the middle-classes, of genteel city ladies, and well-to-do men.

Then, in 1898, a German pharmacologist, Herr Dreser, managed to isolate a potent new substance from morphine. He named this diace-tylmorphine, soon to be known in the popular parlance as "heroin." It was three times stronger than morphine, and, at least from evidence presented by early experiments, it appeared to lack the addictive prop-erties that the medical community had recently come to realize the weaker opiate possessed. Indeed, in much the same way as Sigmund Freud, at about the same time, was promoting cocaine as a wonder drug lacking any harmful side effects, so medical opinion in Germany and America, according to Duster, initially embraced heroin "as a cure for morphine addiction."[11]

Of course, it wasn't true. And, as heroin entered the American med-ical market, so tens of thousands more people found themselves inno-cently hooked on a powerfully addictive narcotic.

By the beginning of the twentieth century, a political groundswell was developing to regulate the drug industry. America was changing. The hard-drinking, drug-ingesting frontier culture was under siege by the burgeoning Temperance movement; by campaigners such as the redoubtable Carrie Nation, who fused old-time, barn-storming religious sentiments with a determined opposition to the intake of booze and drugs, and by the formidably well-organized forces of the Anti-Saloon League of America. Doctors, newly sensitive to the impact of addiction, were also urging a reining in of the quack-medicine industry. And pro-gressive political reformers were pushing the federal government to ex-ercise regulatory control over the vast industrial and financial empires that had grown up in the latter decades of the previous century.

In the first years of the 1900s, several states, with New York leading the way, passed legislation to control the sale of narcotic substances. Finally, in 1906, Congress voted for the Pure Food and Drug Act, setting standards and regulations for the production and selling of food and medicines, and forcing producers to inform consumers as to the content of the medicines they were buying over the counter. It was the death knell for the morphine- and heroin-based miracle-cure industry. From that moment on, writes Duster, opiate addiction became a "vice" of the lower classes rather than a sickness or neurosis of the bourgeoisie. And increasingly, the politically influential viewed a person's reliance on drugs as something to punish rather than to either ignore or submit to medical treatment.

In the six decades between the passage of the Pure Food and Drug Act and Ochoa's slide into addiction, America's governing attitude toward drugs had remained steadfastly conservative. Addiction as a social problem would be solved through punishment rather than through treatment.

Two years after the food and drug legislation, the Great Powers met in Shanghai to discuss the world's opium trade. For more than a hundred years, the western European powers had been saturating China with opium, and Britain had fought several wars with China in the first half of the nineteenth century to keep this lucrative business in place. Now, in 1908, Britain and France opposed cracking down on the opium industry; but America—hoping to gain favor with the Chinese, and to thus improve economic access to the vast country, as much as for any moral reasons—demanded strict international controls.[12] In a sign of changing positions within the global hierarchy, America got her way. Upon their return to the United States, the American delegates set to work pushing for domestic drug-control laws against both heroin and cocaine that would set a precedent on the international stage. One of these men, Dr. Hamilton Wright, pushed the agenda through whipping up Caucasian fear of Black men raping white women while high on cocaine. Wright toured the country, speaking on the dangers of drug addiction and on the societal chaos that would soon result if the politicians in Washington didn't take action to stem this deadly tide.[13] Rumors even began circulating that cocaine or "blowing the birney's"—made Black men bulletproof.[14] And with immigration from Southern and Eastern Europe at its height, and a Protestant reaction beginning to take off against this influx of foreigners, *The New York Times* ran a provocative article linking Jews and Blacks together in the cocaine trade. "The use of 'coke,' is probably much more widely spread among Negroes than among whites," Dr. J. Leonard Corning opined, in the August 2, 1908, issue, seven months after Pete Wilson's grandfather, Michael Callahan, had been killed by cocaine runners. "Heaven Dust, they call it. Its use by Negro field hands in the South has spread with appalling swiftness and results. There is little doubt but that every Jew peddler in the South carries the stuff, although many States have lately made its sale a felony." Soon, the public was demanding a war against this devilish threat to its well-being.

The fight wasn't long in coming. In 1914, as Europe slid into a more traditional form of conflict, one that eventually became a world war, the Harrison Narcotic Act effectively criminalized the use and sale of narcotics in America: it forced those making and selling drugs to register with the government, decreed that such people had to pay taxes on their products—thus putting drug control under the jurisdiction of the Treasury Department—and stated that only doctors could distribute drugs, and that they could do so solely for "legitimate" reasons. Paradoxically, because doctors feared that in the newly hostile political climate, *no* drug distribution would be seen as being legitimate and any such activity would open them up to prosecution and prison sentences, most began abstaining altogether from prescribing drugs.

Taken together, the provisions of the Harrison Narcotic Act had the effect of overnight denying hundreds of thousands of addicts access to their drug supplies, without which they could not function. Within a span of months, an active, aggressive black market—similar to that which emerged a few years later when alcohol was criminalized—had sprung up to fill this void, and an entire section of the population, most of whom were otherwise law-abiding, productive citizens, were driven into criminal transactions to support their long-standing addictions.

As the years went on, a vast underground drug economy flourished, and a similarly epic government campaign to wipe out the industry evolved. Like the war in Europe, however, America's drug war proved impossible to limit. Once let out of the bottle, this was a genie with infinite capacity for damage. Congressmen such as Richmond Pearson Hobson took to the newly popularized radio airwaves to inform the fearful electorate that, in Hobson's inimical words, alcohol and drugs made Blacks, in particular, "degenerate to the level of the cannibal."[15] Preachers denounced the moral evil of the drug world.

Soon, thousands of people were being arrested by state and federal agents and imprisoned for their use of drugs. Heroin heads, cocaine snorters. The few doctors brave enough to continue prescribing drugs to addicted patients found themselves harassed, even incarcerated. The further underground the drug trade was driven, the more the number of people caught up within the criminal justice system escalated. In 1918, federal agents arrested 888 people on drug-related charges. By 1925, that figure had risen to more than 10,000.[16] "In 1900," the author Mike Gray wrote, in his 1998 history of America's drug wars, *Drug Crazy*, "the country had looked upon addicts as unfortunate citizens with a medical problem. By 1920, they had become 'drug fiends,' twisted, immoral, untrustworthy. Like vampires, they infected everything they touched. There was no room for compassion here. The only way to get rid of a vampire is to drive a stake through its heart."

By the middle of the decade, the drug wars had grown to include marijuana. In 1925, Louisiana became the first state in the union to make the possession and use of pot a felony offense. Soon, police officers in several states across the nation were confiscating reefer and slamming its users in jail.

————

Of course, by this time alcohol too was one of America's banned substances, and federal agents were actively engaged in fighting the evils of moonshine and the distribution networks by which it reached the thirsty customers. For, as the world war ended, the peace treaties were signed, and nations got back to the more mundane business of everyday living, a political battle waged over the legality of alcohol. Through the course of two and a half years, from the tail end of the murderous fighting in Europe through the onset of international calm, national and state legislatures argued, voted, and passed legislation on from one branch of government to the next. Eventually, two-thirds of the members of Congress in Washington and three-quarters of the state legislatures, would vote to ban the sale of alcoholic substances for anything other than medicinal usage. Indeed, not only was alcohol prohibited, but it was done so by passage of the Eighteenth Amendment to the Constitution of the United States, and the specifics of implementing the ban were outlined in great detail with Congress's passage of the Volstead Act.[17] That way, supporters hoped, the change would be locked into the founding documents of the land and, like the laws repealing slavery, would prove impossible to reverse.

Reluctantly, on January 16, 1920, with but a year left of his presidency, after vetoing the measure first time around, Democratic president Woodrow Wilson signed the Volstead Act into law and America officially went Dry. It was "a noble experiment"—moralistic in tone, devastating in its public policy impact—that would hang over America for fourteen years and three Republican presidents, until another Democrat, Franklin Roosevelt, successfully pushed through a Constitutional Amendment that undid the laws of Prohibition.

Three times in the Republic's history, anti-alcohol movements, fueled by religious revivalism, had swept through the country, with localities and states going Dry in their wake. Between 1846 and 1855, thirteen states, including liberal New England ones like New York and Massachusetts, had banned alcohol only to see the bans repealed a few years later. Again in the early 1880s, following the creation of the Prohibition Party and the Women's Christian Temperance Union, the cow towns of Kansas and other heartland states banned liquor, only to see the movement stall in the saloons and beer houses of the large industrial cities. The third, and most successful movement, began in 1893, when anti-alcohol activists met in Oberlin, Ohio, to establish the Anti-Saloon League.[18] Using churches as pulpits, carefully developing media contacts and flexing their growing political muscle in elections, the League's members spent the next two and half decades building one of the most effective political movements in the country's history. Soon, one state after another was passing laws either restricting, or banning outright, liquor, beer and wine sales. And, by 1913, with nine states already in their camp, the League felt confident enough to begin advocating a federal constitutional amendment completely banishing alcohol from the streets and homes of America.

On the cold winter morning in 1920 when the Volstead Act went into effect, the League saw their dream fulfilled. Finally, after decades of struggle, local anti-saloon campaigns and legislation passed by individual states, temperance had triumphed and, with the backing of its democratic institutions, America had become officially Dry. In the big cities of America, saloons and hotels held theatrical wakes for their lost drinking rights. But, wrote the historian of prohibition Thomas Coffey in 1975, in many small towns "thousands of Protestant churches held thanksgiving prayer meetings. To many of the people who attended, prohibition represented the triumph of America's towns and rural districts over the sinful cities."[19]

Not surprisingly, however, in much the same way as the Harrison Act had failed to remove heroin and cocaine from American life, so Prohibition didn't turn the country's millions of drinkers into bastions of sobriety. (Contemporaries report cars, taxis, wagons burdened down with bottles of liquor bought up by drinkers in the days before the Volstead Act kicked in.[20]) What it did do was to drive drinking underground, to create vast networks of speakeasies and mob-controlled businesses, in short to criminalize millions of drinkers and to provide law enforcement agents with a vastly tempting opportunity for graft and corruption. By the late 1920s, the estimates were that nationwide half a million speakeasies were in operation, mostly condoned or tacitly accepted by local authorities; and in New York City alone, some thirty-two thousand such joints were doling out every brand of liquor from the meanest rotgut moonshine to the highest-quality French champagnes.[21] And this despite the fact that the eighteen thousand agents from the Bureau of Prohibition[22] had upped their seizures of hard liquor from under half a million gallons in 1921 to well over one million four years later; had increased the amount of beer interdicted by 50 percent; and had gone from destroying less than half a million gallons of wine, cider, mash, and pomace in 1921 to destroying over ten million gallons in 1925.[23] Despite the fact that more than forty thousand men and women were arrested for violating the Prohibition laws in 1922, and a mammoth sixty-eight thousand in 1924.[24]

And so, as the 1920s unfolded, a decade strangely combining the illicit good life of the Jazz Age, as embodied in F. Scott Fitzgerald's *The Great Gatsby*, with the religious precepts of Prohibition, the prisons filled up: with small-time alcohol bootleggers, with gangsters involved in the ruthless and murderous underground trades that Prohibition brought into being, with drug addicts and dealers, and, in some areas, with casual marijuana smokers. And, as Prohibition failed to curtail drinking, so, in much the same way as later drug wars unfolded, the penalties for operating speakeasies and moonshine stalls intensified. Theoretically, writes Mike Gray, even though most of those charged under the Prohibition laws had to pay relatively small fines and serve a few days in jail, "by 1929 you could get five years and a $10,000 fine for selling one drink."

In this climate gangs flourished, and crime bosses such as Al Capone became multimillionaires. By the 1930s, entire city governments were in the pay of the mob. And, in response to this increasingly bloody challenge to the country's law code, so more and more highly secure prisons were built to contain the criminals mass-produced by Prohibition.

In October 1933, after years of planning, Attorney General Homer S. Cummings announced that the Federal Bureau of Prisons was buying the island of Alcatraz in the bay off the city of San Francisco from the military, and converting it into a super-maximum-security prison for the country's most hard-core felons. It was to this cold, windswept, island, separated from the mainland by impossible-to-swim currents, that Capone and other equally notorious killers, gangsters, and racketeers would be transported—many of them to remain there until the prison's closing some three decades later. Thus it came about that, as the battle against alcohol wound down, and barely two months before the Twenty-first Amendment, repealing Prohibition, passed into law, the name of "Alcatraz" became added to those of Leavenworth, San Quentin, Attica, and the other state and federal prisons that had acquired almost mythic status in American culture during the course of the country's prison-building over the past one and a half centuries.

But, Alcatraz or no Alcatraz, Prohibition was proving not just unworkable but disastrous. In most regions, so many people were drinking that it proved simply impossible to enforce the laws. And, even when arrests *were* made, many judges allowed defendants to plead guilty during "bargain days," when the stiff mandatory sentences would be replaced by generally small fines. Arguably, Prohibition's greatest impact wasn't in stopping people from drinking, but in preventing the Treasury Department from collecting taxes on the vast alcohol trade and instead channeling those dollars into the bank accounts of the Mafia. Now, with a catastrophic economic Depression raging, there were cogent economic reasons to legalize anew "Demon Rum." And with Franklin Roosevelt—himself a friend of the nightly cocktail hour—in the White House, the end to the noble experiment soon arrived. In December 1933, the last of the thirty-six states needed to pass a constitutional amendment did so, and alcohol was once more a legal drink.

As Prohibition withered away, though, so the fight against other drugs, in particular the newly identified evil of marijuana, intensified. Even before the Twenty-first Amendment, in July 1930, Congress created the Federal Bureau of Narcotics, and appointed the thirty-eight-year-old Pennsylvanian Harry Anslinger to run it. Anslinger had begun his career as a railway cop, but his star hadn't really risen until Prohibition. During those years he had moved on to being U.S. Consul to the Bahamas at a time when the Bahamas was known as an essential step on the liquor smugglers' route, and from that role, had been promoted to head the Prohibition Unit's foreign control division.[25] He soon established a reputation for himself as a hard-hitting law enforcer with an almost missionary prohibitionist zeal. Finally, during Herbert Hoover's presidency, the tough young officer, now equipped with a law degree from George Washington University, had gotten himself transferred to the Narcotics Division of the Prohibition Unit, and, when Congress created the autonomous narcotics bureau a few months later, the one-time railway lawman seemed the perfect commissioner for the job.

For the next three decades, Anslinger, a large, bald, no-nonsense officer, sat atop the nation's drug war in much the same way J. Edgar Hoover ran the more general war on crime from his position at the head of the Federal Bureau of Investigation. Hoover, himself one of the great crime propagandists in American history, had always been reluctant to involve his agents in the fight against drugs—believing it an unwinnable struggle, like that of Prohibition, more likely to lead his men into quagmires of corruption than into grand avenues of success. He preferred to wow the country with daring exploits such as that of his agents chasing and gunning down Public Enemy Number One John Dillinger. The head of the Narcotics Bureau, however, had no such reservations.

Harry Anslinger was an empire builder. And he rapidly discovered that the best way to expand his domain was to make as many hysterical antidrug pronouncements as possible, and to whip up such fear in the electorate that no Congress would dare to stand in the way of the Bureau of Narcotics. So Anslinger set to work. Cocaine and heroin had already been taken care of by the Harrison Narcotics Act twenty years earlier. But marijuana, the wild plant that grew as a weed in fields and abandoned lots throughout the states, was another matter. Long popular among Native American tribes and peasant farmers south of the Mexican border, the era of jazz was seeing an increasing number of Black,

Latino, and white youngsters smoking marijuana joints. In the mid-1930s, Roosevelt's drug chief launched a masterful propaganda campaign that would sustain him throughout the rest of his career. Invoking images of Black sexual predators carousing through the American night and of innocent white youngsters driven to heinous murder, Anslinger urged Congress to outlaw the killer weed. Years later, the aging boss summed up his ideas in the book *The Traffic in Narcotics*.[26] "Marihuana [sic] is only and always a scourge which undermines its victims and degrades them mentally, morally, and physically," he told his readers. "A small dose taken by one subject may bring about intense intoxication, raving fits, criminal assaults. Another subject can consume large amounts without experiencing any reaction except stupefaction. It is this unpredictable effect which makes of marihuana [sic] one of the most dangerous drugs known." As if these warnings weren't fearful enough, Anslinger went even further. "The will power is destroyed and inhibitions and restraints are released; the moral barricades are broken down and often debauchery and sexuality results."

In 1937, as public opinion swung against this new, and until recently only little known, menace, Congress clicked into gear. With the passage of HR6385, the Taxation of Marijuana Act, the last commonly used subculture narcotic was effectively illegalized. From then on, a line would be drawn between the socially acceptable drugs alcohol and tobacco and the "deviant," illegal, narcotics marijuana, cocaine, and heroin.

And, by and large, that was how the drug war stood for the next decade and a half, through the tail end of the Great Depression, through World War II and into the Cold War and early rock 'n' roll years. And there Anslinger remained, a massively powerful figure with a perfect understanding of the politics of fear. When a blue-ribbon panel appointed by the reforming New York City administration of Mayor Fiorello LaGuardia found, in a report issued shortly after the end of the world war, that marijuana had few if any of the harmful consequences Anslinger attributed to it, the Bureau of Narcotics fought back. His team issued reams of distorted scientific data to back up their claims that marijuana turned juveniles into criminals; they accused commission members of undermining American society; and they issued a series of challenges that attacked the "dangerous" nature of members of the panel.[27] "Anslinger understood one thing these other fellows didn't. If the issue is complex, you don't have to win the debate, you just have to raise enough dust," the above-mentioned drug war expert Mike Gray wrote of this event.[28] "Harry Anslinger was on a mission from God. If he had to cut a few throats to accomplish the Lord's work, so be it."

But the antidrug wars still had a ways to go. A few years after World War II ended, as the world divided into Communist and Capitalist blocs, Anslinger again pumped up the political rhetoric. Chairman Mao, whose revolutionary army had recently driven the nationalist forces of Chiang Kai-Shek off the Chinese mainland and into exile in Taiwan, was, Anslinger opined, using opiates to weaken the West and thereby hasten his way to world supremacy. "Today," the Bureau chief declared, "it is the Communists of Red China who are exploiting the poppy, who are financing and fostering aggressive warfare through depravity and human misery."[29] To respond to this emergency, Anslinger demanded "strong laws, good enforcement, stiff sentences, and a proper [and compulsory] hospitalization program." He urged the country to adopt against drug users and dealers "penalties that are swift, sure, and stringent."[30]

Already pushed into a hysterical, intolerant, political climate by Senator Joseph McCarthy's House Un-American Activities Committee and supporters of the Red-baiter such as the young Richard Nixon, America was only too happy to buy Anslinger's warnings. To the crusty old agent's delight, Congress quickly doubled the Federal Bureau of Narcotics' budget. In quick order, the political leadership in Washington, D.C., then followed up on this by passing what came to be known as the Boggs Amendment.

Congressman Hale Boggs was another of those mid-century crusaders who had realized the enormous potential of the drug wars for stirring up the millions of voters who constituted the building blocks of America's vast democracy. He was a tough-talking Louisianan with ambitions to be governor. He was also a fervent Cold War warrior. In April 1951, in the twilight of Harry Truman's presidency, Congressman Boggs convened three days of hearings into the drug menace facing the United States. Armed with Anslinger's broadsides suggesting that dope dealers constituted a Communist Fifth Column, Hale Boggs accused the nation's judges of turning a blind eye to drug peddling, and of refusing to sentence offenders to the hard time that they deserved. By the end of the spring, Boggs had convinced Congress to remove sentencing discretion from the judges, and to introduce an array of tough mandatory sentences for drug dealers. Two years for first time offenders; five for a second offense; not less than twenty for a third.[31] Five years later, bang smack in the middle of President Dwight D. Eisenhower's tenure in the White House, the largely symbolic Narcotic Drug Control Act created more headlines by allowing for judges to impose the death penalty against dealers convicted of selling drugs to minors.

Although only enforced against a relatively few people, Boggs's mandatory sentencing legislation had set America on a course that would eventually swell the prison population to a size beyond the wildest dreams or nightmares of any mid-century law enforcement officers. In many ways, the Three Strikes laws and web of strict mandatory sentences that emerged four decades later were the direct heirs of Anslinger's rantings on marijuana and Boggs's Cold War–influenced congressional hearings.

SEVEN

There was, however, one rather large flaw in the Anslinger-Boggs strategy. And that was that it didn't work. There might not have been as high a percentage of the population who were literally addicted to drugs as at the end of the nineteenth century, but the raw numbers dallying with chemical substances were still huge. No matter how severe the penalties, an ever-wider array of drugs continued to make their way into the community and a steady stream of new users continued to sample these contraband wares. Beat writers like Jack Kerouac and Allen Ginsberg and bebop jazz musicians such as Charlie "Bird" Parker popularized marijuana, and lesser-known drugs such as benzedrine, amongst the avant-garde and middle-classes. Mystic philosophers like Aldous Huxley and then psychiatrists such as Harvard's Timothy Leary began introducing their followers to the hallucinogenic experiences of LSD and magic mushrooms, to drugs so newly introduced into the American scene that laws did not yet exist criminalizing their use.[1] And an increasing number of inner-city residents—peers of Billy Ochoa, his cousin Jamie, and the street acquaintances they scored off—smoked or injected heroin as their particular drug of choice. By the end of the 1950s, of all the leading bête noire drugs, only cocaine, relegated to being a stimulant of the society rich, appeared to have been largely removed from the country's drug scene.

America was changing. After the vicious years of McCarthyism, the country had settled into a sullen apathy—a determined attempt to avoid discussing the great political and cultural issues of the age. Now, however, like buds feeling for the spring air after a long, cold winter, a new liberalism was coming to the fore. In November 1960, the young Massachusetts Senator John F. Kennedy had beaten Vice President Richard Nixon in the race for the White House; and in January of the following year, he had replaced Eisenhower as president. For the first time, the political elite was made up of men and women born in the twentieth century.

Sometimes transformation is as much about image as it is substance. And, in the brief years between John Kennedy's election and his assassination in Dallas on November 22, 1963, it was the picture that America presented to itself that changed most dramatically. The Kennedy family was glamorous, sexy. By extension, in contrast to the staid old statesmen who preceded them, Kennedy's mainly young entourage— the cabinet members and advisers the Bostonian brought to Washington—talked and acted with an air of dynamism and hope. They exuded an almost contagious optimism. It was, in terms of image, the difference between color television and black-and-white. Social problems such as poverty and addiction, according to the new ethos, could all be solved, if only America were to concentrate the might of its massive scientific and economic energies on these tasks. What came to be known as the Camelot presidency may have been short on concrete policy reforms, but its mere existence opened up the doors to more profound, far-reaching, reinventions of the nation's soul. "One could," writes social historian Todd Gitlin, "anticipate a thaw, a sense of the possible. What had been underground flowed to the surface. After all the prologues and precursors, an insurgency materialized, and the climate of opinion began to shift."[2] Suddenly—despite Kennedy's reappointing them, in a doff of the hat to tradition and an acknowledgement of the boundaries set by real politik—men such as Harry Anslinger appeared relics from a very different world.

The newfound liberalism of Washington gelled with other forces transforming the country. In the south, a young preacher named Martin Luther King, Jr. had spent the latter part of the Eisenhower years leading a powerful civil rights movement, fighting for an equality before the law promised by the lofty rhetoric of American democracy but never previously delivered. In the north, campus organizations such as Students for a Democratic Society (SDS) began delivering first a liberal, and then, as the decade developed, a radical critique of America's status quo. A second feminist movement—heir to the suffragettes of two generations previously—was stirring. And, increasingly, the cultural voices shaping American art, music, drama, were the voices of the young. At first slowly, then with the force and speed of an accelerating train, the country transformed itself.

As these youth subcultures developed, so drug use took on increasingly political meanings. Marijuana and LSD in particular came to be seen not simply as accoutrements of hedonism, but also as tools of insurgency. Both those who used and those who opposed use understood it in this way: taking these drugs was thumbing one's nose at the Establishment, and depending on one's point of view, that was either a worthy act or a shameful one. In the later 1960s, as the Vietnam War intensified during Lyndon Johnson's presidency, a lifestyle that revolved around frequent drug ingesting could all too easily be passed off as an antiwar statement and as a rejection of the "mainstream" values that had led to the country's military adventures in Southeast Asia. And as more people threw off their allegiance to those values, so more people began experimenting with one or another psychedelic substance. Marijuana smoking, and the taking of harder, more addictive narcotics, often implied a certain set of views on civil rights, the Vietnam War, sexual mores, religion, tradition, respect for law and order. Increasingly, drug usage, and arguments over how to treat addiction, reflected far broader, deeper divides in American society—divides that would eventually fuel both the War on Crime and the War on Drugs in the decades to come.

As the 1960s matured and then gave way to the 1970s, Billy Ochoa seemed to be enjoying life. The addiction had whittled away his body fat, leaving him fashionably skinny—his taut, angular face almost poetic. His wardrobe reflected the times: shiny gold shirts, flared pants, pointy leather boots.[3] He had a large record collection, and could sing along to Del Viking, The Platters, and any number of R & B groups. He still had some of his Elvis records from his teenage years in the 1950s, and, of course, some Beatles vinyls. On occasion, Billy would visit nightclubs, but LSD wasn't a drug he had any interest in, and so he preferred to stay away from the psychedelic scene. He liked instead to just relax on the sands of Huntington Beach, to sit at home and listen to his records, or to get into his car, the upholstery remodeled into a tuck 'n' roll, and cruise up and down the L.A. freeways, just watching the world zoom by.[4]

Everyone seemed to be on heroin these days — rock stars such as Janis Joplin and Jim Morrison, middle-class kids from the suburbs as well as friends from the barrios and ghettos of L.A. — and, within the heroin world, Billy was keeping his act together as well as most. Some months, Billy would even cobble together enough money to rent an apartment, and he seemed to make an honest effort to gain more stable employment. He was entering a new stage of his life. No longer was he taking heroin for kicks. Now, it was more a matter of necessity: without the drug, he was a quivering, sickened wreck. With it, he could function with a semblance of normality.

During these years a steady stream of good-looking women passed into, and out of, Billy's life. "Mostly just dope fiend broads," cousin Jamie opines. Skinny addicts waiting for their next fix. But one woman stood out. In 1966, Billy had met, and fallen hard for, Laura Camina. [*Author's note: "Laura Camina" is a pseudonym rather than her real name.*[5]] She was, family legend has it, "dark and wild looking," as glamorous as the circumstances of East L.A. poverty allowed. Billy had met her through a friend of a friend of a cousin of a friend of Laura's. Or something complicated like that.

Laura had two young children, one of whom was a boy with Down Syndrome. She was on welfare and living in a small apartment not too far from the Ochoa family house. Unlike most of Billy's girls, however, Laura wasn't a junkie.

For the first time in his life, Billy began feeling some responsibility.

He moved in with Laura and began helping to care for her disabled child.

Unfortunately for Laura's lover, shortly afterward, in June 1967, the LAPD caught him burgling a house. It was the first time he'd been nabbed at this rather lucrative activity, and it marked the beginning of a new stage in Billy's ongoing relationship with the California criminal justice system. Because it was a first offense, Ochoa was released on bail. In quick succession, however, the young man was arrested in Orange County on a separate burglary beef, and so, with the summer paling into autumn, Ochoa found himself a pretrial detainee, shuttling between Orange County jail to the south and L.A. County jail, atop the old courthouse on Broadway, slightly to the north in order to attend his various hearings. It wasn't too bad a life; he'd get up late in the morning and stroll out of the cell he lived in and onto the communal walkways to talk with pals. He played dominoes with groups of inmates. Even the food was okay, though if he had had to choose, Billy preferred Orange County—they gave him little side dishes of salsa to go with his meals there, and sometimes the kitchens served up his favorite dessert: a nice large slab of strawberry shortcake.

Eventually, he pled guilty to both charges and negotiated that he would only have to face one term of incarceration. On November 7, 1967, while Flower Power seemed to be converting much of middle-class America into a psychedelic lovefest, and LSD-inspired albums such as the Beatles' *Sergeant Pepper* dominated the pop-culture scene, Ochoa went down to the Central Courthouse to hear his sentence: convicted of burglary in the second degree, he was sentenced to six months in the county jail. Thus it was that as 1967 gave way to the tumultuous year following—a year of political assassinations, campus occupations, massacres in Vietnam and urban rioting across the country—Billy whiled away his time behind bars. He was in jail when the North Vietnamese stormed the American Embassy compound in Saigon during the Tet offensive; when Martin Luther King was shot on April 4. He was sitting in jail throughout the riots that followed. And he was still there in June, when Bobby Kennedy was murdered in Los Angeles, not that many miles from the jail, after having just won California's Democratic primary in the race for the presidential nomination.

"Doing my sentence in L.A. County wasn't to [sic] bad," Billy wrote from CSP-SAC thirty-three years later. "Nothing like coming to jail and prison now." Perhaps it was even good for him. For during his time at County, away from the temptations of street life, Billy stayed relatively clean.

Not until that summer, as antiwar protestors at the Democrats' Chicago convention were being beaten and tear-gassed by the Windy City's finest to chants of "the whole world is watching," was Ochoa let out of jail. He hit the streets at just about the time that Richard Nixon—once more the Republican nominee for president—was hitting his stride.

In addition to the high-profile assassination victims, the chaos of 1968 had claimed another political scalp: that of President Lyndon Johnson. In April, Johnson had stunned the nation by announcing that he would not seek reelection. Now, as summer gave way to fall, Richard Nixon and Johnson's Vice President, Hubert Humphrey, were duking it out for the highest office in the land.

For the past five years, ever since he had assumed power in the chaotic moments after Kennedy's death, Lyndon Johnson had been pushing his Great Society programs, his advisers urging huge government interventions to defeat, once and for all, the plagues of poverty, slum housing, and crime. Generally, these liberal analysts believed, people weren't innately bad; they were simply forced by circumstances larger than themselves into doing bad things, and putting them in prison wouldn't really help matters. Indeed, in 1967, the President's Crime Commission had reported that too many people were being locked away by a system using the prisons "as a rug under which disturbing problems and people can be swept."[6]

The War on Poverty that Johnson had declared was premised on the belief that a rationally ordered federal bureaucracy, coupled with imaginative social engineering, could radically transform the social and economic landscape of America's fifty states. Raise enough taxes, pump enough money into a problem, put enough good brains to work on solutions, and develop enough computers to work coordinating information flows between different local, state, and federal agencies, and no problem was too great for this generation of decision makers. After all, over the past quarter century, hadn't American brainpower split the atom, won a world war, put men into space, created prosperity the like of which had never been seen before? NASA was preparing to land men on the moon. Surely it wasn't too utopian to expect that American brains could also solve the social ills of modern, industrial living.

To this end, in addition to creating institutions of the modern welfare state such as Medicaid and Medicare, and dramatically expanding programs such as Aid to Families with Dependent Children that had originally been created during the Roosevelt years, Johnson's administration also developed two powerful crime-fighting institutions: the Bureau of Narcotics and Dangerous Drugs (BNDD), and the Law Enforcement Assistance Administration (LEAA). The former was intended to coordinate state drug interdiction efforts. The latter was a federal organization designed to channel money to local law enforcement agencies and to aid in breaking local criminal networks and solving local crimes. Together, these two organizations supplemented the FBI and the Bureau of Narcotics — both of which had been founded in the years between the two world wars, and had long been dominated by two men: J. Edgar Hoover at the FBI, and Harry Anslinger at the Bureau of Narcotics.

On the surface, the creation of these agencies ought to have played to the Democrats' advantage. After all, in a period of domestic upheaval not seen since the Civil War over a century earlier, surely they indicated the Democrats were taking "the crime problem" — and all the generational and racial tensions wrapped up in these three deceptively simple words — seriously. But, Richard Nixon knew that oftentimes when a population is fearful, all that the creation of new agencies like this does is to stoke the fear: *if the government felt compelled to create the BNDD and the LEAA, did that not signify the country's leaders were running scared?* Instead of it being taken as a sign that things were being brought under control, did it not smack of panic? Moreover, if you promised grandiose results—a rapid end to poverty, the reining in of crime, victory in the war against drug addiction and so forth—and then failed to deliver, the populace rapidly grew restive. Candidate Nixon believed that at a time like this, the best thing he could possibly do was to stoke up this fear, to whip people up, to make them believe that only he, Richard Milhouse Nixon, was capable of introducing the really tough measures needed to reclaim the country from the dope peddlers, the political militants, and the flag burners. If white working-class voters feared and resented radical Black movements like the Panthers, and associated Black political aspirations with rising crime, then, if this would help him get elected second time around, Nixon wasn't averse to pandering to their prejudices. Moreover, if he didn't woo these voters for the Republican Party, he risked being outflanked by the southern segregationist candidate George Wallace. And that was a sure-fire method of once again losing the election to a liberal Democrat.

"I have found great audience response to this [law and order] theme in all parts of the country," Nixon wrote to his one-time boss, an ailing ex-President Dwight Eisenhower, during the campaign. "Including areas like New Hampshire where there is virtually no race problem and relatively little crime."[7]

And no criminal activity produced a greater reaction, Nixon found, than that of drugs. "Drug use was the perfect crime on which to focus," the author Dan Baum wrote in his book *Smoke and Mirrors: The War on Drugs and the Politics of Failure*.[8] "In the War on Drugs, users would come to provide a bottomless well of villains and scapegoats for administrations looking to unburden the electorate of taxes, shed federal responsibilities, and divert attention from their own failures." The more attention Nixon's team devoted to crime and drugs, the more the media would cover the issue; and the more time the evening news spent on crime, the more the populace would fear it. And the more the populace feared crime, the more he, Richard Nixon, could bulk up his opinion poll numbers by generating seriously hard-hitting new anticrime initiatives. In many ways, it was little more than a repeat of the anti-

Communist campaign Nixon had made himself so large a part of back in the late 1940s and early 1950s, when he was a young member of Congress and Senator Joe McCarthy was busy whipping the country up into paroxysms of anti-Red terror. During the McCarthy years, Nixon had made his career by going after State Department employee Alger Hiss, accusing him of being a Communist and driving him out of office. He had taken part in televised hearings in which cabals of supposed Reds were exposed, caught in the act of nefariously undermining everything the Constitution held sacred. Soon, Richard Nixon was one of the best-known politicians around. And in 1952, Dwight D. Eisenhower had made him Vice President.

Waiting in the wings in 1968 Nixon had a raft of men just itching to get down to business after the November election. Men like John Mitchell, shortly to become Attorney General; H. R. Haldeman, soon to be appointed White House Chief of Staff; Donald Santarelli, who was slated to take over, and massively expand, the LEAA; and Nixon's adviser, John. D. Ehrlichman. After Nixon won the presidency, the team got to work.

These men believed, like Nixon, that the country needed a massive law-and-order clampdown. Once in power, following the Republican victory in November, they successfully lobbied Congress to raise the LEAA's budget from $75 million to more than $500 million.[9] They channeled $90 million into a massive expansion of the National Crime Information Center's computer databases; by 1974, the NCIC computers contained nearly 5 million entries.[10] In 1970 they oversaw Congress's passage of the Organized Crime Control Act, designed to expand the power of government agencies fighting to curb the power of the Mafia and organized drug cartels such as the notorious French Connection heroin ring. And they encouraged local police forces to work with members of the community to establish secretive surveillance networks that would promote anonymous tip-offs against those thought to be engaged in criminal activities.[11]

Not surprisingly, as the government focused more attention on crime, so the public grew more nervous. Shortly after Nixon's inauguration, polls showed that only 3 percent of Americans believed drugs were the most serious problem facing the country; and this despite the vast usage of psychedelics, uppers, downers, and everything else the Baby Boom generation was indulging in. By May of 1971, however, 23 percent viewed drugs as the number one problem. And by July of that same year, as Nixon's team cranked up the rhetoric, more people ranked drugs as the worst societal ill than any other problem.[12]

At this point, Nixon needed to show that, unlike the Democrats who preceded him, he could now take the decisive action the country was demanding. So, without consulting the established antidrug agencies, the president used his executive authority to create an entirely new organization: the Office of Drug Abuse Law Enforcement, led by a man named Myles Ambrose. Over the coming years, ODALE agents would make a name for themselves by their paramilitary tactics, by using overwhelming force to break up street-dealing drug gangs, and by smashing their way into private homes—oftentimes with TV crews accompanying them—and then rampaging through the properties, guns drawn, in a search for drugs. Sure, some innocent people had their homes destroyed, a few were even shot dead by the agents, but generally it made for great viewing. *Here was an administration prepared to really take the action necessary to make America safe again*, the images seemed to be saying. So determined was the president to really strike against criminals that at one point the White House went so far as to ask the Bureau of Narcotics and Dangerous Drugs to prepare a plan for "clandestine law enforcement" that some took to mean a program of assassinations to be carried out against major drug traffickers.[13]

Two years later, with Nixon demanding long mandatory sentences for drug dealers and preparing to declare a "national emergency" caused by rising heroin usage,[14] and Nixon's aides encouraging the CIA to get involved in the "war" against drugs, Congress merged the old Bureau of Narcotics and Dangerous Drugs with the new ODALE. Thus was born the all-powerful Drug Enforcement Administration (DEA). From then on in, the numbers of nonviolent prisoners in America convicted only of drug-related crimes began to rise. And once started, the growth in the prison numbers proved impossible to stop. As the author and journalist Edward Epstein wrote in 1977, in his book *Agency of Fear,* "If Americans could be persuaded that their lives and the lives of their children were being threatened by a rampant epidemic of narcotics addiction, Nixon's advisers presumed they would not object to decisive government actions, such as no-knock warrants, pretrial detention, wiretaps, and unorthodox strike forces."[15]

When Billy was released in mid-1968, however, all this was still in the future. Laura took him back into her apartment. Maybe she ordered her man to sort himself out; or perhaps it was just that county jail hadn't agreed with Billy this time. Either way, the burglar decided it was time to sample a more legitimate occupation. Once more, he went to his father, and once again William Ochoa pulled favors—this time at the tortilla shop he worked at—and got Billy enrolled with him in the delivery department. William was a loyal fan of owner Tony Del La Reyas's double bass playing and would always go down to the bar named Michael's Place where Reyas's band played.[16] For Reyas, bringing Billy on board was just returning the favor to his old drinking buddy. The money was so-so, but at least the large brick building in which El Sol was located was close to the pretty little pink adobe bungalow on Judson Street, overlooking the recently opened San Bernardino Freeway, that Laura, and now Billy, was renting an apartment in at the time. Perhaps, William hoped, if Billy could only hold down the job for a while, he'd finally be able to kick the drugs and go on the straight and narrow. He wore a beige El Sol T-shirt with a picture of the sun radiating off the back and a pair of gabardine slacks. "You've got to look good when you deliver tortillas, you know," William Senior explains matter-of-factly. Every day, Billy would arrive at 5 A.M., pick up one of the company trucks, and set off on his rounds.

But work or no work, Ochoa just couldn't kick the habit. "[Laura] tried to get me to stop using heroin, but I like the high to [sic] much," Billy explained. He would, his father believes, arrive at work already shot full of heroin. For by then, Billy's body simply couldn't function without the drug. The good news, though, was that he'd stay on the job the full seven hours.

El Sol was, in fact, the only long-term job that Billy would ever hold. He held it four years, until the owner, Tony Del La Reyas was shot dead, right through the eye, by a hit man, and the company swiftly went out of business.

Or rather, to be more accurate, he started work in 1968 and he finished with El Sol in late 1971. But he didn't work for forty-eight months straight. The drug addiction was just too powerful, and no matter how many tortilla runs Billy drove, he couldn't earn enough to fund the habit. He even got Laura started on the drug. She was standing at the stove making tacos one day when she burned her hand. The pain was excruciating. "I told her I could stop the pain with a little heroin," Billy recalled sadly. "She said, 'just make the pain stop.' I gave her a little heroin. She liked it. In her own words she said, 'I never thought it would be like this.' One day, she told me 'if you are going to use, then I am going to use;' so she started getting high with me."[17] Now, Billy had two habits to support. And so, after a few months' hiatus, he began moonlighting again as a cat burglar. And by the summer of 1968, he had picked up a second term in the county jail.

This time the sentence was for 365 days, the maximum possible sentence a judge could impose without sending a defendant into the state prison system. Once again, Ochoa spent his days sleeping, eating, playing cards and dominoes, and just shooting the breeze with the other young toughs and addicts in the tank. Again, he went through cold turkey, the muscle-wrenching, feverish withdrawal from heroin. Through days of nausea followed by the "long gut," the time at the tail end of the turkey when he was so hungry he'd eat anything he could scrounge off his fellow inmates. At least, he consoled himself, he was better off than the poor bastard whose withdrawal pains so destroyed him that he began screaming aloud and smashing his head against the metal bars of his jail cell.[18]

By early in the new year of 1969, however, Billy was out on the street

again and working for El Sol. After all, although he was a chronic offender, on the grand scale of things his crimes were fairly petty. Indeed,
compared to murderers such as the notorious Charles Manson, arrested
at his Death Valley hideout shortly after Billy walked out of the county
jail, Ochoa could scarcely even be considered a real threat to society.
Rather he was a nuisance, an heir to the street-corner beggars and pick-
pockets, gin-drinking fools and blaggards who had plagued the cities of
the world from time immemorial. He was the irredeemable face of
lower-class mischief peering out of a darkened seventeenth-century oil
painting. Or he was the conman and hustler of any number of back
alleyways and seedy courtyards. He was, in the prevailing judicial philosophy of the era, society's failure rather than a serious menace needing
to be locked up for years. In a time of change, when states like Vermont
had started calling their maximum-security inmates "residents" and
hard-core thugs were "treated" with "aversion therapy" rather than being
punished,[19] the idea of locking Ochoa up for decades would have struck
the experts as deeply counterintuitive.

Moreover, quite apart from the philosophical objections, with limited
financial resources and cell space available to departments of corrections, the courts had to determine their priorities. And, as inner-city
violence increased and social strife intensified, a small-timer such as
Billy just wasn't high up on the list of people for whom long prison
sentences were deemed to be the only reasonable option.

Once more, within weeks of his release, the police arrested him for
possession of a hypodermic kit, and Ochoa spent a couple weeks detox-
ing in jail. In the last week of the decade, he was arrested for a traffic
violation. Nine months later he copped another burglary charge and
served ninety days. Shortly after he came out, he was again arrested for
possessing a needle. The sequence was as predictable as it was endless.
Drug cravings followed by a small-time crime to buy his drugs; arrest
followed by a short spell in jail during which Ochoa partially detoxed;
release followed by a return to drugs.

One time, when he was shooting up with pure white heroin, Billy
almost died. He shot the dope into a vein, pulled out the needle, and

suddenly was on the ground. "I went down like a boxer K.O.'ed," he says. The dope was just too strong. After a few minutes, however, Billy felt well enough to crawl into bed and nod off to sleep. But that was only the beginning. In the middle of the night, Laura woke up to the sound of a strange, raspy breathing noise. She turned on the light and found, to her horror, that her man was foaming from his nose and mouth. *Oh no! He's dying*, she must have thought as, terrified, she dialed for an ambulance and anxiously waited out the minutes until the paramedics arrived. When the doctors at the hospital examined him, they found that his lungs had begun filling up with water, and his blood pressure had fallen to catastrophically low levels. Another couple hours, and Ochoa would have been just one more dead addict. Instead, a doctor took a large needle, injected it through Ochoa's chest cavity and into his lungs, and sucked out the water. *Don't go to sleep for another few hours*, he warned his patient, *or you might not wake up again*. Breathing shallowly and with each breath an agony, Ochoa heeded the medical advice . . . just long enough to get home and to scrabble under the house to find the packets of heroin that Laura had thrown away in a rage upon finding her lover frothing at the mouth next to her in the dark.

By 1971, Laura had had more than enough of Billy's foibles. Unlike her boyfriend Laura was tired of heroin, and she was fed up with having to come visit Billy in jail. It was clear that things couldn't go on like this.

As luck would have it, Laura was spared the final heartbreak of a formal breakup. For in late 1971, the state of California finally realized that jailing Billy Ochoa for weeks, or even months at a time, wasn't doing anyone any good. He needed more intensive intervention. And so, on December 20, following yet another arrest for possession of heroin, Billy was committed to the California Rehabilitation Center.

In 1971 — as in previous eras of criminal justice reform — ambitious sentiments regarding curing the criminal ills of the soul were in vogue among penologists and sociologists, and even among some politicians. The 1960s had dramatically altered America's cultural and political landscape, and criminal justice policy had undergone change along with most other aspects of governance. Many judges across America, influenced by the radical currents of the previous few years, were deciding that prisons weren't the best place for nonviolent offenders such as Billy Ochoa. A year previously, Congress had even passed a law repealing the federal mandatory sentences that had been on the books for drug offenders since the days of the Hale Boggs Act two decades earlier.

The California Rehabilitation Center was an institution committed to the best rehabilitation ideals of the age, one dedicated to weaning addicts off their fix rather than to punishing them for it. There, instead of being given a California Department of Corrections number and treated as a common criminal, Ochoa was labeled with an "N," as in narcotics, tag, and, for the first time in his life, offered some form of psychiatric help.

The Rehabilitation Center's buildings, located in the Norco-Corona Hills near the small town of Riverside an hour and half southeast of Los Angeles, had a varied history. Originally, they had formed part of an upscale resort catering to California's wealthy elite in the early years of the century. By the time World War II came around, however, the resort was in decline, and following Pearl Harbor the buildings were appropriated by the military and converted into army barracks. Fifteen years after the end of the war, the military having long vacated the premises, the property had morphed into its latest incarnation. By the time Ochoa was committed by the courts to undergo treatment there, the California Rehabilitation Center had been running for more than eleven years.

Around 1,100 men were housed in the old barracks buildings, 60 men in each unit, along with 250 women, who lived in a nearby dormitory. Each of the units had its own counselor, a therapist who was employed to work with the inmates—referred to by the more genial nomenclature of "residents"—eight hours a day, five days a week.[20]

At the CRC, Billy's story was fairly standard. Over half of the residents were Mexican American. Two-thirds came from Los Angeles County.

Most had been convicted of burglaries, robberies, or drug sales and then remanded to the Center for treatment by the judge in charge of their case. The remainder had been committed for treatment without being formally convicted of the crimes for which they had been arrested. Most of the men and women had been sent to CRC for an indeterminate period of time ranging from a year all the way up to ten years. If they behaved, if they cooperated with the therapists, if they participated in group activities, there was a good chance they could regain their freedom within three years.

"N numbers had to attend a group session twice a day and talk about their drug problem," Ochoa wrote from his maximum-security prison nearly thirty years later. "CRC is a group talking program to get a person off of drugs and to keep them off of drugs; very much as the AA program. This really didn't work, but it's the only drug program the state had."[21] Each day, Ochoa and his fellow residents had to spend four hours either working, taking part in job training activities, or attending high-school or college-level classes. On top of this, they had to spend another four hours in group therapy, in cleaning up their dormitories, and in recreational activity. Keep the residents busy, the theory went, and they would eventually cease to crave their drugs so heartily.

Oftentimes, the Center seemed more like a summer camp than a detention facility. Ochoa and his fellow residents were free to roam the vast yard, in the footsteps of an earlier generation of soldiers who had stomped up and down what must have once been a parade ground. Near the women's unit, an Olympic-sized swimming pool remained in place from the facility's previous incarnations. The male and female inmates took turns in the water. When they weren't in class or in therapy, the residents were free to visit friends in other barracks buildings sprinkled across the complex. "There was what I would call more freedom than most of [sic] other state institutions," Ochoa recalls, somewhat fondly. "N numbers had a few privileges that inmates didn't have. It use [sic] to be a place where it was relax [sic] to do a sentence." Staff would even host weekend dances and Christmas parties for their wards. On occasion, Ochoa was even sent as part of a work crew to the nearby

California Institute for Women. He got to know three of the Manson girls. "They really looked young and inecent [sic]," he remembers thinking.

The therapy sessions were huge and infused with much of the fashionable psychological rhetoric of the time. All the sixty occupants of a barracks would attend, and individual residents would be called upon to discuss the reasons for their addiction. If conflicts had arisen between residents in the barracks, they were expected to be talked through and solved during these hour-long rituals. Even minor infractions of the rules merited prolonged conversation, the argument being that the addicts needed to learn, almost from scratch, to abide by the legal and moral structures of the outside world. "If a pen is stolen from a counselor the session will be devoted to recovering it and encouraging others to snitch on the thief," the sociologist Troy Duster wrote, with more than a hint of frustration, after his work at the Center. "If someone working in the kitchen gives a bit of extra food to friends it becomes a huge cause for concern."[22]

Participation in these sessions was key. Duster found that the addicts quickly learned to pander to what their therapists wanted to hear. "The residents are poignantly aware," he reported, "that one of the most important criteria for being released is to demonstrate in group sessions that one is aware of the psychic disturbance that the staff feels brought about the narcotic delinquency, and what is more important, that one is able to express in some kind of searching, groping, or perhaps articulate fashion that this is the case." Conning the earnest but nonstreetwise staff became almost a rite of passage. "If you wanta walk, you gotta talk," became the informal barracks' motto.

Despite President Nixon's extremely tough law-and-order message, an interregnum prevailed. Caught somewhere between the heady, radical experiments of the recent past and a more conservative, unforgiving future, the criminal justice system oscillated between the ideas of "treating" and "punishing" those who came before the courts. On the one hand, judges had to take into account the growing reaction by middle-America, the voices advocating a clampdown against what they saw as a law-breaking subculture, the ordinary Joes who had voted Nixon into office. But at the same time, many of these same judges had been appointed to the bench during the more liberal presidencies of Lyndon Johnson and John Kennedy. They believed in rehabilitation strategies, and felt that no matter how severe the sentences, crime could not be dealt with in the absence of major social policy interventions. Many judges had also come to believe that institutes such as the CRC provided better opportunities for rehabilitation than did the traditional prison setting. In the early 1970s, a complicated interweaving of these two contradictory trends was occurring.

And Nixon himself had gone a long way toward encouraging this ambivalence. True, he had won power, and maintained himself in power, at least in part through molding himself as a law-and-order leader. But, behind the scenes, Nixon had proven to be a true pragmatist. When his young adviser Egil Krogh had stumbled upon experimental addiction-treatment programs that used the synthetic chemical methadone to wean people off heroin, he had been struck by the potential for reducing drug-related crimes such as burglaries and muggings. During the first half of Richard Nixon's first term, Krogh worked on inner-circle confidants like John Ehrlichman to persuade them that the epidemic of addictions warranted a full-blown national treatment program, and he nurtured a pilot program in crime-ridden Washington, D.C., that soon produced significant drops in crime. Initially, though, the focus of Nixon's team remained on punishment, until April 1971, when the two congressmen, Robert Steele and Morgan Murphy, issued their report on the huge numbers of soldiers returning from Vietnam completely dependent upon heroin. Here was a huge problem for the drug warriors: how could young men, drafted to fight a war for their country, be treated as common criminals after developing a drug habit in the hellish conditions of bloody jungle warfare? These boys might be sick, Nixon's war-supporting constituents would think, but surely they didn't deserve to be shipped off to prison.

Two months later, Richard Nixon called a press conference in the White House and announced the creation of an entirely new office —

unsnappily titled the Special Action Office for Drug Abuse Prevention (SAODAP)—to be headed by a Chicago medic named Dr. Jerome Jaffe. Jaffe had spent the previous few years building up a large methadone treatment program in Illinois, and his work had resulted in marked reductions in property crimes throughout the South Side of Chicago.

Now, as Nixon declared that drug addiction was "public enemy number one in the United States," he announced that Jaffe would be moving to Washington to head the new organization. He also told reporters that more than $100 million of the $155 million that he was requesting in federal money to fight drugs would be devoted to drug treatment programs. "As with China and the environment," the journalist Michael Massing opined, "Nixon's ideological convictions on drugs were tempered by a strong dose of pragmatism."[23] Within a year, Congress had authorized $420 million for SAODAP, and Dr. Jaffe, the psychiatrist from Chicago, suddenly was in a position to create drug-treatment centers and programs all over America. Soon, the FBI was reporting that 94 of the nation's 154 largest cities had seen a fall in crime during 1972.[24]

Thus it was that at the very same time Myles Ambrose's ODALE was grabbing the headlines with its pyrotechnic home invasions and street sweeps, behind the scenes, tens of thousands of heroin addicts were being treated in government-funded clinics and residential programs. And, despite the warlike rhetoric, in reality two-thirds of federal drug money under Nixon was allotted to treatment rather than to the interdiction of drugs and the imprisonment of drug offenders.

The California Rehabilitation Center of the early 1970s was a classic example of this merging of punishment and rehabilitation. It was designed to treat addicts, yet it was based around incarceration. It didn't classify narcotics cases as simply criminal, yet it punished inmates for the pettiest infractions of house rules. And, while it didn't prescribe methadone to its residents—Ochoa only ever went on to the synthetic drug once, for a twenty-one-day period, when he was applying for a job as an X-ray technician at a southern California hospital—it utilized the "therapeutic community model" in abundance. The residents could practically *talk* their addictions into the ground.

The talk sessions were in keeping with the age. For if the Nixon years represented any single criminal justice model, it was arguably a sort of totalitarian therapy system. To illustrate this, Princeton sociologists Joan Smith and William Fried describe how in April 1970 President Nixon passed on to the department of Health, Education and Welfare [HEW] for consideration the advice of his personal physician: "All children be tested at age six to identify criminal potential; and that the potential criminals be 'treated' by being placed in state-run camps."[25] Nothing came of the suggestion, but it did reflect a growing body of opinion: that if the underlying social causes of criminal behavior couldn't be eradicated, at least individuals could be "cured" of their criminal inclinations.

After spending a little under a year inside the Rehabilitation Center, Billy was sent back to Los Angeles. He was a smooth talker and had also shown an ability to stay away from drugs while off the streets. There was no good reason to keep him committed. He reemerged into a strange new political climate. Richard Nixon had been reelected in November 1972, defeating the liberal antiwar Democrat George McGovern in an eighteen-million-vote landslide. But now his administration was in turmoil, with accusations that he had ordered the bugging of Democrat campaign headquarters, that he had compiled "enemies lists," and that his operatives, guided by the dedicated Egil Krogh, were responsible for politically motivated burglaries, smear tactics, the disruption of opposition rallies and a host of other dubious activities. These election campaign shenanigans, it appeared, had been paid for by a secret slush fund run by an organization named the Committee to Re-Elect the President (CREEP) and had been carried out by a team of fixers known as "the plumbers."

Now, as Nixon's White House disintegrated amid a welter of public accusations, and as Congress began the long investigations that would eventually lead to a recommendation to impeach the president, and to Nixon's resignation, so the national Wars on Crime and Drugs faded into the background. True, in a desperate attempt to regain his political momentum, Nixon embraced New York's Rockefeller drug laws and proposed harsh mandatory sentences of his own. And in late March 1973, the beleaguered president created the Drug Enforcement Administration, an organization that would soon become the most powerful government agency in America's increasingly potent War on Drugs. But, for the moment, the nation's fixation on drugs—and on the competing issues of treatment versus punishment—ebbed as the sordid and illegal deeds of the Nixon White House were exposed in all their raw detail before the world. By the end of May, fearing that his treatment program was stagnating, and his philosophy was being sacrificed both to Nixon's need to appear tough and to the broader political squabbles, Dr. Jaffe tendered his resignation as head of SAODAP. Within two years, while the huge federal antidrug bureaucracy that Nixon had created remained in place, the spending priorities of that bureaucracy had moved decisively away from treatment and toward a more traditional law enforcement approach to drugs.

While all this was unfolding, shortly after his release, in 1973 Billy turned thirty. It wasn't the happiest birthday of his life. Laura wanted nothing more to do with him, his father wouldn't let him stay in his house, his siblings were embarrassed and disgusted by his lifestyle, and his mother—although always happy to welcome her boy home—was, by now, desperately sick. Once again, the recently released inmate made what was by his rather modest standards a concerted effort to find employment.

Always, however, the weight of Ochoa's history—all the mistakes and wrong choices he'd made down the years—came back to haunt him; always the street life, the lure of easily available heroin, called him back. He worked for a month in the quiet suburb of Monterey Park, just east of Downtown as a punch press operator, at a fairly decent wage of $3 an hour.[26] Then he quit. He roamed north through California and worked for a while at a car wash in Sacramento. He returned to Los Angeles and got himself another punch press gig, this time working for the American Labor Corporation in Huntington Park. Once more, a few weeks in, Ochoa cashed in his chips. Again the details are hazy. Perhaps Billy just couldn't deal with the routine, with getting up early every morning and driving to work. Perhaps he got tangled up in another web of drug taking and buying. Maybe the corporation found out about his criminal record and concocted a convenient reason to dismiss him. Either way, the thirty-year-old was left to his own devices again. He got a job as a maintenance man for the Times Mirror Press newspapers, and for four or five months pulled down $3.80 an hour. And then he upped and left. After so many years of drifting in and out of drug abuse, of being placed into juvenile camps, jails, and the Rehabilitation Center, it was almost as if Ochoa now found it impossible to function on the outside, to live beyond the confines imposed by a state institution.

Somewhere during this time, Billy found a woman to fill the emotional void left by Laura's rejection of him. She was called Eleanor [Author's note: her name has been changed and a pseudonym substituted] and her friends referred to her as Elsie. Like Billy, Elsie was a heroin-hype. She was originally from Sacramento, but these days had taken to living in the more pleasing, sunny climes of Southern California. Billy had first met her at the California Institute for Women when he was doing chores with his Rehabilitation Center work crew. She had been released about a week before him. But she'd returned to Sacramento and he hadn't thought any more about her. "I was running free and wild," Ochoa recalls. He wasn't about to chase a broad four hundred miles up the spine of the state. But then he got arrested again and went back to jail. One day, just because he was bored, Billy started recalling old flings. He thought of Elsie. *Maybe she's also gone back to jail.* On a whim, he wrote her at the Institute for Women. And sure enough, a couple weeks later, a letter came back. *Yes, she also had flunked parole and was back behind bars. Perhaps Billy would like to visit her if he got released soon.*

And so he did. Shortly after getting out of jail, Billy decided to visit

Elsie at the Institute for Women. "I just went there, I didn't need any paperwork." They began a courtship, and, when it came time for Elsie to be released, Billy was waiting for her. "So I pick-up her from prison in February 1974 and I flew back to Sacramento with her," he recalls. Several years younger than Billy, she was short and chubby. And, being addicted to the same dope as Billy, she was a perfect foil for him. Soon afterward, when he went back to L.A., Elsie followed.

Soon, the two hypes had shacked up together in the old room in Josie's house on Matthews Street that Billy had shared with his brother Ken when they were both boys. "Every time I'd go over there," William Senior says, remembering his occasional visits to his ex-wife's house, "they used to be there. Sitting in the living room. Just hanging out." Most of the time, it seemed, neither of them had any form of legitimate employment.

Jamie saw them periodically. Still as addicted as ever, the older cousin's life had also become one long journey into and out of California's penal institutions. When he wasn't in prison, Jamie would sometimes score drugs with Billy and his girlfriend. They shared their crime sagas with each other. Elsie, Billy confided in his cousin, would drive a getaway car, speeding Ochoa away from houses he had just burgled. They were a good team, robbing houses, selling the stolen property, buying dope and getting high together.

But then one day, Elsie disappeared. William Senior remembers being told that the young woman had finally decided to get clean, once and for all, and that she had left Billy behind as a no-good reminder of her wasted years. Jamie, though, recalls it somewhat differently. In his mind, Billy and Elsie had taken a road trip up to her hometown of Sacramento, four hundred miles to the north. They'd spent some time up there, hanging out with her friends and breaking into a whole new hunting ground of houses. After a while, the local police had caught up with them, and both had been arrested for residential burglary. Somehow, though, while Elsie had copped four years in a women's correctional facility, this time around lady luck had shone on Billy and he had avoided a prison sentence. In a hurry, Billy left Sacramento and skedaddled back to Los Angeles. And that, Jamie recalls matter-of-factly, was that. Billy wrote to his moll occasionally, even sent her some spending money to make life on the inside a little easier. Well before her sentence ended, however, the young addict had become but a faded memory filed somewhere in Billy's chaotic past. He saw her once more, in 1982, when he'd again been admitted to the California Rehabilitation Center. He had a job in the visiting room, and one day there she was. She was a prisoner in the women's unit. After that, though, he lost all contact with her.

One day Gloria came to the house to visit Josie. She'd left school a few years before and had a job in the neighborhood. Oftentimes, she'd come home, to have lunch at the house in which she'd grown up. By now, the Ochoa matriarch was seriously ill, her prematurely aged body ravaged by diabetes. Barely fifty, she was a chronic invalid, housebound and dependent on her children's help.

Gloria turned her key in the lock and opened the door. Her brother Billy was sitting in the living room with a woman. Lolling around, doing nothing in particular. Both were hyped up on heroin. Gloria said hi, and started to settle down. Then she heard something. In another corner of the tiny house, Josie was desperately trying to breathe, choking on her own phlegm. Frantically signaling to somebody, anybody, to come to her rescue.

In a panic, Josie's youngest daughter snatched up the telephone and dialed for an ambulance. And within a few minutes, the paramedics were kneeling next to the frail, prematurely decrepit woman, bringing her back to life, helping her to once again fill up her lungs with air. Billy still sat in the living room. Helpless. Pathetic. His brain was so fried he hadn't even realized that his mother was close to dying.

EIGHT

Diabetes finally did claim the life of Billy's mother, Josie, in 1977. In the last few months, her eyesight had failed and her legs had become virtually useless. She'd gone on to dialysis to try to jump-start her crippled kidneys, but that had only prolonged her agony. When she knew she was going to die, she'd gathered up all her strength for one last visit to her wayward firstborn son.

That year, Billy was doing a short spell in Tehachapi prison, near the city of Bakersfield, in an area of the state Californians referred to as the Inland Empire. And when Josie visited him, in the large communal visiting area, he saw his mother—the only person in the world whom he really loved—sitting in a wheelchair, almost completely blind. He knew he'd never see her alive again. And given the pain she was in, he wasn't sure he even wanted to. After all, he'd always believed that life was only worth living if it could be enjoyed. Nevertheless, when his brother Ken phoned the prison to tell them that Josie had died, and when the prison chaplain came to his cell to convey the news to Billy, the burglar broke down in tears. For two days, he couldn't stop sobbing. He kept thinking about how she'd tolerated his excesses; about how she'd even eventually learned to accept his addiction and to love him regardless. He even thought that she'd loved him the most of all her four children because she knew that, deep down, Billy was the weakest; he was the one who needed his mother the most.

Because Ochoa was classified as a minimum-security inmate, the prison officials allowed him to journey to Los Angeles for Josie's funeral.

After all this was the mid-1970s, and—despite Nixon's tough law-and-order rhetoric from earlier in the decade—in the years after Nixon's resignation the prevailing governmental philosophy toward incarceration had returned to being determinedly, if temporarily, liberal. Despite rising crime rates, the incarceration rate hovered at barely 100 per 100,000 people (just over a fifth the rate it would be two decades later). Moreover, with the country still stunned by the break-ins, the smear campaigns, the violence against opponents, committed by the Nixon administration and exposed during the Watergate hearings, the public's fear of crime in the mid-1970s seemed to be at least balanced by its suspicion of government and its unwillingness to expand the coercive arms of that government. The crises that would soon shatter America's basically optimistic liberalism and usher in a far more conservative, unforgiving, and fearful politics were still a couple years into the future.

In such a climate, criminals such as Ochoa—whose crimes were a by-product of their drug abuse—weren't treated as the full-blown, irredeemable public enemies they would soon become. Four years earlier, Oregon had decriminalized the possession of pot, and over the coming years, it had been joined by Alaska, California, Colorado, Maine, Minnesota, and Ohio. President Carter himself, as well as his drug czar, the outspoken Englishman Dr. Peter Bourne, had come out in favor of decriminalizing marijuana. Bourne had even begun attending parties in Washington, D.C., hosted by the National Organization to Reform Marijuana Laws (NORML),[1] and had spoken sympathetically about experimenting with legalizing the harder drugs.

Thus it was that, when Josie died, Billy was given a temporary leave from prison. The condition was that the family paid for the cost of an off-duty cop to escort him to L.A. and back to Tehachapi again. And so they scrabbled together $125 and Billy went home. He watched his mother's coffin being buried and then the cop and he went to Ken's home for the traditional wake. The cop, he recalled, seemed to be embarrassed by the whole thing, unwilling to eat any of Ken's food, yet nervous lest the family feel he was intruding. Billy almost felt sorry for him.[2]

In the years since Josie's death, and following his release from Te-hachapi, Ochoa really hadn't been able to call anywhere his home. His mother's old house on Matthews Street had at least been a refuge of sorts. Now he was reduced to sleeping on friends' floors; or on occasion to begging favors from the few family members still on speaking terms with him. One day, his aunt, cousin Patty's mom, agreed to let him stay in the empty old house in South Los Angeles that she had inherited from her father. Over the next few weeks, Billy made friends with the man next door. But Billy's selfishness was now overbearing, and for him friendship was about gaining access to things. One day, when the old man was out somewhere, Billy snuck into his house and stole some of his possessions. "My mother got *so* mad!" Patty says sadly. By now she was coming to believe that Billy was *sick*, that he was a kleptomaniac, that he needed psychiatric attention rather than endless short spells be-hind bars. But the attention wasn't forthcoming. And, in the meantime, the only way she could think to keep her cousin out of trouble was to try to find work for him. It was the least she could do, Patty figured, to honor the memory of her beloved dead aunt Josie.

Patty was a secretary at a local television station. They were always looking for casual laborers there. And so the young woman brought Billy in and introduced him to the person in charge of hiring furniture mov-ers. It was an undemanding job, and the company could always use an extra hand. Billy was hired, no questions asked. And, briefly, Patty breathed a little easier about the relative she loved who was causing her such heartache. But even though he seemed to be staying out of trouble, Patty kept hearing stories about how her cousin was talking up his jail time, trying to prove to his coworkers that he was a big-time bad guy, that he wasn't someone to be messed with. The other furniture movers got a little nervous. True, it was probably all made up, but you never knew these days. There were an awful lot of wackos out there ready to explode at the slightest provocation.

Not too long after he'd started promoting his jailbird image, the building manager accused Billy of stealing his prescription glasses. Billy said he'd just moved them from their perch on a wall to stop them from getting lost, or dirty, or some such excuse. He quickly produced the spectacles, and the matter was dropped. Perhaps he really *had* just been looking out for his manager. But a few days later, some pieces of equipment went missing from a stage set, and, since Billy had made it clear to all and sundry that he knew about stealing, he found himself summarily dismissed from the station. The ironic thing was that Billy really *was* innocent of this particular crime. Later on, Patty heard that the equipment had been found in the possession of one of her bosses' sons. But by then Billy, rebuffed in his latest attempts to make a go of it with a real job, had returned to the world of petty theft with which he was more familiar. He'd left the watchful eye of one cousin and returned to more nebulous activities with another, to stealing with his cousin Jamie.

And then Jamie and he had gotten arrested with someone else's RCA television in their car.

At 4.09 P.M. on the afternoon of December 20, 1979, Officer Jimmy Holland of the South Pasadena police pulled Billy and his cousin Jamie over at the intersection of State and Raymondale, near one of the on-ramps to the Fair Oaks and Pasadena freeway. A few minutes previously, Holland had received a radio message to look out for a green car, license plate number 277DFC, that was a possible getaway car in a burglary.

The officer saw this vehicle coming toward him, and he decided to make a traffic stop. He called for backup, and a minute later another officer, one by the name of Hearn, arrived. The two policemen approached the car. They asked the two men to step out, and after they had done so, one of the officers began searching the car. Inside, on the backseat of the Chevy Oldsmobile, partially hidden by a brown overcoat, was a thirteen-inch RCA color television. Ochoa claimed the television belonged to him, that it was a gift from one of his sisters. But the police didn't believe him and Billy and Jamie once more found themselves under arrest and on their way to the precinct.

A little over an hour earlier, a woman who lived in a building on Raymond Hill Road had been doing chores about her house. Wandering into her living room, the windows of which looked out onto the street, she had been startled to see a man standing with his hands on the window peering into her home. The man was even more startled. He had, she later declared, literally fallen off the raised ledge on which he'd been standing, looking in her window.[3] Soon, however, the Peeping Tom had recovered enough to try to cover his tracks. He walked over to the woman's front door, knocked on it and told her, through the wood, that he was a social worker looking for one Richard Garcia. There was, of course, no Garcia in the building. But, upon being told this, the man proceeded to get into quite a flap, stating how important it was that he find him. *Sorry*, she repeated, *there is no Garcia here*. After a while, hoping that he had convinced the woman regarding the legitimate nature of his mission, Jamie—for that is who it was—strode off.

But the neighbor wasn't convinced. She maintained her post at the living room window, and when, a short time later, the man returned up the hill with a television, and got into a car which quickly speeded off, she called the police. When her neighbor Mr. Hamer returned to his home, several houses down the hill, an hour and a half later, he found that his front door had been forced open while he was at work. He rushed inside. In the living room, where his television usually stood, was a space. In the bathroom, his medicine cabinet had been flung open and the contents rifled through, as if somebody were looking for drugs. Hamer phoned the police. Ten minutes later they were at his house, taking down the details of the crime. Luckily for the burglary victim, he had bought the television only a few weeks before, from a nearby Safeway, and he had kept the $317 receipt.[4] He had also written down the serial number: 928701547.

Hamer was more than a little surprised when the police told him they already had the suspects in custody, along with a television sporting the same serial number that they had rescued from the back of Jamie and Billy's Chevy. The police had also removed from the car, as evidence, a pair of channel lock pliers, a boning knife with a wooden handle, a large screwdriver, and a pair of vise grips. All the important tools for a team of burglars.

Nothing was going right for the United States in the last months of the 1970s. The Iranian revolution had not only brought political chaos to the Middle East, it had also led to a catastrophic oil shortage as production temporarily dried up in the new Islamic republic. By the summer of 1979, America was wilting under a combination of gas shortages and inflation. In much of the country, a rationing system meant that drivers could only fill up their tanks on certain days of the week. It was almost bad enough that you could pull your car into one of the burgeoning lines at a gas station only to find the price of a gallon had soared in the half hour it took you to reach the pump. Even before the events in Iran had unfolded, ongoing oil shortages throughout the 1970s had nudged President Carter into making speeches about how the "energy crisis" was a national security problem of the highest importance. On a moral par, he declared as early as 1977, with a military emergency. Now, as the oil crisis mounted, Carter's support plummeted. By June, only 28 percent of the electorate approved of how he was running the country.[5]

It wasn't just economic problems gnawing at the country's self-confidence. America's last troops had pulled out of Vietnam four years previously in the most humiliating of circumstances—the final helicopters flying out of Saigon minutes before the Communist forces of North Vietnam poured into the heart of the southern capital. Now, to cap America's growing sense of impotence, Islamic revolutionaries, led by the firebrand cleric, Ayatollah Khomeini, had seized control of the strategically vital oil-producing Iran, and, along with the resulting gas shortages, radical students were holding American citizens hostage in their embassy, mocking an enemy they termed "the Great Satan," and threatening to kill their terrified captives. The hostage crisis began in early November 1979. And at the time of the presidential election, one year later, most of the Americans were still being held captive. Attempts to send in U.S. helicopters in the spring had resulted in dismal failure: the craft crashed into the desert in full view of television audiences around the world, not even getting near enough to Tehran to mount any sort of rescue effort. So, as the months wore on, the hostage crisis continued to dominate the news. Arguably at no time since Pearl Harbor had America looked so vulnerable, its presence overseas so open to ridicule, or, worse, to armed attack.

"I felt the anger of that crowd and saw it etched on every face," wrote Carter aide Hamilton Jordan, about American demonstrators protesting Iran's holding of hostages. "Their rage, their very presence seemed to be saying 'We've had enough! After Vietnam and OPEC price increases and gasoline lines, we've had enough. This is the last straw.' "[6]

Adding insult to injury, however, and magnifying the country's malaise, from 1977 onward, crimes of all kind had been on the increase, and, more frightening to many, by decade's end violent crime was rising to record levels across America.[7] Tied in with this trend, the quality of urban living was deteriorating. Gang warfare was raging throughout the inner cities, made all the more deadly by easily accessible semiautomatic weapons flooding the gun market. More and more teenagers were being arrested for astonishingly violent and bloody crimes. And entire neighborhoods, such as New York's South Bronx, were being set afire by absentee landlords who found it easier to collect insurance money on destroyed real estate than to gather in rent from the tenants occupying their slum dwellings. With jobs drying up, welfare rolls rising, and the tax base shriveling, New York City had teetered on the brink of bankruptcy in 1976. And when the city had sought a federal bailout, President Gerald Ford had, in the famous *Daily News* headline, told it to "drop dead." Crime rates and drug addiction were so bad in the slums of Detroit that the Michigan Assembly had been pushed into passing the draconian HB 4190 in 1978; a bill that introduced mandatory life without parole sentences for possession or distribution of over 650 grams of hard drugs. Even though it was largely the low-level drug couriers known as "mules" who were caught up in this law, it at least reflected the sense of mounting frustration that more and more people were experiencing.[8] For many ordinary citizens it appeared that something fundamentally wrong was eating away at the nation's fabric and that the system was becoming stacked against the little man who minded his own business, went to work, paid his bills, obeyed the law.

In a myriad of ways, both cultural and political, the United States had changed dramatically in the past twenty years, had become a more complicated society. What had once seemed so simple — that America would be a melting pot, in which origins and ancestries would meld into a generally white-bread, Protestant notion of identity — was now no longer universally accepted. It had gone through a civil rights revolution, the birth of the Black Panthers, the rise of the American Indian Movement (AIM). Hippies had subverted dress codes, hair standards, even — with terms like "far out, man" — the basic norms of language. Feminism was transforming the workplace and also the family. Abortion had been legalized in 1973. Drug use was commonplace. Religious participation was declining. Sexual mores had dramatically shifted. Teenage pregnancies were rising and gays were coming out of the closet. The ways in which America had altered in the span of so few years was positively mind-blowing. Almost as if all the ingredients that went to make up the huge land had been squeezed into a ball, heated up to tremendous temperatures, and then allowed to coalesce again into entirely new and unpredictable arrangements.

And it wasn't just a matter of manners either. Politically, the liberal impulses that had resulted in Kennedy's election had, among the young, evolved into something very different. *Radicalism.* A revolutionary critique of the foundation principles and myths of "America" itself. From the early 1960s on, the country had been rift by every hew of demonstration in the books: peaceful, violent, provocative; political, drug-related, anti-war, anti-segregation. During the course of the decade, and into the 1970s, practically every city and university campus worth their salt had exploded into rioting. Students had repeatedly occupied university grounds from Berkeley, in California's Bay Area, to Columbia, on Manhattan's Upper West Side. Black ghettos had erupted in anger after Martin Luther's King's murder in Memphis, and by the end of the decade millions of white home owners in the cities had sold out and migrated suburb-ward.

As every aspect of society took on political auras and every action acquired political significance, even the prison inmates had mobilized; *common criminals*, the lowest of the low, were demanding reform of the institutions that held them captive and were threatening violence if their demands were not met. Many were declaring their solidarity with revolutionary organizations such as the Black Panthers and with the emerging post-colonial governments of Africa and Asia.

From the case of the Soledad Brothers in California through to the infamous Attica uprising of September 1971, prisoners, supported by networks of activists on the outside, had been rebelling. Ever since convicted armed robber and sexual assaulter Caryl Chessman had made an international name for himself back in the 1950s through writing a series of powerful autobiographical books while awaiting execution on California's Death Row in San Quentin prison, a prisoners-rights movement had been percolating. It had gained steam in the spring of 1960, when, despite an emotional international campaign, and demonstrations around the world, Chessman had been executed by cyanide asphyxiation in his state's gas chamber. And throughout the following decade, like so many other aspects of the American stage, the country's prisons and prisoners had become increasingly politicized. Inmates who'd gone into prison illiterate practically learned to read through studying radical, even revolutionary texts. Prison writers and activists such as Eldridge Cleaver and George Jackson became icons for much of the radical left. And as the inmates immersed themselves in political literature, so more and more prisoners came to see their battles behind bars as being but an extension of the wider struggles being waged throughout the country.

Sometimes these prisoners' wish lists were run of the mill: more nutritional food, access to showers more often than once a week, better exercise facilities, and expanded visiting rights. Often, however, they were distinctly political and even utopian — ranging from demands for more Black and Hispanic prison guards, to the prisoners being able to choose their own wardens; even, in some cases, for prisoners to be granted asylum in socialist Third World countries. They published their own underground newspapers, launched massive lawsuits against departments of corrections, struck for higher wages at prison workshops and, with increasing frequency, took guards hostages and occupied prison buildings when their grievances were not addressed in a timely enough fashion.

When, in September 1971, the more than 1,200 prisoners inside New York State's maximum-security prison of Attica, the vast majority of whom were Black or Hispanic, took over their institution and seized 38 hostages, it appeared to many, on all sides of the political spectrum, that the country really was careening out of control. To a large part of the left, it seemed as if the chickens were finally coming home to roost for a repressive and racist political system. To the observers such as radical lawyer Bill Kunstler, Congressman Herman Badillo, and journalists such as Tom Wicker of *The New York Times*, called in to oversee the tense negotiations between the correctional authorities and the prisoners, many of the inmates' demands appeared eminently reasonable. Less reasonable were the prisoners' tactics—holding blindfolded and terrified hostages, setting fire to buildings, issuing ultimatums to the Commissioner of the Department of Corrections to fire the prison's warden. The observers were hoping they could convince both sides to put their weapons down and start negotiating. To much of the public, however, and to the armed guards and troopers waiting outside the barricaded prison, even the idea of negotiating with over a thousand rebellious criminals made no sense. How could thieves, drug dealers, rapists, murderers be dictating terms to the very society that had ordered their imprisonment? Governor Nelson Rockefeller agreed. And, on the morning of September 13, four days into the uprising, he ordered in the troops and helicopters. Within a few minutes, as clouds of tear gas spread throughout the complex, as the copters dropped pepper gas into the yards, and as hundreds of troopers stormed inside Attica, 39 inmates and 9 hostages lay dead, and nearly a hundred more inmates were seriously wounded—most by bullets sprayed around the prison yards by the infuriated officers.[9]

Attica was America's most bloody prison uprising. And, while the causes of both the uprising and the massacre that ended it were extremely complicated, the emotions many apolitical citizens felt were more straightforward. According to Dick Edwards of the Harlem newspaper *The Amsterdam News*, white bystanders shouted to the observer Tom Wicker, who had written sympathetically of the prisoners, that he was a "Nigger-lover!" a "sonofabitch," and a "dirty double-crossing bastard" who ought to be strung up.[10]

Not surprisingly, these years were, for large numbers of all political persuasions, a deeply frightening and unsettling time. For the conservative Joe Everyman, they were becoming etched into consciousness as a time to scurry from.

And even as the radical politics had waned in the latter part of the 1970s, the riots died down and the revolutionary political organizations of the campuses, the ghettos, and the prisons, splintered or dissolved, the cultural legacy of the 1960s remained. In sexual behavior, in drugs of choice, in dress mores and music fashions. And, on the political stage, in the broader move to identity politics. Toward the politics of gay liberation, of ethnic nationalisms, environmentalism, and feminism.

Caught up in this uncertain *zeitgeist* many were apt to lump the good with the bad, to equate campaigns for social justice with a breakdown in law and order, and to oppose both with equal vehemence. By late 1980, Democratic President Jimmy Carter was discovering that a groundswell of support was building for the conservative B movie actor and ex-governor of California, Ronald Reagan. Working-class voters, whose families had for generations cast their support to the Democrats, were abandoning their party for the more optimistic and soothingly backward-looking message espoused by "Dutch" Reagan.

As the election campaign wore on, support for the Republican candidate rose. There were, however, so many other things for the American public to worry about that crime didn't even make the top five. Gallup polls asked questions about fear of nuclear war with the Soviets, about race relations, about unemployment and inflation, the Iranian hostage crisis, falling faith in the government's ability to handle major problems, the energy crisis. Even as crime rose and public nervousness increased, as late as October 2, 60 percent of respondents to a Gallup survey listed inflation as America's number one problem.[11] Under the surface, however, the voting public was clearly bothered by other issues that politicians could link to crime should they so desire. Race relations. Moral decline. Poverty. Inner-city decay. The increasing numbers of people living on welfare. And as Reagan began talking more about crime and drugs, so more people began registering their fears, began articulating their belief that the legal order was crumbling.

In many ways, Reagan's appeal was simple. Taxes were bad, welfare spending was worse. The country needed to spend more money on its military and more on its police. Traditional moral codes had to be reimposed on the drug-ingesting, hairy young. Indeed, in 1966, shortly after Reagan had been elected governor of California, he'd made one of his more famous quips. "A hippie," Reagan sneered, "is someone who dresses like Tarzan, has hair like Jane, and smells like Cheetah."[12] Criminals had to be locked up for longer, and the prisons in which they were kept had to be made harsher, but, in other spheres, the role of the government had to be drastically reduced. Follow these prescriptions, Reagan promised, and America's sunniest moments lay ahead. Essentially, his message could be put as follows: *Give me your trust and I will show you that both overseas and within America's boundaries, American righteousness can, and will, still prevail.*

And trust they did. Archie Bunker–type hard hats who twenty, even ten, years earlier would have laughed at the merest mention of voting for a Republican, flocked to Ronald Reagan's message. They didn't term themselves "Republicans," rather they were "Reagan Democrats." Alienated from the counterculture, from the Democrats' embrace of the civil rights movement, from kids burning American flags and middle-class elites making excuses for the criminal behavior rampant in so many cities, working-class white voters stood up and walked over to the Grand Old Party. In some ways, it was merely a replay of Richard Nixon's 1968 victory over Democrat Hubert Humphrey. But while 1968 might have been seen as an aberration, as the product of a year of unprecedented upheaval, 1980, the commentators agreed, represented a deeper, longer-lasting political realignment, ushering in what the journalists Rowland Evans and Robert Novak promptly termed "the most revolutionary administration since Franklin Roosevelt's."[13]

In this climate, the voices of men such as James Q. Wilson loudly reverberated. "Increasingly, the central city is coming to be made up of persons who have no interest, or who face special disabilities, in creating and maintaining a sense of community," wrote Wilson, who was a leading Harvard sociologist at the time, and, as importantly, one of those rare figures, a public intellectual. "If the lower class has focal concerns that make crime attractive or even inevitable, it is not clear how government would supply 'the lower class' with a new set of values consistent with law-abidingness." Wilson argued that those in power who emphasized the social causes of crime were naively led into "a preference for the rehabilitative (or reformation) theory of corrections over the deterrence or incapacitation theories."[14] Both welfare and rehabilitation, two of the leading pillars of recent liberal social thought, were clear failures, according to this school of thinking; and worse, they were failures with devastating consequences. It was time for public intellectuals such as himself to come out and say the hard truths: that welfare was creating a "user" mentality, and that people never taught the virtues of hard work and responsibility were only too likely to take up lives of crime. Instead of shying away from imprisonment, judges should use this potent tool to ratchet up the *cost* to individuals of breaking society's laws.

The arguments struck a commonsense chord, and in the newly conservative halls of power, academics such as James Wilson and the anti-welfare theorist Charles Murray were suddenly being quoted with a whole lot of fanfare. Soon President Reagan was talking about "running up the battle flag" in the wars against crime and drugs.

By January 1982, nearly a year before Pete Wilson got elected to the Senate, twenty-nine senators had come together to form the bipartisan Senate Drug Enforcement Caucus, calling for the military to get involved in eradicating overseas sources of drugs, the CIA to spy on drug cartels, twenty-year sentences to be imposed on first-time heroin traffickers, forty years for second-time traffickers, and five years for a first marijuana conviction.[15]

Against men like Ochoa, and the seedy, miserable world they inhabited, war had indeed been declared.

Unable to raise bail at the tail end of 1979, in what would turn out to be the second-to-last year Democrats controlled the White House for twelve years, Billy and Jamie spent New Year's Eve in the Los Angeles County Central Jail. It was a new facility, built on Bauchet Street, near the great art deco railway terminus of Union Station. Built to replace the old jail on Broadway, housed many floors up, above a now-defunct courthouse. For both of them, going to L.A. County — even a new one — was almost like a homecoming. The one on Broadway was a place to which they each had been delivered numerous times in the 1960s and 1970s, and, despite the new premises, the Bauchet Street jail seemed extremely familiar. They could still sleep until noon if they wanted, they could warm their snacks on a communal hotplate, and shoot the breeze, play dominoes, or try their luck at cards with the other inmates in the "tank." There were still the corners where they could sit and shiver as their bodies shifted from hot to cold and back again with the onset of their heroin withdrawal symptoms. And there was still the communal eating area where they could barter items of food with the other inmates. Like in the old jail, in Bauchet the inmates wore the standard prison blues.

A month later, on January 22, the two cousins filed into Judge Samuel L. Laidig's room at the Municipal Court in Pasadena for their preliminary hearing. Billy was represented by a public defender. Jamie had a private attorney. Not surprisingly, Laidig found that there was enough evidence to proceed to trial, and he set bail at one thousand dollars. Since neither cousin could come up with anywhere near that sum, back to jail they went. Interviewed by probation officers preparing a character report for the court, Jamie flippantly told them that his only hobby was "tropical fish."

Three months into this stint in jail, Ochoa got fed up with sitting around all day, with waiting for a trial set for far into the spring, with the endless routine of life on the inside. And so he joined a protest. It was hardly an Attica; but, with the traumatic uprisings of a decade earlier still deeply scarred into the public's mind, it *was* enough to ruffle the feathers of the authorities.

On April 19, Captain Robert T. Grimm reported "a major disturbance" at his jail. Ochoa and twenty-five other *pro term* inmates—jailies awaiting trial who were representing themselves in court—wanted some attention paid to three major complaints: that they were being denied access to the showers, that the sheriffs weren't permitting them to see visitors, and that the facility's staff were denying them the law library access that they needed in order to prepare for their appearances before the judges. To get this attention, the inmates refused to enter their cells when told to do so. Instead, they loitered on the open walkways lining the two tiers of cells to which they were supposed to be confined.

Soon a fierce melee broke out between guards and inmates. Unarmed sheriff's deputies had poured onto the walkways, hoping to manhandle the twenty-six renegades into compliance. But the young *pro term* inmates had given as good as they'd got, punching and kicking, and after a few minutes the staff had retreated off the tier. The hotheads were jubilant; but Ochoa—already at nearly thirty-seven an experienced old-timer—warned them the deputies would soon be back. And, of course, he was right. Within minutes, scores of uniformed officers were flooding back onto the cell block, this time clad in riot gear and wielding hefty metal flashlights as weapons. Ochoa, standing near the front of the group, was one of the first to fall under the blows of the infuriated deputies.

By the time all the inmates had been subdued, many hours later, four prisoners and seven lawmen had been injured.[16] Ochoa claimed that he was "severely beaten over the head and body by Los Angeles

County Sheriff Deputy's [sic]."[17] They had, he declared, repeatedly struck him with metal flashlights, causing so much blood to flow from two wounds to his head, that a doctor had had to sew him up with sixteen stitches.

As a result of this fracas, Ochoa had to spend two days in the county medical center, and another eleven recuperating at the county jail hospital on Bauchet Street. As the lawyers prepared to argue their cases, Ochoa filed a motion calling on the judge to dismiss charges. As a result of the beating, the burglar stated, he had serious brain damage, he was having severe memory-recall problems, and he thus regarded himself as incompetent to stand trial.

Not surprisingly, the judge dismissed Ochoa's motion, and, miraculously, Ochoa's brain damage promptly disappeared. Soon afterward, he was found guilty of burglary in the second degree. On the morning of June 30, Ochoa appeared before Judge Gilbert C. Alston to hear his sentence. The result was somewhat pleasing. Two years in a state prison, with a pretrial credit of 273 days. What made Ochoa even happier was that, despite Captain Grimm's written intervention informing the court of Ochoa's role in the jail disturbance, Alston had arrived at the figure of 273 through adding 92 days of "good time" credit to the 181 that Ochoa had actually spent in jail.

He served his time in the California Institution for Men, Chino, a large medium-security prison an hour's drive east of Los Angeles. As prisons went, it wasn't bad. He got himself a job as a "hobby clerk," writing up files on which inmates made what products in woodwork class or any of the other trade classes they partook in. And when he wasn't working, he was free to roam around the walkways, talking with other inmates and playing games. Best of all, when he went to sleep at night, he could stretch out on a mattress that was actually supported by proper bedsprings. As institutions went, this one was practically *comfortable*. A few months into his sentence, Ronald Reagan was elected president. Billy, not much interested in politics, hardly even took note of the event. He also didn't follow the ever-tougher rhetoric uttered by senators such as Pete Wilson in the newly declared War on Crime.

After Chino, Ochoa was once again committed to his old alma mater, the California Rehabilitation Center, for a couple years, before being released back to L.A. It was an arrangement that suited him down to the ground. Because the CRC was now being used more like a regular prison, Billy was no longer required to attend the therapy sessions to convince the well-meaning staff that he could kick off the chains of drug addiction. Instead, he worked as a clerk in the visiting rooms, and, as he later told it, under the benignly turned eyes of some of the correctional officers, soon established a nice little sideline smuggling powder cocaine and heroin between visitors and "residents." The little packages of cling film–wrapped drugs fit snugly into the sides of cigarette packets, and soon Ochoa had become a respected middleman. The only thing he asked in return was a cut of the narcotics.[18]

And so it came about that Ochoa, who for twenty years had taken heroin and not much else, began snorting cocaine. It gave him a buzz, energy, and Billy liked the sensation. When he came back to Los Angeles, Billy began seeking out dealers from whom he could buy this newly discovered tonic.

Meanwhile, while Ochoa was in prison, the country's political mood, which had already hardened during the disastrous last half of Carter's presidency, was, under Ronald Reagan's leadership, swinging ever farther rightward, and the support offered to its poorest individuals was declining. In 1975, according to Harvard University sociologist William Julius Wilson, a little under one-third of the people in America listed as "poor" had "incomes below fifty percent of the amount officially designated as the poverty line; in 1992, forty percent did so. Among Blacks, the increase was even sharper, from thirty-two percent in 1975 to nearly half (forty-nine percent) in 1992. Moreover, the overall poverty rate actually increased after 1978."[19] In other words, the poor in America were getting ever poorer, more people were becoming poor, and despair was increasing amongst those without access to legitimate income. But, at the same time, as the top tax rate was slashed and government regulations on corporations were weakened, the wealthy were also getting far wealthier. Caught between the extremes was a middle class struggling to make it and increasingly unsympathetic to the hard-luck stories of those on the bottom of the heap.

Three thousand miles across the Atlantic, similar political trends were unfolding in the United Kingdom, a country whose political, economic, cultural, and military fortunes were inextricably linked with those of the United States. In 1978–9, Britain had experienced a "winter of discontent." With the double nightmare of spiraling inflation and unemployment ravaging the economy, and with tax rates inching up by the month, trade unions had struck for higher wages against the Labour Party government led by Prime Minister James Callaghan. It was an unmistakable sign that the post–World War II social compact—built around high taxes and a semicontrolled economy in exchange for comprehensive government programs such as universal health care, and lifetime job security—was breaking down. And that Keynesianism, the economic philosophy that advocated governments support employment through large-scale public spending, was withering on the vine after a thirty-year ascendancy. Carter's problems in America were replicated for Callaghan in Britain. Throughout the winter of 1979, public services had come to a standstill, with uncollected garbage clogging the streets, and even—according to some sensational accounts—unburied bodies taking up space in the mortuaries of industrial cities like Liverpool because the gravediggers were out on strike. "Each night the television screens carried film of bearded men in duffle coats huddled around braziers," wrote the Chancellor of the Exchequer, Dennis Healey. "Nervous viewers thought the Revolution had already begun."[20] Britain might have won World War II, but, scoffed many, it was now "the sick man of Europe."

By the spring of 1979, Britain's electorate had had enough. In the general election called for May 3, the Conservative Party, led by Margaret Thatcher, swept into power on a program of economic change known as "monetarism," championed by Chicago economist Milton Friedman: privatization of state-owned industries, tax cuts, the dismantling of large numbers of antipoverty social programs, and an increased emphasis on military expenditures. The party also advocated a reinvigorated approach to crime. *No more would politicians and bureaucrats fumble around looking for "root causes" of criminal behavior. Instead, they would get serious about making ordinary citizens feel safe again.* In the new economy that was soon to establish roots, unemployment would soar from one million to over three million, as inefficient old businesses were permitted to decay in the name of laissez-faire capitalism. To counter the rising crime that followed this explosion in poverty, Britain's police forces were beefed up and new "boot camps" were created for young offenders.

It was a model for transformation of a sluggish system, and for a newly aggressive state clampdown on crime, that Ronald Reagan's economic advisers and policy analysts in Washington, D.C., would soon embrace.

When Reagan was first elected, a year and a half after Maggie Thatcher's rise to power, slightly over half the country supported capital punishment. Three months later, fully two-thirds supported the death penalty.[21] And when, at the end of March 1981, the mentally unstable John Hinckley shot Reagan in the stomach in a failed assassination attempt, the country's support for toughening up the criminal justice system became practically airborne. Soon, opinion polls had three-quarters of the public demanding that murderers be put to death. And the anger wasn't restricted to murderers, to the worst of the worst. A year after Reagan was shot, nearly six in ten voters favored building more prisons in their state to house criminals of all stripes.[22] Amazingly, given the reigning hostility to Big Government, almost half of all those questioned said they would be willing to pay higher taxes in order to fund such an expansion of the country's prison system.

In retrospect, however, the first years of the new administration were still the early days of an escalating battle. In opinion polls, fewer than 10 percent listed crime as the worst problem confronting America. And, despite all the increased government activity against marijuana and cocaine production, it wasn't until June 23, 1985, that drugs even made the nation's "most important problem list," weighing in at a somewhat tepid 6 percent. After all, there were other things to worry about: rising unemployment, for starters. And increasing nuclear tensions with the Russians.

But even though crime and drugs didn't initially rank top of the list, attitudes *were* indeed changing. In 1977, when President Carter and many of his aides had openly contemplated decriminalizing marijuana, only four in ten Americans believed in prosecuting small-time pot smokers. By 1985, half favored prosecution. And, by September 1986, the month that Ronald Reagan called for a "national crusade against drugs," over two-thirds wanted the courts to punish users.[23] The early days were morphing into all-out war.

The launching of Reagan's "crusade" was timed to perfection. Timed to distract the public from what was just coming to be known as the Iran-Contra affair; intended to draw attention away from the allegations of money being channeled by elements of the administration to the Nicaraguan Contras despite a congressional vote barring such aid; to turn ears and eyes from the stories of high officials journeying clandestinely to Iran on illicit arms-sales trips that would raise millions of dollars for the guerrilla wars of Latin America. How better to erase those troubling opinion polls that showed 70 percent of the public thought the president was lying when he proclaimed his ignorance of all these shadowy goings-on? And, since crack was just then proving its utter destructiveness to individuals and communities alike, who could possibly criticize the Gipper for trying to save America from the clear calamity of a full-blown multimillion-addict rock-cocaine invasion?

And then, to add fuel to the flames, the president's wife stepped in and turned up the volume on a campaign she had first launched in 1984. First Lady Nancy Reagan looked into the television cameras and blessed her husband's crusade with a tag line, built around three concise words, words that she had been delivering to crowds of schoolchildren across America. "Just Say No." It was simple and to the point; and it completely ignored the complexities of the issue. Wrapped up in those three words were a whole host of unspoken commands: *Don't ask why people take drugs; don't give me excuses about why you take drugs. Don't ask for antipoverty programs to provide legitimate jobs outside of the drug gangs. Just don't do it.* It reduced all the chaos, heartbreak, peer pressure, poverty, loneliness, and everything else that presaged an individual's drug use and community disintegration to a three-word commandment: "Just Say No." It sounded so easy. *And if you can't even follow something as straightforward as this, then why should taxpayers spend their hard-earned money helping you out with social workers, detox clinics, and the like?*

By 1987, a Harris Poll was finding that the majority of Americans favored prison sentences of over ten years for cocaine dealers, and, more surprisingly at least five years for personal users.[24] Three years later, according to journalist Dan Baum, more than four in five people stated that they would turn in drug-using family members to the police.[25] During the decade, federal courts had increased the length of the sentences they were doling out for drug-related crimes by an average of 59 percent. And state courts, too, had dramatically upped their sentences.[26]

Criminologist Diana Gordon summed it up this way: "Where drug law violations were formerly treated in district courts like property crimes, they are now treated like violent crimes."[27] In 1989 alone, an estimated one thousand people received life sentences for drug offenses.[28]

But that was only part of the story. For, as cases like Ochoa's would show over the coming years, by the late 1980s the courts were also doling out an increasing number of sentences for relatively minor property crimes that in previous decades would have been reserved only for violent criminals. As the country's fear about crime grew to almost hysterical proportions, so the nuances within the criminal justice system, the ability to distinguish between more and less serious offenses, waned. By the late 1980s, with open drug bazaars, graffiti-tagged buildings, streets littered with crack vials and other detritus of the trade, and the increasing prevalence of "ho stros"—"whore strolls" populated by desperate female crackheads—much of America's urban landscape was collapsing into near-total chaos. So deadly had the gang wars and crack battles become that by the latter part of the decade, murder was the leading cause of death for Black men aged between eighteen and twenty-nine.[29] In 1989, in New York alone, nearly two thousand people were dispatched by the violence of others.[30] And, from California to Miami, the public was confronted by the scary spectacle of gangs possessing, and using, heavier firepower than the police who were supposed to be preserving law and order.

Primed by two decades of tough-on-crime rhetoric, the public response to the very real and terrifying wave of violent crime generated by the crack epidemic was to demand ever-tougher laws, legislation that would deal not only with the murderers and the top traffickers, but with *everybody* who in any way stepped over the line into the unpleasant, drug-infested world of crime. And when those laws didn't make them feel safe, they demanded still tougher ones from their political representatives. And, not surprisingly, elected officials were only too happy to oblige. North Carolina Senator Jesse Helms pushed a law through Congress providing for a five-year prison sentence for possession of a mere five grams of crack — approximately one day's supply for a regular user.[31] And by 1989 incoming President George Bush's new Drug Czar, William Bennett, was announcing to the public that "a massive wave of arrests is a top priority for the War on Drugs."[32] He argued on Capitol Hill that punishment should be "moral, to exact a price for transgressing the rights of others," rather than rehabilitative.[33] Bennett and his advisers believed that the only way to curb the plague of drugs was to go after the casual users. After all, these were the people who touted drugs to their peers, who made narcotics appear sexy, hip, cool. Put enough people in prison, Bennett argued, and you'd soon see progress.

A year later, in 1990, Texas Senator Phil Gramm and a then-relatively-unknown Republican representative from Georgia named Newt Gingrich even tried to convince Congress to pass a National Drugs and Crime Emergency Act that would have converted unused army bases, made redundant by the fall of the Berlin Wall and the ongoing disintegration of the Soviet Union, into "detention centers" for drug offenders. At least on this occasion, however, Congress balked at such an extraordinary action.

But even without a National Emergency Act, in practice huge numbers were already being shipped off to detention. In the 1980s, according to *The Corrections Yearbook*, almost six hundred prisons and jails opened across America.[34] To fund these projects, state politicians were devising increasingly creative schemes: in New York State Governor Mario Cuomo was tapping into Urban Development Corporation moneys, raised through the issuance of state bonds, to build prisons. It was easier that way, since prison bonds had to be voted on by the public, whereas UDC bonds didn't need to be validated at the ballot box. Seven billion dollars was spent in ten years.[35] In Alabama the Department of Corrections had just begun a spending spree that would eventually balloon its expenditures from a 4 percent share in the general funds budget to a whopping 16 percent.[36] And then, of course, there was George Deukmejian's California, busily building the largest prison system in the land. Even in low-crime, liberal states such as Minnesota, prison spending was in the process of quadrupling as the 1980s sped along. The same held in Connecticut, where a $400-million prison-building spree resulted in cuts in education budgets in many localities. And, at the federal level, as the 1990s got underway, William Bennett was calling for 130 percent increases in prison expenditures.

In many ways it was an endless cycle, what Colorado-based journalist Joel Dyer has labeled a "perpetual prisoner machine." Rising poverty was generating more crime, more violent cynicism, and more drug addicts. As the wider public experienced more crime firsthand, and, as important, read more about crime in the newspapers and watched television news programs increasingly dominated by violent crime reportage, so fear increased. The fear led to political movements to toughen up the criminal codes. In response, politicians from both major parties embraced concepts such as Truth-in-Sentencing, mandatory minimums, and, eventually, Three Strikes. And then the prison population increased. The problem was, once this cycle had been established the intertwined spirals of fear and tough political responses proved very hard to break. And so, even when the crime rate began to decline in the early 1990s, the prison population continued to rise.

Ochoa was approaching his fortieth birthday by the time he got out of prison; no longer was he a young man with feelings of immortality. In fact, when he looked in the mirror, nothing more than a run-down, middle-aged heroin addict, with an impressive list of crimes behind him and a family that had long ceased to hold out any hope for his rehabilitation, stared back.

There isn't much a forty-something-year-old ex-con with a major drug problem can do in the legitimate economy, especially in one busy shedding the jobs that traditionally employed its millions of unskilled workers. After all, admitting to extensive knowledge of the penal system doesn't really make up for those large gaps, those missing years on one's résumé. So once more, Billy Ochoa returned to the career he knew best: burgling houses. He had no steady girlfriend. His mother was dead. There was no one else who would simply and undemandingly love him for who he was. If Billy had stopped to contemplate his life, he wouldn't have found it a particularly rewarding existence. But Ochoa wasn't one for contemplation. He had always lived for the moment.

In the middle of October 1984, he got out his pliers and his screwdriver, and the various other tools of his trade, and broke into yet another dwelling. But, like the burglary of Hamer's house five years earlier, this was another of those unlucky moments that presaged prison; those moments now strung like beads on a cheap necklace across the decades of time from Ochoa's first arrests as a juvenile back in the 1950s. The police caught him in the act and, once more, took him off to yet another precinct house. In one respect, however, Ochoa caught a break. It was a precinct he hadn't previously had any run-ins with, and none of the officers knew who he was. Billy had no identification on him, and he told the police that his name was Richard Gutierrez. When he appeared in court, using this false alias, he told the judge that this was the first burglary he had been involved in and that he had no prior record. There was nothing to prove otherwise, for Ochoa had indeed never previously been booked under the name of Gutierrez, and somehow, perhaps because the police were so busy with catching more violent criminals, his fingerprints weren't sent off for any comparative analysis. And so, perhaps for the last time in his life, Ochoa wriggled out of major trouble. Instead of sentencing him to yet another term in prison, the court put Billy on probation. Screw up, however, the judge informed him, and "Gutierrez" would be heading straight to the pen.

Of course, drug addiction being what it was, eventually "Gutierrez" did indeed screw up.

Once introduced to cocaine at the Rehabilitation Center, his desire for the drug had ballooned. But cocaine was an expensive drug, and no matter how many houses he might burgle, Billy couldn't afford regular binges on cocaine in addition to sustaining his more powerful heroin addiction. But then, in 1985, the dealers had started selling a new, far cheaper, variant: crack cocaine. Unlike the powder variant that had to be snorted, crack was smokable, and a small amount would produce an intense, and instant, high. Instead of cocaine deals involving hundreds of dollars, crack created the drug market's equivalent of the eponymous 99-cent store. Within an astonishingly short period of time, it became the new drug of choice for America's desperate urban poor. Billy Ochoa, and countless others like him, could now afford cocaine on a daily basis.

For Billy, who had taken to living in the dangerous halfway houses on L.A.'s skid row, crack opened up a whole new world. He would ready a hypodermic needle full of heroin and would then inhale a lungful of crack from a pipe. He'd hold his breath and, while his lungs were still full of the crack smoke, he would take the needle and plunge the heroin into a vein. Then he'd breathe out, and the smoke would curl out of his mouth and float up into the air. It was a perfect combination. The cocaine would produce a god-almighty rush, and, then, just when the high was getting too much to bear, just when he felt his brain was about to explode, the heroin would bring him right back down again.

He'd buy the crack late at night, in the bleak, drug-infested Macarthur Park. It was always an adventure. "Waddya want, pops?" the teenage dealers would cry out to him. *Nothing, nothing,* Billy would mumble. He was afraid of appearing too eager, of appearing like he was carrying money on him. After all, these young kids would just as soon rob and kill an old man like Billy as sell him dope. He'd shuffle through the park wearing his most beat-up, shabby clothes, several days' growth of stubble adorning his face. He'd smile his broken-toothed smile and hope that they thought he was too poor to bother. Then he'd seat himself on a bench and watch, trying to work out who was doing the most business, who was selling the best "screen." He even had tricks to convince potentially violent onlookers that he really was penniless. "Downtown, your life is worth nothing," Billy asserts. "If you have twenty dollars and you're not willing to part with it, they'll cut your throat." So, Billy would shuffle through the young dealers, approach one and take a broken watch out of one of his tattered pockets. *The watch for five dollars worth of crack,* he'd plead in a loud voice, making sure that the young men loitering nearby saw the whole scene and comprehended when the dealer turned him away contemptuously. Then, and only then, would Ochoa go off to a less frequented part of the park, catch the attention of a dealer, if possible a woman dealer less likely to attack him, make sure no one was watching, and then take his money out from inside his hat or shoe, or wherever else he was using as a hiding place that night. When he wanted to buy a donut late at night, he'd pull a similar stunt. If a donut cost fifty cents, he'd bring forty seven with him to the late-night outlet. Then, when it came time to pay, he'd beg the remaining three cents off some of the other bums hanging around the entrance to the store. Sometimes, he'd pretend to be a Spanish-speaking immigrant with nothing to his name apart from the clothes on his back. That way, Billy figured, he wasn't likely to get all cut-up—like a well-dressed friend of his had been after removing a wallet from his pants' pocket to pay for some food. You had to be smart if you wanted to survive in this particular environment.

Ochoa would take his rocks of crack back to whatever roach-infested halfway house he was crashing in that night. And then he'd scout around for a woman who might want to share his high with him. They were all over the streets these days—young girls so dependent on crack that they'd have sex with strangers in exchange for a couple hits from their crack pipe. For the old-time prostitutes, the women who charged twenty dollars and up for their services, these new addicts were proving disastrous. After all, why would a man like Billy Ochoa part with twenty bucks, when all he had to do was approach a girl in the lobby of a sleazy hotel, whisper the word "screen" and, despite his grotty teeth and air of decay, she'd be all over him in a New York minute. He could find them in the lobbies, in the elevators, in the dorm rooms they shared with other girls of the street. He could strike up a conversation, noncommittally mention that he had some crack, drop his room number into the mix, return to his room, and a few minutes later, there the girl would be, knocking on his door, practically tearing her panties off in her hurry to get a hold of the drug.[37]

But, this was another party that couldn't last. In early 1987, the law once again broke in upon this crack and heroin fantasy, and Ochoa was arrested for being under the influence of drugs. Since he had a record a mile long under his original name, Billy again told the police that he was Richard Gutierrez. This time, however, the scam was figured out, and the befuddled addict was hauled back to court under his real name. Prosecutor Kenneth Jeffers, once he had acquainted himself with Gutierrez's true background, was outraged that the burglar had avoided prison back in 1985, and now he demanded that the court get tough. "I had to take my shoes off to count the pages on the rap sheet on this particular case," the lawyer informed the judge in the most dramatic of tones. "It's one of the longest records I've ever seen."

Yes, Ochoa's court-appointed attorney agreed, *it is bad, but there's a reason*. The defense lawyer, Jane Marpet went on to point out that her client was "obviously a hype. His problem is obviously drugs. That's why he's committing burglaries. And it doesn't look to me like he's gotten any breaks. All he's done is go to prison his whole life." Marpet was, however, not convincing anybody. After all the years of liberal experimentation with various rehabilitation programs, after all the money poured into antipoverty programs throughout the 1960s and 1970s, after all the promises that criminals such as Ochoa just needed the right nurturing environment, America was fed up. Sure, Ochoa might have grown up poor. Sure he'd always had it tough. Sure he had outgrown violence at about the time his teenage acne had disappeared and he'd reached legal adulthood. All of this paled before the undeniable fact that Ochoa kept committing small-time crimes in order to buy a drug that the overwhelming majority of the population viewed with absolute disgust and loathing. If he was too weak to beat the addiction, well that was nobody's fault but his own. With crack tearing apart entire cities, and the murder rate spiraling, the population was demanding action.

In early 1987, Ochoa was sentenced to six years in prison for violating the probation conditions that had been imposed on him following the 1984 burglary. It was by far the harshest sentence ever handed down to him, and it demonstrated the extent to which views of crime and punishment were changing. As America lost patience with its troublesome underclasses, the net was closing around men like Billy.

NINE

Since the summer of 1986, and the frenzied response to the arrival of crack in America, crime and drugs had been at the top of the country's domestic political agenda. The 1986 Anti-Drug Abuse Act had chan-neled billions of dollars into law-enforcement and eradication efforts; and, because drugs had been deemed a threat to national security, the way was opened for the military to get involved in fighting drug traf-fickers, especially in the mountainous terrain of Latin America. For those in positions of power, milking the fear of crack was proving an electoral godsend, with no publicity gimmick too coarse to be indulged in. In August of that year, during what the academic and drug war critic Arnold S. Trebach termed "the scared summer,"[1] President Reagan, Vice President Bush, and seventy White House staffers had even gone so far as to offer up urine samples to prove to the world that the country's leadership was indeed free of drugs and practicing the abstinence that it preached. And, to back up the words with action, Attorney General Edwin Meese III was urging that the federal, state, and local police forces should join together to form twenty-four crack task forces that would spread out through the largest metropolitan areas rooting out dealers and users wherever they were found.[2] The anticrack fight would be similar to that of Operation Delta-9, launched by more than two thousand armed police the previous summer to search out and destroy marijuana crops in all fifty states of the union.

The public's fear of crack, and the more general, and growing, anx-iety about all forms of crime, had been used to perfection by George

Bush in his successful bid to win the presidency in 1988. And, while Reagan had offered up jars of urine to prove his mettle in the War on Drugs, Bush's team orchestrated the arrest of a teenage crack dealer in Lafayette Park, just across from the White House, shortly after his inauguration in order to convince the country that this was indeed a plague demanding extraordinary measures. In one fell swoop they also ratcheted up the federal antidrug funds from six to ten billion dollars.

Despite the release of statistics indicating that casual drug use actually *declined* by 40 percent between 1985 and 1988, as a hard core of clinically addicted users came to dominate America's drug scene, and with opinion polls showing that 64 percent of Americans viewed drugs as the country's most serious problem, it was politically convenient for Bush to focus on the image of a spreading narcotic plague.[3] And to do this job, the incoming president shifted Education Secretary William Bennett into a new role—that of Drug Czar.

Bill Bennett was a latter-day version of Hale Boggs and Harry Anslinger, a large man prone to talking about how culture wars were raging for control of the country's soul, to lambasting liberal intellectual elites for systematically undermining everything ordinary Americans held dear. Like Anslinger decades earlier, the one-time professor was also a master of lurid, almost purple prose. Crack, he subsequently wrote in his book *The De-Valuing of America*, was leading women to give birth to infants "weighing a pound or two, with a bulb head and Popsicle limbs. These infants are so tiny and vulnerable that they look barely human." He went on to write about crack houses populated by "people sprawled out on their high, or 'crashing' afterward. Food and garbage are littered everywhere. Often human excrement and puddles of urine are found around the room."[4]

Tall, rugged, and hammer-voiced, fancying himself a philosopher of rank—the New Yorker–come–North Carolinian possessed both a doctorate in political philosophy and a law degree—he believed that drugs were destroying America's moral fabric, and he favored a near-religious crusade to banish these substances from the country's cultural landscape, and to ruthlessly punish those who continued to use or sell such substances. Having made his name in the early 1980s as a ruggedly conservative chair of the National Endowment for the Humanities, and having solidified his reputation as a bare-knuckles fighter through his attacks on teachers' unions in the second Reagan administration and his calls for "demolition squads" to solve the problem of under-accomplishing schools,[5] Bennett relished the opportunity to tackle the country's drug problem. After all, it had been a perennial favorite of his even while at the Department of Education. There, he had called for teachers caught using drugs to immediately resign, and for students nabbed in the act of getting high to be summarily expelled.

The new Drug Czar argued that "small quantities, even so-called personal amounts should be punished," and he demanded "swift and certain punishment" for dealers.[6] He advocated more inspections of international mail and cargo shipments, hoping to break down cross-border smuggling routes, the building of more prisons to house drug dealers, and, time and again, the use of the military against both drug producers overseas and drug traffickers coming into America.[7] Appearing on the CNN show Larry King Live, Bennett even embraced a caller's plea for the beheading of drug dealers, saying such an idea, while perhaps impractical from a constitutional point of view, was nevertheless perfectly acceptable from a moral viewpoint.[8]

In such a climate, only talking tough counted. A year into Bush's term of office, Bennett could crow that there was "a palpably different spirit in the nation. We had undergone the great American change of mind about drugs."[9]

Shortly afterward, however, exhausted by the pace of his war and looking to return to private life, Bennett decided to step down. He had only been the nation's Drug Czar for twenty months. But, in those months, he had moved the country ever farther down the path toward mass incarceration, and he had personally championed an extraordinary expansion of the country's already bulging prison population.

By the time the 1992 election rolled around, even though a sagging economy had once again displaced drugs and crime as the problem identified in polls as America's number one problem, the country was still fearful and angry enough that the Democrats had also come to believe that only through talking the talk on crime could they hope to get elected. Luckily in Bill Clinton the party's elite believed they had found just the man for the job.

Unlike Dukakis in 1988, Governor Clinton was a man firmly committed to the death penalty, not afraid of promising more police on the streets and more dollars to be channeled into prison building and not averse to waging whatever drug wars the people wanted waged. Coming out of the Democratic Leadership Council, which was committed to move the party toward the political center and away from its more liberal constituents, as Bill Clinton, the man from Hope, saw it no matter where your core sympathies lay if you wanted to play the rough-and-tumble game of politics, you had to appeal to that great Silent Majority that Richard Nixon had so successfully identified in 1968 and Reagan had spoken to in 1980. And so, like all his recent predecessors, Bill Clinton was pouring money into law enforcement. (Indeed, by the end of his tenure in office, the federal antidrug budget would have soared to close to twenty billion dollars per year—up from just over one billion when Ronald Reagan had first entered the White House two decades earlier.[10])

Thus it was that by the mid-1990s, with crimes such as the Polly Klaas murder and the Long Island Railroad massacre hogging the headlines and once more raising the public's level of anger, the politics around crime and drug abuse had been largely reduced to a battle of sound bites: who could successfully communicate their toughness to voters clamoring for harsher punishments. And, on the West Coast, the answer was emerging loud and clear: Governor Pete Wilson.

By March of 1994, Pete Wilson's team had successfully turned the gubernatorial election in California into a referendum on three issues: California's approach to illegal immigration; California's attitude toward welfare recipients; and California's methods of dealing with crime and punishment. Kathleen Brown was still ahead in the polls, but the huge lead the Democrats had enjoyed going into the election cycle was shrinking by the day. Throughout the spring, the summer, and the fall of 1994, Wilson made speech after speech on these three themes, using ever more incendiary language to describe the criminals, illegal immigrants, and welfare recipients living within his state. He attended one funeral or memorial after another for police officers killed in the line of duty, and he addressed every gathering he could of crime victims and their families. Whenever an invitation to one of these events was sent to his office—such as the one inviting him to speak at Officer Richard Maxwell's memorial in Bakersfield, at the Canyon Hills Assembly of God Church—an aide would scrawl on the top, "This is a must do," and sure enough it was done.

The electorate of California wasn't just voting for its political leaders in 1994, it was also voting on several important ballot initiatives. Two in particular stood out. The first was Mike Reynolds's Three Strikes initiative, Proposition 184. And the second was Proposition 187, which, if voted into law, would deny illegal immigrants access to *all* public services: health care, public schooling, even vaccinations for their babies.

The arguments behind Proposition 187 appeared fairly straightforward: if someone was in the country illegally, why should the taxpayers of California have to pick up the tab for looking after them? Of course, what went unsaid was that many of those very same outraged taxpayers had encouraged illegal immigration in the first place through hiring these Spanish-speaking workers as low-paid gardeners, babysitters, and casual day-laborers. Practically every bookstore in L.A. sold Spanish phrase books that taught readers how to tell the home help what to clean and when to do it. Moreover, if illegal immigrants remained in America but had no access to education or to health care, there were serious risks of creating a desperately uneducated and diseased substrata living in the heart of the largest states and cities in the land, and—as the AIDS epidemic had shown only too clearly—once started, public health disasters obeyed no social or class boundaries. But, with unemployment stubbornly high and the fabled Californian optimism evaporating in the desert heat, it was becoming increasingly popular to blame illegal immigrants for all of the state's woes and to demand tough, albeit simplistic, action to rout them out.

Soon Pete Wilson—the same man who as senator less than a decade earlier had worked with Californian agribusiness to allow *more* casual farm laborers into the United States from Mexico—had reinvented himself as one of the country's preeminent crusaders in what was coming to be seen as a *war* against illegal immigration. He visited one jail after another, denouncing the federal government for not stepping in to foot the costs of California's incarceration of close to twenty thousand illegal immigrants—many of whom were in prison as a result of the increasingly tough-on-crime politics that Wilson himself was espousing, and who had been convicted under U.S. laws, in U.S. courts, and were thus serving time in U.S. prisons. Time after time, he spoke about criminal aliens, playing to that age-old fear of the country being beset by foreign criminal hordes; the same fear that the LAPD had played to in the run-up to the zoot-suit riots; the same fear Harry Anslinger had alluded to in his panegyrics on the Chinese subverting America through drugs. He visited hospitals in San Diego and East Los Angeles and talked with doctors and administrators about the crippling costs associated with treating paperless aliens. He demanded that President Bill Clinton declare an "immigration emergency" in California. He visited El Paso to see how their zero-tolerance "Operation Hold The Line" approach was battening down the border crossings. He released funds for the Border Patrol to hire more officers. He flew to Washington, D.C., to testify before a Senate hearing on illegal immigration.[11] He filed three lawsuits against the federal government to get them to toughen up their immigration policies and he proposed a constitutional amendment to deny citizenship to children of illegal immigrants who were born in the United States.

When it came to welfare—with the public clamoring for an end to "welfare as we know it"—Wilson was equally severe. Over the past few years, the governor had almost doubled the number of welfare fraud investigators employed by the state. Now he coined another sporting slogan. "One strike and you're off," he told his audiences. Commit welfare fraud once, and you will never again be eligible for any public assistance. He also began to talk about imposing time limits for welfare recipients. It was a theme that Wilson was planning to spend more time on once the business of the election was over.

With Newt Gingrich heading a resurgent Republican Party in its bid to take over the federal Congress, and with Republican gubernatorial candidates leading in close to two-thirds of the states, Wilson was finding that the tougher his messages on these topics the more his support rose. And why not? After all, this was a year of hyperbole; it was the period in which the South Carolinian mother Susan Smith had drowned her two young children in a lake, and Gingrich had gone on television to tell voters that if they were fed up with crimes such as Smith's—for some reason he specifically focused on her act of infanticide—they should vote for the Grand Old Party.

For a man who had started off as a centrist, moderate Republican in the 1960s, Wilson had come a long way. Unlike his opposition to the tax-cutting Proposition 13, in 1978, the career politician was now absolutely determined to be on the right side of every popular insurgency that the volatile Californian, and by extension national, political system could throw up. And unlike the moderate mayor whose Crime Commission had deliberately downplayed the effectiveness of mass incarceration for criminals, now Wilson couldn't stress his toughness fast enough. For he knew too well the cost of putting himself on the wrong side of the zeitgeist.

State Treasurer Kathleen Brown had started her run for governor opposing both Propositions 184 and 187. Soon, however, as the political tide turned against her, Brown—the scion of a liberal family that had already had two members serve as California governors in the past forty years—was desperately trying to reinvent herself as a tough-on-crime convert. In the second week of March, just a few days after Wilson had signed Three Strikes, her aides tried to trump the governor by claiming that the Department of Corrections was irresponsibly releasing from prison a serial rapist by the name of Melvin Carter. It wasn't too hard to see that Brown was trying to turn Carter into Wilson's Willie Horton. The Republican, however, promptly squashed this attempt to outflank him on his favorite issue. Yes, he replied, Carter was being released. And yes, this was a terrible thing. But the reason he was being released was because of a dangerously liberal sentencing code that allowed a monster like Carter to gain good-time credits through working while in prison.[12] And many of those liberal laws, Wilson charged, were instituted by Kathleen Brown's father, Edmund, and brother, Jerry, during their terms as governor. Surely it was better to elect a Republican pledged to overhaul these laws rather than another Brown with the same liberal credentials as the other members of her illustrious family. "Indeed, while you and I and victims' groups have been working for years to change the law and make California safe," Wilson told a group of sheriffs, "Kathleen Brown has been a non-participant."

From that point on, Brown was playing a losing game of catch-up. Having accepted that the election would be fought on Wilson's territory, the Democrat never could quite find her way back onto the offensive. For every time Brown tried to appear tough-on-crime, her opponent would simply declare a need for even tougher rules. "This new 'Three Strikes' law isn't an end to reform," Wilson promised an audience of police officers and district attorneys, "it's just a beginning. California's peace officers *still* need additional resources and backup to put violent career criminals behind bars. And California's prosecutors *still* need tougher laws to keep these useless thugs there for as long as they deserve."[13]

Despite passage of Three Strikes by the legislature, murder victim Kimber Reynolds's father Mike was still pushing his November Three Strikes ballot initiative, encouraging the electorate to lock the new sentencing code into place to prevent politicians in Sacramento from watering down the law once the political spotlight had shifted onto other issues. The Three Strikes You're Out Criminal Justice Committee, of which Reynolds was a leading figure, was, by now, raking in huge political contributions. On November 23, for example, the prison guards' union had made out a check to the committee for fifty thousand dollars. In February, they sent another fifty thousand dollars Mike Reynolds's way.[14]

In the meantime, as the initiative campaign gained momentum, Pete Wilson was doing everything he could to keep the political spotlight right where it was, and the California Correctional Peace Officers Association was rewarding both him and Attorney General Dan Lungren with enormous donations. By the time the election was over, Wilson would have received well over half a million dollars from the union, making it his biggest single political contributor. Lungren would have garnered close to one hundred thousand dollars.[15] By contrast, the trade union gave Kathleen Brown a mere twelve hundred fifty dollars.

In late April 1994 Wilson's long-time mentor, ex–President Richard Nixon, died. Ever since the early 1960s, when the ex–Vice President had hired the fresh lawyer as a staffer, the younger man had looked up to Nixon as a mentor, almost it seemed at times, as a surrogate father. Nixon had been one of the first to encourage Pete to run for the State Assembly, and, even at the height of the Watergate crisis, he had found the time to write friendly notes to his long-time Californian protégé. Wilson regarded the older man as the preeminent politician of his generation, as a man who had understood the roads to power and who had connected with the American electorate at the most basic, most instinctual, of levels.

Now, deep into his reelection campaign, Wilson took time out from the rat race to work on a eulogy for his old boss. The governor didn't usually write his own speeches, but on this occasion he wanted to make the tribute as personal as he possibly could. It wasn't just a matter of dropping kind words on behalf of a departed friend: he also hoped to tap into the wealth of belated respect that Richard Nixon was reaping now that he was no longer alive. In collaboration with a handful of his best writers, he wrote draft after draft for a speech that, according to the schedule, was supposed to last only four minutes; he put researchers to work looking up old newspaper clippings; he studied articles and books that Nixon had written. On April 26, the day before Wilson was to read the eulogy at the Nixon Library in Yorba Linda, one of his aides sent the speech to Ronald Reagan's speechwriter Peggy Noonan to look over. Noonan sent a memo back to the aide. "By explaining Nixon as a human being, his generosity to Pete Wilson, how he helped and encouraged a young kid [Pete Wilson] getting his start in politics will show the warm and funny side of Pete Wilson," Noonan wrote. "By talking about Nixon the political fighter who stayed in the arena and picked himself up off the mat—the real and original comeback kid—the analogy to Pete Wilson is obvious—fighting for what you believe in, etc."

The next day, Governor Wilson addressed the somber crowd at Yorba Linda. Quoting Nixon, he told the crowd that "idealism without pragmatism is impotent. Pragmatism without idealism is meaningless. The key to effective leadership is pragmatic idealism." It was, he hoped, a quote that would reflect equally the belief system of the speaker. Nixon, he intoned, "was a hero who honored their [ordinary Americans'] belief in working hard, worshipping God, loving their families, and saluting the flag. He called them the 'silent majority.' "[16]

Twelve hours later, Wilson headed south to the dry, dusty border with Mexico, just south of his old home town of San Diego, to stoke some of the fears that the 'silent majority' was now wracked by. For Wilson, like Nixon before him, was proving himself a master at manipulating public opinion. This time around, the topic, in a state still suffering close to 10 percent unemployment and the squeeze of budget cuts, and casting around for groups to blame, was immigration. California, he announced, had just that morning filed suit against the federal government demanding that they reimburse California for the costs of imprisoning the thousands of illegal immigrants clogging up the state's prisons. It was the first of a series of lawsuits that Wilson would bring over the coming months.

Then, in early May, Wilson started pushing a new catchy slogan to that angered silent majority. "One strike, you're in . . . for life!" he told one audience after another, from San Diego in the south to Sacramento in the north, referring to his new plan for rapists and sexual predators to automatically receive life sentences. He signed an executive order releasing seven million dollars for anti-graffiti efforts and told a crowd in the conservative Los Angeles suburb of Glendale that graffiti was "the first sign that a virus is spreading into our communities, a virus of drugs and gangs and crime." Then, in front of the television cameras, the ex-marine rolled up his shirt sleeves and set to work with a crowd of volunteers painting over walls sprayed with gang graffiti tags. He toured gang turf in Fresno with the California Highway Patrol, with Mike Reynolds and D.A. Ed Hunt, and, with steel in his voice, informed reporters that "we're not going to sit by and let the Central Valley become another death valley." In front of a meeting of California District Attorneys in the picturesque waterfront community of Newport Beach, a triumphant Wilson told the prosecutors that "the people of California, and all of America, are clearly behind us. Even Governor Cuomo recently said he'd allow the death penalty in New York if the people approved a referendum. Justice should be swift and sure. The number one cause of death for Death Row inmates shouldn't be old age."

Behind all of Pete Wilson's cranked-up rhetoric about a crime epidemic, however, the California Department of Justice's Division of Law Enforcement was sitting on some rather interesting statistics. Adult murder rates in the state had actually peaked in 1990, and by 1992 murders were down 15 percent from those highs. The trend had continued into 1994. Similarly, the categories of property offenses, burglaries, thefts, car thefts, and drug offenses, had all peaked between 1989 and 1991, and had fallen considerably in the years since then.[17] Even among juveniles, a category Pete Wilson was soon to turn the heat of popular fear onto, violent crimes, while still far higher than in 1987 when juvenile crime began to spiral upward, had begun falling by the 1994 election campaign. Indeed, by late 1995, according to journalist Joseph McNamara, as the trend continued beyond the election, the FBI's uniform crime report along with census bureau victimization studies were indicating that national crime rates were actually at their *lowest* levels since 1975.[18]

None of this information mattered. For years, television and newspaper coverage had stressed the increasing prevalence of violence. The *perception* was that a crime epidemic was advancing throughout the state, and Wilson, like Nixon writing about New Hampshire in 1968, knew that it was perception that generally determined elections. "Experience has taught us that we know at least two strong ways to prevent crime," he told a gathering of Republican women that April. "Put more cops on the street and put more thugs behind bars—and keep them there." In the same speech, Wilson castigated Brown for her opposition to the death penalty for carjackers and her hostility to the idea of trying fourteen-year-olds accused of violent crimes as adults. He also played to his audience's antipathy toward both immigrants and welfare recipients. "California," he told them, "shouldn't be compelled to finance a welfare system for the world."[19]

As the campaign unfolded, Pete Wilson worked his way into a rhythm. He'd make speeches about crime, and then he'd make a speech about immigration. He'd tap into the growing national resentment against people on welfare by attacking teenage mothers or those who thought welfare was a way of life. And then he would return to the crime issue. Hardly anything else was worthy of attention. In June, with Washington still refusing to pony up the billions of dollars that Wilson was demanding as reimbursement for California's expenditures on illegal immigrants, the Republican announced a series of symbolic spending cuts. Because of Congress's intransigence, the governor declared, he had no choice but to end the provision of dental services to poor women and the elderly covered under the Medi-Cal program. He was going to cut back an important drug treatment program for pregnant women. The increases in funding that the state universities were demanding would have to be put on hold. And he would have to cap the number of women eligible to take part in a state-funded prenatal care program. All these cuts, Wilson and his finance director Russ Gould stressed, were because California had too many illegal immigrants and the Clinton administration wasn't addressing the problem. Reelect Wilson, however, and, through lawsuits and popular anger, he would force Washington to come up with the cash.[20] Then, to assuage fears that the budget cuts would impinge upon law enforcement, a week later Wilson was in Monterey to address the State Sheriffs' Association. "This year, we again face tight budgets throughout California," the governor intoned to his favorite audience. "But let me assure you, one thing we won't cut is funding for public safety. I've proposed an *increase* in funding for Corrections to finance locking up the career criminals convicted by our 'Three Strikes' law."

By July, as public fear about the twin evils of crime and illegal immigration grew in tandem with the governor's rhetoric, the *Los Angeles Times* was reporting on its front page that Wilson had narrowed his twenty-three-point deficit in the polls to a mere 5 percent, almost a statistical dead heat.[21]

And now, as he had done so successfully at the end of 1993 and beginning of 1994, the governor again began a war of words against his own legislature, positioning himself at the head of a popular rebellion against the go-slow politicians up in Sacramento. On August 8, he announced, he would lead a public safety rally on the steps of the capitol to demand enactment of the "one-strike" law and a raft of other tough-on-crime statutes. As the big day approached, fliers went up around Sacramento. "No More Victims!" the notices blared. "The Public Safety Rally August 8, 1994." And then, in splashy letters on the middle of the page: " 'Every Californian has a fundamental right not to become a crime victim, and not to live in fear. I urge you to join me to fight for this right.'—Pete Wilson." Again, since no one in their right mind would *oppose* the utopian idea of ridding the state of all criminal activity, through posturing Wilson had, for the second time in under a year, placed his crime legislation right at the heart of the political process.

On the steps of the Capitol, flanked by Polly Klaas's father Marc, by Mike Reynolds, and Manson victim Sharon Tate's sister Patty, Wilson addressed the crowd. "Today, together, we're going to march through the halls of this Capitol," the ex-marine promised. "And we're going to convince the Legislature to lock sexual predators away so that there will be no more victims. Starting tomorrow, and for the next two weeks, the Legislature will be considering our anti-crime package of eighteen bills. Seven of our eighteen bills—including our one-strike and our death penalty bill—are currently in the Assembly Committee on Public Safety. Today, four Assemblymen stand between us and criminal reform. They need to hear our message: NO MORE VICTIMS!" He paused to allow the crowd to join in the chant. "NO MORE VICTIMS! NO MORE VICTIMS!"

It was a bold promise, and an unrealizable one, but, in the height of what was still a close election race, a bit of hyperbole never hurt. *Vote for me*, the governor seemed to be saying, *and I will end crime in this great state. Vote for my proposals, and you will never be victimized again.* And it gelled well with the latest television commercial the Wilson campaign was putting out.

Wilson's ad opened with black-and-white footage of a woman being grabbed from behind by a would-be rapist, while a voice intoned: "Rape. An ugly word, a devastating crime." Then the rapist's image was replaced by color footage of a forceful Pete Wilson telling his viewers that "the victim does life, and yet the average rapist in California spends less than five years behind bars." As the image cut back to the rapist being handcuffed and led away by police, the first voice came back: "Wilson has pushed for a tough one-strike law. Life in prison for rapists and child molesters on their first conviction." The screen returned to Wilson, saying "Three strikes, that's two too many for some crimes." Once more the announcer came on. "Kathleen Brown," he told the audience, "thinks differently. She opposed Wilson's one-strike law even though rapists and child molesters are the worst repeat offenders." The advertisement switched over to a statement from Carol Rose, a deputy district attorney from L.A. County. "It's unconscionable that Kathleen Brown could oppose the one-strike bill." Finally, the unseen voice dramatically intoned four more words. "Where do *you* stand?"[22]

In fact, Brown had already declared her support for a modified version of the one-strike bill that doubled the existing sentences for rape and child molestation and imposed a mandatory twenty-five-to-life on rapists who had seriously injured their victims or threatened them with a deadly weapon. But, in the new California, even this was considered as being irremediably weak on the hot-button issue of crime. Like a punctured air balloon, Kathleen Brown was rapidly sinking back to earth.

In keeping with tradition, the final countdown to the election began immediately after Labor Day, after the last of the summer barbecues and the end of the school vacations. And, for the incumbent governor, heading into the home stretch things couldn't have been going any better. He was now safely ahead in the polls and Kathleen Brown's campaign was proving so muddled that even seasoned Democratic veterans such as Assembly Speaker Willie Brown (no relation) were already all but declaring Wilson the winner. The Democrat had failed to offer voters any clear vision she had for California, and, like Dukakis's staffers in the 1988 election, her team had been thoroughly outflanked on the emotional issue of crime. Now, with Republicans across the country beginning to dominate their various political races—hammering home on voters' concerns about crime, immigration, and welfare, the three signature issues Wilson had already made his own—political pundits were even beginning to talk about the California governor as a presidential candidate for 1996.

Already, in the weeks since the Public Safety Rally, Wilson had journeyed around his huge state at breakneck pace, visiting round table discussions on juvenile crime hosted by law enforcement officials; popping in on meetings of crime victims; hosting events in which he announced that the reward offered for information leading to the arrest of cop killers would be doubled from fifty to one hundred thousand dollars. At a conference held by the Doris Tate Crime Victims Bureau, the governor had presented awards to seven people who had worked extensively with victims of crime. Finally, at the end of August, as it became clear that the legislature was once again going to pass most of the bills he had demanded, the experienced politician decided to reap the fruits of his campaign: he declared "victory" in the fight for reform. "The people have spoken," he declared, "and the Legislature did its job. I will now do my job and sign these tough crime bills into law."

In the second week of September, the series of laws that the August 8 demonstrators had demanded passed their final legislative hurdles. And, as each one reached his desk, Wilson was ready for the signing ceremony. On the eighth, the governor was in the LAPD precinct house in suburban Van Nuys, surrounded by police and representatives from victims' rights groups, signing SB26X, the one-strike law for which he had lobbied so fiercely throughout the summer. On the ninth, with Attorney General Lungren on one side and California Peace Officers Association president Maury Hannigan on the other, he signed AB560, allowing for fourteen-year-olds charged with serious and violent felonies to be tried as adults. That same day, he signed SB23X, sponsored by his old ally Bill Leonard, that would allow those juveniles tried as adults to be committed to state prison when they turned twenty-five, should their sentence extend beyond their twenty-fifth birthday. Senate Bill 1539, providing for eighteen-to-twenty-year-olds to be sent to prison rather than to the California Youth Authority, was also signed with a flourish. That evening, Wilson titled his weekly television address "Unprecedented Progress in the War on Violent Crime." He told his constituents, up and down California, that "This year, the people of California said 'Enough is enough!' You raised your voices. You rightly demanded the change that would make California a safe and civilized state. And you showed what the will of the people can accomplish."

Three days later, the governor traveled down to the prison at Chino—the same facility in which Billy Ochoa had been incarcerated in the early 1980s, the prison he had remembered fondly for its bed-springs—where, surrounded by prison guards, he signed SB1260, re-pealing the Jerry Brown–era Inmates Bill of Rights. "We're here today to take a landmark step in rolling back the perks, privileges, and profits of crime," Wilson told his delighted followers. "In the 1970s, misguided liberals became more concerned about the rights of criminals than the rights of victims. But dangerous thugs don't deserve the right to pump iron while in prison—while the rest of us pay for the privilege at a local health club. Criminals don't deserve their very own Bill of Rights."

A couple weeks after that, he signed a bill strengthening the penalties against spousal abusers.

Now, opinion polls showed Wilson far ahead of a fading Brown. The more he talked the talk, the more the public—so recently hostile to the fiscally strapped Wilson administration—responded with their favor. *After all*, Wilson kept telling them, *I'm only doing what you are demanding of me.*

By Election Day, November 8, Wilson was home free. The weekend before, Kathleen Brown's team had even had to pull its television commercials after running out of money.[23] He was so far ahead in the polls that the vote itself was a virtual formality. That night, as Republicans gained control of the U.S. Senate and the U.S. House of Representatives, as tough-on-crime, tough-on-welfare gubernatorial candidates across America were swept into state office, as liberal icons such as New York's Governor Mario Cuomo gave way to a new breed of conservatives, Wilson watched the results come in from across California. Despite a low turnout, the vote was even more lopsided than the pundits had predicted. In practically every county, Wilson came out ahead. Propositions 184 and 187 were supported by almost every demographic group in almost all regions of the state apart from the traditionally liberal Bay Area. Dan Lungren won his race for attorney general. And the G.O.P. took control of the State Assembly. Wilson himself had come out ahead of Brown by a staggering 15 percent, winning 4,357,713 votes to the Democrat's 3,191,428. As a new Republican "revolution" dawned, Wilson was suddenly one of the most influential political figures in all America.

Soon he was crisscrossing the country, drumming up support for a possible presidential run. In Washington, D.C., he addressed a luncheon at the conservative Heritage Foundation think tank. Success, he told the audience, had come to him because he had taken on the question of illegal immigration. (In the latter weeks of the campaign, the Wilson team had repeated their use of grainy black-and-white mock-documentary footage in a television commercial; this time, as the screen showed immigrants crossing the border illegally, a doom-and-gloom voice had intoned, "They keep on coming.") A week after the D.C. event, he was telling a group of Republican politicians at the National Policy Forum in Williamsburg, Virginia, that "The reason we were able to turn a twenty-three-point deficit into a fifteen-point victory is simple. We focused our campaign on the truly historic reforms we've been able to make to turn California around in the toughest times we've faced since the Great Depression. This is especially true when it comes to crime."[24]

The triumphalism continued into the new year. For his inaugural gala, on January 6, Wilson's aides rented out the 4,000-seat Arco Arena, home of the Sacramento Kings basketball team. Natalie Cole was the featured entertainer. Other musical treats were provided by the Sacramento Symphony Orchestra, the Twelfth Marine Corps District honor guard, and a Marine band from San Diego. As Pete and Gayle Wilson entered the arena and walked toward their box, the band struck up "California Here I Come" and the thousands of spectators cheered wildly. Who knew, but maybe Wilson's next inauguration party would take place far across the country, in Washington, D.C.

Not surprisingly, Pete Wilson's inaugural address the next day carried a dramatically different message from the visionary sentences he had intoned four years previously. Wilson had his eyes set on the presidency, and, as the voting public had made so clear, the country's mood in 1994 was a fearful and angry mood; and the politicians who fared best in such a climate were those who adapted their language accordingly. "Citizens ask," he told the nation, "why do our laws put dangerous criminals back on our streets and put us behind barred windows and locked doors?" "We must choose whether California will be the Golden State—or a welfare state. It can't be both," he averred. "Is it fair that the welfare system taxes working people who can't afford children and pays people who don't work for having more children? We will make clear that welfare is to be a safety net, not a hammock—and absolutely not a permanent way of life." It was a theme the national Republican Party was pushing for all it was worth, with their Personal Responsibility Act proposing to overhaul AFDC, replace welfare with workfare, and set strict time limits on how long a recipient would be eligible for cash handouts. In the heady early winter days of victory, House Speaker Gingrich was even floating the idea of forcibly removing children from teen mothers and placing them into orphanages.

A couple days after the inauguration festivities, in his annual State of the State speech Governor Wilson again went after women on welfare, this time slamming teenagers who got pregnant in order to become eligible for AFDC checks. "She must learn that her options do not remotely fulfill her fantasy," California's leader thundered. "*Before* she gets pregnant, she needs to know that *after* she is, she will live with her baby in her parents' home, or in a group home with other teen mothers." In the same oration, ignoring statistics suggesting the crime wave was already flowing back out to sea, he launched a new war against what he called "the scourge" of juvenile crime.

The stump speeches soon followed. At Sheriff's Headquarters in San Diego, he talked about the "cancer" of juvenile crime, and demanded that teenagers convicted of serious crimes serve "hard time" and "experience the terror that can only come from being locked in a real prison environment.[25] He began calling for curfews to be imposed against teenagers. He called for the creation of a juvenile justice code "that is as unforgiving as the terrorism that's been inflicted on innocent victims for too long now." And, at a Washington luncheon to celebrate the Republican Party's congressional victories, Wilson used his national podium to again attack illegal immigrants, welfare recipients, and lenient criminal justice codes.

Shortly afterward, in mid-February, in the snowy, bitterly cold winter of the Colorado Rockies, Wilson huddled at a retreat with some of his closest friends and advisers. *It's looking good*, they told the Comeback Kid. *You ought to start seriously considering a run for the White House.*

Two months later, Wilson set up an exploratory committee and announced to the nation that he was in the race for the presidency.

TEN

Early in the year 2000, Cal Trehune was thinking over the crime problem.[1] Trehune was the Director of California's Department of Corrections, the man responsible for the smooth running of its forty-three prisons and camps, and the well-being of the more than 160,000 inmates and 46,000 staff within this vast system. Like all prison officials, the Director had worried, in the weeks leading up to the New Year, about what the "millennium bug" might do to the computers operating the doors, the security gates, the alarm systems, the hospitals, and everything else inside his empire. With hindsight, the fear might have seemed overblown, comical even, but in the last few months of 1999, with warnings that electric grids could fail and communications networks collapse, nobody in charge of secure institutions such as prisons was taking the threat of computer chaos lightly. Trehune had set up an emergency operations center at Folsom Prison and, as the twelve o'clock hour approached, his representatives were in constant communication with the Governor's Office of Emergency Services, vital players in a California Y2K response team named "Follow the Sun."[2] As midnight passed without cell doors swinging open and security cameras switching themselves off, the sixty-something-year-old, brought out of retirement by Governor Wilson in 1997 to run a department in the throes of scandal, must have breathed one huge sigh of relief. After all, the outcry that would have resulted from a Y2K prison failure would have dwarfed the allegations of institutionalized violence at the Pelican Bay and Corcoran prisons that had led Wilson to call his old friend Cal back to Sacramento three years earlier.

Now Trehune was sitting in his comfortable Sixteenth Street office reminiscing about his life in the field of criminal justice. He'd first begun working for the Department of Corrections way back in 1955 when he was a student parole officer. Then he'd gone back to college for a few years, gotten himself an MA in social work, and once more returned into the correctional fold. Over the decades, the soft-spoken, almost academic-sounding Trehune had been promoted into the upper echelons of the Golden State's penal hierarchy. He served as the super-intendent of five different California Youth Authority facilities. He was the deputy director of institutions and parole, and finally he'd become the director of institutions. That was the position he retired from in 1991, when he decided he wanted to spend more time in his home town of Ione. By the time he got the phone call from Wilson, six years later, Trehune had forged a new career as the mayor of Ione and he wasn't at all sure that he wanted to resign this post and return to Sacramento.

But Wilson's arguments were persuasive and simple. *Trehune, a man respected for his humane leadership, was needed.* The *Los Angeles Times* and other large newspapers were running stories on an almost daily basis about the sometimes deadly "gladiatorial combats" between rival gang members which guards had been organizing, and had been betting money on, in the small triangular concrete exercise yards at Corcoran throughout the 1990s. And then there were those allegations, substantiated by medical officials, coming out of Pelican Bay about the psychotic African American prisoner who had been almost boiled alive by a team of sadistic white guards.

Wilson had appealed to his old buddy's sense of institutional loyalty to the Department of Corrections. And, somewhat reluctantly, Trehune had responded to the call. To be fair, in the years since, he'd done a remarkable job in crisis management. Within weeks, the administrations at both troubled prisons had been thoroughly overhauled, and new wardens brought in. More generally new training practices were adopted for the 46,000 employees throughout California's mammoth prison sys-

tem. "Ninety-nine percent of the staff are good people," Trehune
thought. But nevertheless, clearly they needed some serious retraining.
Now, three years later, Trehune, still serving under the new Democratic
governor Gray Davis, felt he had something to be proud of. "We've cut
down the use of deadly force. We haven't fired a lethal round in twenty
months now, which is a life-time record," he declared with obvious
relief.

But now that the worst, most spectacular, abuses *within* the prisons
had been tackled, there was something else bothering the old man. And
that was life on the *outside*. "People still feel unsafe," he mused. "Crime
does have a high visibility on our evening news. It really does. I'm not
saying that's the sole source of the uneasiness, but that's all you see, all
you read about. If crime's down, you should see a reduction in coverage.
But you don't. It sells well." Trehune knew only too well that crime
rates were tumbling. And he also knew that the prison system he presided over was still growing. Over the nearly half century he'd worked
in criminal justice, he'd seen a sea change in the public's response to
crime. "People aren't as forgiving today as they were before. In the old
days you could open a parole office, a halfway house—people might be
a little concerned but you could work it out. Today, the thought of
opening a new parole office is very difficult. People just do not want
parolees in their community." Instead of looking to rehabilitate ex-cons,
the public seemed to want to make more and more people cons in the
first place. Entire classes of offenders were being condemned as "incor-
rigibles," and pushed into prison. Juvenile delinquents, nonviolent drug
users, shoplifters. "God help us," Trehune prayed. "If we turn 'em out
meaner and more vicious than when they come in, we've done nothing
to help."

As was only to be expected given the current state of public opinion,
the old bureaucrat's private warnings had gone largely unheeded, and
extraordinary sentences continued to be imposed by the courts of California. A few months after the Y2K crisis management sessions, Trehune, once again, retired.

Billy Ochoa had, by now, been locked up in the high-security prison twenty miles east of downtown Sacramento for over three years. He only had another 323 to go. Originally, when the high-tech institution opened in October 1986, it had been known as New Folsom, and had been under the control of Old Folsom's warden. Then, in 1992, Old Folsom having made the transition to a medium-security prison and shipped its more dangerous inmates out to other centers, it had gained full institutional independence, and, now with its own warden, had received a new name: California State Prison, Sacramento, or CSP-SAC. Its mission was to "house maximum-security inmates serving long sentences or those who have proved to be a management problem at other institutions."[3]

CSP-SAC sprawled out across 1,200 acres, had more than 2,000 staff guarding prisoners and otherwise operating the facility, and cost over $80 million per year to run. When Ochoa first arrived, it housed more than 3,100 inmates, close to twice as many as the prison had been designed to hold.[4] It was, almost literally, busting at the seams. Ninety percent of the maximum-security prisoners — murderers, rapists, psychopathic gang members, along with the nonviolent inmates like Ochoa — were double-bunked in their tiny cells and even the solitary confinement unit was so packed that an overflow crowd was being housed in improvised solitary in another of the prison's concrete units. A total of 443 of the inmates were like Billy, criminals convicted of crimes against property. Another 300 or so were doing time for drugs. Because of the overcrowding, they all lived intermingled with the 1,000 murderers and miscellaneous other violent inmates that CSP-SAC was housing.[5]

Like Corcoran and Pelican Bay, like the newly built maximum-security institutions in so many other states, and like the new supermax federal prison in Florence, Colorado, no expense had been spared in the escape-proofing of CSP-SAC. The entire perimeter was surrounded by swathes of electrified fencing. Outside the electrified fencing was another chain-link barrier, topped off with rolls of the nastiest, deadliest razor wire around. Gun towers spaced at regular intervals monitored the open ground between the cell blocks and the perimeters, and skinny palm tree–like towers flowered out on top with banks of powerful flood-lights. All entrance points into and out of the prison had multiple se-curity checks. And all doors were computer operated.[6] Just to be extra-safe, antennae capable of detecting the slightest movement in unauthorized areas, and similar to those used along the Israeli border, had been buried several inches underground at strategic points through-out the facility.[7]

So far the strategy had worked. Not a single prisoner had ever escaped from Billy Ochoa's new home. In fact, the few dozen guards and family members who lived in the picturesque, almost surreally suburban early-twentieth-century housing, originally built to house Old Folsom guards just on the other side of the electrified fencing, felt that their community was one of the safest in the country. After all, if the inmates couldn't get out and outside criminals proved reluctant to prey on buildings at-tached to a secure prison, then the quaint steeple-roofed bungalows lining the three streets of "The Valley" were practically invulnerable. You could almost leave your front door unlocked. Hell, at $500 a month rent for a nice two-bedroom, lawn out front and back, free gardening work provided by nearby minimum-security inmates, and yellow school buses available to pick up the kids for school, this was one of the best deals in all of northern California.

At Old Folsom, San Quentin, and all the other older penitentiaries that had acquired almost folkloric status over the decades, prisoners were housed in vast buildings, crammed with cells facing onto central walk-ways. Old Folsom had had the largest of these, a cavernous block on the north side of the prison yard, lined with two facing walls of five tiers of cells, one layer atop another, soaring up over one hundred feet to the prefab ceiling above. Each cell held two inmates behind the painted steel bars that substituted for doors. When the 1,200 men living in this one building started a disturbance, banging the metal bars with their plates or cups or whatever else came to hand, the noise was deafening. Like being caught in the middle of a battleground. Or a nineteenth-century bedlam. In the 1930s, during a particularly bloody prison riot, inmates had even managed to stab to death the warden. And in the 1970s, violence was so rampant that the mere threat of "Folsom" was enough to send a shiver down the spines of all but the very toughest of criminals. Even today, the enormous prison yard was informally divided into territories. One of the basketball courts was dominated by the Crips. Another area was lorded over by the Black Guerillas. A third space was for the Southern Hispanics. One more for the Whites. Somewhere else were the Northern Mexicans. Another spot was where sex offenders congregated together to try to prevent the other inmates from beating them. And so on. Endless permutations of identity, exponentially multiplying possibilities for conflict.

The newer prisons were designed very differently. When Ochoa arrived at CSP-SAC, he found a prison the like of which he had never experienced in all his years of crime. There were three "facilities," A, B, and C. Each of these three areas contained eight concrete blocks, built around an exercise yard designed to service the inmates of the eight buildings. In the yard for A facility, where the Administrative Segregation inmates were held, a series of outdoor cages, like the cages in an old-styled zoo, were lined up next to each other. These cages were where the most disturbed of the Ad Seg prisoners, the mentally ill inmates imprisoned within the Psychological Services Unit, got their fresh air. As likely as not, at any given moment, several of them were howling like loons, spitting, cursing the world, or just rambling incoherently at the other inmates around them. All told, about 330 inmates lived in the A facility. They spent more than twenty-three hours a day locked up in their minuscule, barren cells. Exercise was limited, visits were rationed to the occasional glimpse of a loved one on the other side of a thick bulletproof glass window. The inmates of A facility were even given their meals through a slot in the door of their cell. You could end up in Ad Seg for self-protection; for example, if you were a child molester and feared being attacked by inmates in the other two facilities. Or, you could end up there through breaking prison rules—fighting with other inmates, swearing at a guard, joining a prison gang. Sometimes, inmates claimed they were put there simply because a guard didn't like them. The internal process by which inmates were removed to solitary was so vague that almost any excuse would suffice.

Over fifteen hundred miles away, Texas was beginning to use solitary confinement as an almost routine system of imprisonment. The Estelle Unit of the Huntsville prison complex, seventy miles north of Houston, opened the summer after Ochoa had been sentenced in California, and within months was housing 660 inmates in the most austere conditions of any prison in America. Some prisoners here were only let out of their cells to exercise for three hours a week, and were allowed a mere two hours of visits per month. Other than that, they remained in their cells. Even the showers, which in prisons such as CSP-SAC were communal spaces, had been built inside the cells of Estelle. When prisoners broke any of the rules, or began going crazy under the strain of constant isolation, they were punished and humiliated. If prisoners refused to eat, or to return their meal trays through the slots in their doors, they were put on rations and fed "food bricks" made up of an almost inedible combination of all of the day's ingredients. If they ripped up their prison-issue uniforms, they were made to dress up in paper gowns. When isolated prisoners "self-mutilated," as they often did, minimum-security inmates from another unit within Huntsville would be called in with sponges, mops, and buckets of soapy water to clean up the bloody mess from the floors, the walls, and oftentimes the ceilings too.

Yet, despite these results, Estelle was being judged a success, and five more purely supermax units, designed to house another 3,000 inmates, were being built. Another 8,000 inmates spread throughout the Texas prison system were also already being held in some form of Administrative Segregation.[8] After all, even if isolation didn't rehabilitate inmates, it prevented prisoners from escaping. "The security here," explained Larry Fitzgerald, public relations officer for the Texas Department of Criminal Justice, "is better than Alcatraz. Alcatraz didn't have the electronic things we have now. The art of incarceration has definitely improved."[9]

"You've got some superbad people out there," declared Representative Bill McCollum, (R, FL), chair of the House Crime Subcommittee in justifying the increased use of solitary confinement throughout the United States. "You not only have to provide for their safety, but for the safety of the corrections officers. Rehabilitation is not the purpose here."[10] Indeed, in California, the penal code had been formally amended to no longer mention the goal of rehabilitation. Containment and punishment were now the official orders of the day.

The concrete exteriors of the CSP-SAC buildings through which Ochoa was being led were unpainted, and the drab-gray anticolor exuded bleakness. Dotting the gray at regular intervals were narrow window slits, perhaps six inches wide and a couple feet high. They looked somewhat like the narrowed eyeholes in the heavy metal of a medieval knight's facial armor. These slots, deliberately designed to minimize the inmates' ability to see other residents, were the prisoners' one access point to the world outside their cells.

The green-uniformed guards took Billy, in handcuffs, into one of the general facility buildings. Each of the eight units attached to a facility contained sixty-four cells. In the parlance of modern penal architecture, these structures were designed as "pods." A two-story control booth occupied central position, and small tentacle-like lines of cells radiated outward from the booth in a half circle. Each tentacle had two tiers of cells: eight on bottom, ten on top, with a single tiled shower at the end of each tier. The correctional officer manning all the computers and communications equipment behind the bulletproof glass walls of the central booth had a perfect 180-degree view of the entire pod, of every single cell under his control. Like the utopian "panopticon" prison written about by the English philosopher Jeremy Bentham two centuries earlier, CSP-SAC had successfully managed to eliminate the dangerous blind spots that had plagued prison administrators throughout the ages. In the open space surrounding the control towers, awkwardly worded signs were posted. "Warning. No warning shots will be fired in this area—Warden." In other words, if by some remote chance, a prisoner escaped his cell and descended on the booth, officers were under orders to shoot to wound or even kill.

Billy was marched to one of the cells. At one of the solid steel doors, the institutional green paint broken only by a narrow plexiglass slit window and a cell number painted in white above the metal handle, they stopped. This was to be Billy's abode. They opened the door and their prisoner stepped inside. The cell, which the fifty-three-year-old was to share with another inmate, was eight feet by eight feet. A dull industrial strip light, attached to the ceiling, illuminated a green metal bunk bed, the stainless-steel toilet/sink installation attached to the wall, a metal plank protruding from the wall opposite the bunk that served as a primitive desk, and a couple green metal bookshelves. The walls were a mottled brown concrete variant on the gray outside.

Each inmate, according to the prison rules that Billy had to familiarize himself with, was allowed only six cubic feet of property — the equivalent of a box measuring three feet by two feet by one foot: and that included clothes, books, and a television. The inmates here wore coarse blue cotton shirts and loose-fitting jeans: their prison blues.

The general population inmates of B and C facilities ate in elongated common dining areas. Their food was prepared by inmates in the C facility kitchens, who, over the course of a day, had to prepare approximately 28,000 meals, to feed all the inmates at CSP-SAC, Old Folsom, and the minimum-security Community Correction Facility that lay perched on the edges of the CSP grounds. Both the B and the C sections contained four such dining rooms.

Like everything at CSP-SAC, eating was an uncomfortable, overwhelmingly institutional experience. The rooms had brown linoleum tiled floors. The walls were divided into three horizontal stripes: the base was painted a dull gray; the middle was cream colored — an almost absurd attempt at lightening up the atmosphere; and the top of the wall was just bare, exposed, ugly concrete. Each of these rooms had fifteen octagonal stainless-steel tables, from each of which four metal stools, attached by metal arms to their parent tables, protruded. The inmates ate in turns; groups of up to sixty at a time filing in for the daily prison fare, making a sea of uniform blue at the bottom of the concrete hole.

Underneath the uniform blue, CSP-SAC seethed with violent tensions. As with most high-security prisons, Ochoa's new home bristled with brutal gangs and with regional and racial hatreds. In prison, inmates survive through seeking out the mutual support and protection of others. If you get into a fight on the yard, you need to know somebody will back you up. In a world of homemade shanks and spectacular outbursts of sudden, uncontainable fury, you need others in whom you can place a modicum of trust. And the easiest way of forging ties is through an appeal to geographic or racial loyalties. The neo-Nazi Aryan Nation flourishes among white inmates in prison. So do the Mexican Mafia, the Black Guerillas, the Southern Hispanics, the Northern Mexicans, and a host of other ethnic- and locality-based groupings. Street rivalries—the Bloods and the Crips for example—continue behind bars along with a whole slew of newer permutations.

Ochoa was an older inmate, a nonviolent con who'd left the Midget Dukes gang behind more than thirty years previously. All he wanted was to be left alone, to play the occasional game of handball in the prison yard—"these youngsters make me play hard, and they just can't understand how a [sic] 'old timer' can beat them," Billy wrote to Virginia proudly—and to find himself a prison job that would help him while away the days, the months, the years, the decades, even theoretically the centuries of his incarceration. But both the prison and the inmates insisted on categorizing everybody. Because Billy was ethnically Mexican, and because he had grown up in Los Angeles, prison officials filed him as a "Southern Hispanic." For the same reason, other inmates also regarded him as being either an enemy or an ally. To renounce these loyalties was to invite a swift and bloody retribution. And so, Ochoa hung with the other Southern Hispanics, spoke the street-Spanish he'd picked up over the years, and talked nostalgically about a "motherland" south of the border that he himself had no firsthand knowledge of.

When the rival groups came together on the prison yard, or in the dining areas, bloody fights would frequently erupt. Inmates would fashion blades out of the strangest of objects—melted down and sharpened toothbrushes, tiny bits of metal from television sets, hidden tools stolen from some of the worksites within the prison—and stab other inmates, sometimes for no apparent reason whatsoever. And the prison authorities would respond by putting entire gang-categories into "lockdown." Security was so tight at New Folsom that female visitors weren't even allowed to wear bras containing wire frames—for the guards feared that once inside the prison, the women would take off their bras and surreptitiously hand them to their loved ones, and that those loved ones would fashion the underwear wire into deadly weapons. Neither were women having menstrual periods allowed to bring in extra pads, again because the authorities feared they would be used to smuggle in contraband. Within weeks, as a "Southern Hispanic," Ochoa had been placed on the first of what would come to be many spells in lockdown, confined, with his cellmate, to his cell more than twenty-three hours a day, prevented from attending his job in the prison kitchens, and denied access to the phones which he had been using to make collect calls to his sister, Virginia, four hundred miles away in Los Angeles. The old welfare fraudster, burglar and heroin hype, one of only eighty prisoners in CSP-SAC over the age of fifty-five, repeatedly requested the administration to recategorize him as a prisoner without a gang affiliation. After all, in this tough world, Ochoa was an extremely old man, far too old to be fighting it out in the yard. The prison officials refused his requests.

Soon Virginia's brother was writing her letters, fearful missives about how violent the prison he had been sent to was, about how different things were now compared to when he'd first gone to prison as a young man. Now, Ochoa felt that the young inmates had no respect for age. Perhaps for the first time in his life, Billy felt truly vulnerable. Death seemed to be crowding in on his consciousness. "I am going to try to get closer to L.A.," he wrote his sister with a patina of false hopefulness in September 1998, as if he still had any control over his destiny. "It seems the closer we get to the year 2000, more people that I know are dying." He wrote of his uncle Rudy, "in his later 80's and he has burned the candle at both ends." He began to worry that maybe soon his own health would deteriorate. But, he wrote, as if to reassure himself, "I am glad I can still play a good game of handball; I am the only 55 year old man playing, there was a guy 50 years old who played a little, and sad to say he moved like he was 50." A few months later, he was complaining about dental problems and worrying that his "teeth will have to come out eventually." He suffered from stomach pains, and sometimes came in from the exercise yard so exhausted he could barely move. To get even a partial night's sleep on the hard concrete slab that served as a bed, he had to play up his back pains until the prison authorities reluctantly agreed to give him a second thin mattress to lay out upon his slab. He craved stimuli and told his sister, with joy, about being able to see occasional birds—once even a turkey—from the slit window at the back of his cell. Sometimes he seemed near despair, other times he wrote with passion about how he wouldn't let prison break him. "The most important thing in places like this (the Hole) is to keep your mind busy," he confided, perhaps trying to boost his own flagging spirit. "Many human being [sic] don't know it but they can just about adapte [sic] to anything." Ochoa knew he was somewhere near Sacramento, but, isolated deep within the penitentiary to which he had been transported in the middle of the night, he had no idea if he was north, east, west or south of the state capitol.[12] In lockdown, he spent much of his time sleeping, just waiting for the day when he could go back to the general prison population.

In 1999, a prisoner was beaten to death by his own cellmate. Crazed prisoners in isolation periodically sliced their own arteries, spattering blood from floor to ceiling, in desperate attempts to gain attention. Also in 1999, two prisoners committed suicide.[13]

When he was stabbed in the prison yard over a pair of sneakers, it made Billy realize all the more how fragilely connected to life is an old prisoner in a super-maximum-security prison. "I use to play handball with these youngsters, and they use to mess around by coming up behind me and running their hand across my throat, like getting my throat cut," the old prisoner remembered. "Well anyway I was going in my

building where I was housed; just after yard recall. When I enter the
building my hands were full. As I was walking into my section where
my cell was located, I felt someone grab me from behind and felt there
[sic] hand run across my throat; first I thought someone was messing
around, but when I felt my throat, I felt blood. As I turned around, the
person was running out of the building."

As it happened the cut wasn't too deep, and Billy didn't even fall to
the ground. But it did serve as a wakeup call. Billy was an old man, and
in a young man's world that was not a healthy thing to be. "I realize
you always have to be on your guard," Ochoa wrote. "For this prison
there is a lot of cutting and stabbing. I seen a lot of people get cut and
stab." It made him "mad, real upset, because to have a person sneak up
on you and cut you and run away, is a cowardly move."

Immediately afterward, Billy was removed from the general prison
population and placed, for his own protection, in "the hole." He spent
the next two months there, living alone, eating alone, trying to while
away the endless hours, the endless days in a room the size of a small
walk-in closet.

While Cal Trehune was worrying about his computers crashing in the
first minutes of the year 2000, Pete Wilson had entirely different concerns. He had left office at the end of 1998, after his second term of
governor expired, and now was readjusting to what, for such a public
figure, passed for life as a private citizen. Not since the Lyndon Johnson
years had the politician not held an elected office. Sixty-six years old,
he had recently accepted a part-time managing director's position at the
Pacific Capital Group, a Santa Monica–based organization that leant
venture capital to start-up companies. According to its literature, PCG
Inc. specialized in extending short-term loans in the hundred-thousand-
dollar range to new companies, with the borrowers pledging their stock
as collateral. Wilson had also joined the board of directors of a San
Francisco investment bank. And as if these jobs weren't enough, the ex-
governor had been named a Fellow at the prestigious Stanford

University–based Hoover Institute. Now, as he faded out of the political spotlight, Wilson was commuting between northern and southern California, plying the many political and business connections he had made in his decades at the center of political power.

In many ways, the ex-governor should have been content with his legacy. He hadn't been voted out of office, but rather had been prevented from running for a third time by the state's term limits law. And, despite the electorate's rejection of his hand-picked successor, Dan Lungren, under the leadership of the new Democratic governor, Gray Davis, the state's criminal justice policies were remaining on much the same course that Wilson himself would have wanted. Davis, much like Bill Clinton, was determined not to let the more traditionally liberal wing of his party regain control of the policy debate.

After all, it was Jerry Brown's politics, and his support for controversial laws such as the Inmates Bill of Rights, that had led to Deukmejian and Wilson's four-term stranglehold in Sacramento. In fact, so tuned in to the new anticrime rhetoric was Davis that during the election campaign, Lungren found to his chagrin that crime policy wasn't even a usable election issue. "Because," the ex–attorney general subsequently explained, "we're all tough on crime now." During the election campaign, the Democrat even went so far as to praise the authoritarian regime of Singapore—a country known to use corporal punishment on minor offenders—for its criminal justice system.

And the tough words hadn't merely been election-year posturing. Once elected, Davis made it abundantly clear that he wouldn't tinker with the Three Strikes law, or, for that matter, with any of the other get-tough legislation that his predecessor had pushed the reluctant legislature into passing. So determined was Davis to neutralize this issue that even when the notoriously cautious Board of Prison Terms recommended that he release a handful of middle-aged lifers who had been sentenced decades earlier, the governor made a point of overruling their recommendations, sarcastically noting that the board members were supposed to be toughened-up Republicans. Looking in on the politics behind Davis's decision from his new position as a private citizen and

Conservative talk radio host, even Lungren was amazed at Davis's denial of parole to the lifers. "I thought it was totally inappropriate," he recalls, perhaps just a touch self-servingly. "The obligation of the Governor is to look at the record and see *why* they were recommended for parole."

By the year 2000 California was lavishing a staggering $4.6 billion a year on the Department of Corrections, and for every 100,000 L.A. County residents, amazingly close to 2,000 were in prison.[14]

But, despite the Wilsonizing of California's and, indeed, America's criminal justice system, Pete Wilson himself wasn't entirely happy with how this story had worked out. He had always wanted to be president, and that ambition had ultimately eluded him. All through the winter and spring of 1995, as California's economy improved and voters' optimism bounced back, the governor had juggled mundane gubernatorial duties — addressing the Raisin Growers' Association, attending prayer breakfasts, welcoming business conferences to towns in California — with his need for national coverage. To get that coverage he continued to focus on his holy trinity: crime, welfare, and immigration. He had claimed partial victory in early February, when the new Congress had agreed to set aside more than $3 billion over the course of five years to reimburse states such as California for the costs of incarcerating illegal immigrants. And even though U.S. District Court Judge Judith Keep threw out California's lawsuits against the federal government for full reimbursement for the cost of providing *all* services to illegal immigrants, Wilson scored political points by promising voters that he would fight this decision all the way to the Supreme Court if need be.[15]

The problem was that, using emotional subjects such as crime in such a partisan way, politicians such as Wilson had been too successful for their own good: now *every* serious candidate was proposing tougher laws in these three areas, and at the national level the ex-marine no longer stood out as steelier than his opponents. In fact, by the time the primary season rolled around, Texas Senator Phil Gramm was vowing "to put these people [criminals] in jail and keep them there," and was urging that the federal prisons be turned into "mini-industrial parks, where prisoners work ten hours a day, six days a week."[16] Meanwhile,

House Speaker Newt Gingrich was floating the idea of mass executions of drug traffickers. "You import commercial quantities of drugs in the United States for the purpose of destroying our children, we will kill you," the brash leader asserted.[17] By the summer of 1995, Gingrich had gone even further, this time telling a crowd of footballers and cheerleaders at a camp in Georgia that he would introduce legislation mandating the death penalty even for the lower-level drug *dealers*.[18]

So, to his triumvirate of vote-winning issues a couple months into his presidential campaign the governor added a fourth: he had decided to tackle affirmative action and the employment policies that opinion polls showed white men, in particular, to be so bitterly hostile toward, and was preparing an executive order banishing affirmative action from all state-financed institutions in California. Old-time campaign advisers like Ken Khachigan and Stu Spencer, many of whom had cut their teeth during Reagan's presidency, were helping Wilson to frame his message; and Massachusetts governor William Weld was heading a team trying to drum up the massive injections of cash that Wilson would need if he were going to campaign for the year and a half that remained until the presidential election. They needed a new national issue that Wilson could claim as his own. All through May, memoranda flew over the fax machines and E-mail systems in Sacramento. It was vitally important not to let Republican rivals such as Senators Bob Dole or Phil Gramm get a head start on this. "Let me say at the outset that I am not certain we will be able to drive national news on the executive order announcement itself," Wilson's aide Leslie Goodman wrote. "But we will be able to position you to begin leading the debate as the first public official to take action to end special preferences in government."[19]

Goodman then referred to focus group testing which indicated Wilson needed to stress more that his opposition to affirmative action was "founded in long-standing principles not political ambition." It was, the aide wrote, essential to avoid appearing as if he was "riding the tide of public resentment and 'white male anger' to the presidency. Coupled with illegal immigration, criminal justice reform, and welfare reform they will accuse you of negative tactics — playing the race card and being intentionally divisive for political gain." No matter that that was exactly what Wilson *was* doing; he had to couch his politics in slightly more subtle terms.

Thus it was that when Wilson released an eight-page Open Letter to the People of California on Affirmative Action, on May 31, it was a letter peppered with references to Martin Luther King Jr. and to liberal icons such as former Vice President Hubert Humphrey. It called on the citizens of his state to embrace a new vision of a truly color-blind society, and it demanded diversity founded in "fairness." Surely this would be the magic wand that Wilson could wave to transform himself from just another regional politician into a heavyweight politician with enough national name recognition to unseat Bill Clinton. Surely this would carry him to the Republican Convention in his adopted hometown of San Diego in the summer of 1996, as the party's nominee-in-waiting.

Unfortunately for Pete Wilson, it didn't happen quite like that. Wilson's Republican support base in California felt betrayed by his attempt to jettison Sacramento for Washington after all the hard work they had put into his reelection campaign the previous year. And, in early April the governor's doctors had discovered nodules on his vocal cords that warranted immediate surgery. Thus it was that for two crucial months in the middle of 1995, Wilson couldn't talk aloud. Instead of being able to defend his positions on controversial subjects such as affirmative action, he had to rely on surrogates—on friends, and, increasingly, on his wife, Gayle. When the California Peace Officers Association invited him to speak at their annual conference in Indian Wells, it was Gayle who got up and told the crowd that "as governor, Pete Wilson has overseen the opening of eight prisons. And if keeping prisoners locked up longer to make the public safer means building more prisons, he'll lead the fight to do just that."[20]

That summer, as the governor got into a month-long spat with the state legislature over the size of his proposed tax cuts, welfare cuts, and increases in schools and prison expenditures, Wilson could only speak in a scratchy voice for short periods of time. For the first time since he'd been elected, he lost an argument over correctional spending, and actually had to accept a $125 million *cut* in the Department of Corrections budget.

By the summer, Wilson's embryonic campaign was in deep trouble. The millions of dollars that he had raised in the spring were almost gone, and new funds just weren't flowing in.[21] He could still rely on a terrific audience response when he told a group, such as the California District Attorneys' Association that "we're tearing up the 'get out of jail free' cards and replacing them with lifetime memberships,"[22] but he was faring far less well in the early caucus and primary states of Iowa and New Hampshire. It wasn't that the citizens of these states didn't approve of his tough-on-crime message—indeed, they cheered dutifully when he told them that it was high time to take the fight against criminals that he had launched in California to the rest of the country. It was more that all the candidates were saying these things—because, as the governor told a crowd of district attorneys gathered for a booze-and-schmooze convention in Las Vegas, "the nation is obsessed with public safety. Crime stories lead the evening news not just in my California, but across America"[23]—and Wilson, a Californian, seemed unable to grasp the more specific economic and religious concerns of the conservative, rural heartlands. That was where candidates such as Bob Dole, Lamar Alexander, and the fiery populist Patrick Buchanan did far better.

In a crowded field, the California governor just couldn't gain momentum. Opinion poll after opinion poll showed him mired at 5 percent support, or even less. And, in late October, Wilson swallowed the bitterest political pill of his long career. Flying home from the campaign trail, the governor announced he was withdrawing from the race and endorsed the campaign of his friend Bob Dole. "It's nice to be home after the presidential wars," he told a meeting hosted by the League of California Cities. "I've had some interesting experiences." Then, in a bittersweet talk before his most sympathetic audience, the California Peace Officers Association, meeting in the rolling hills of Napa County, Wilson again said his good-byes to the national scene. "Thank you, my friends in this proud organization, for all of your support throughout my presidential campaign. I wish I'd found the same courtesy in New

Hampshire."[24] Pete Wilson's dream, which he had nurtured ever since he'd been a young man working for Richard Nixon, had fizzled like a damp firework on a rainy day.

And, despite the momentum of his reelection victory the previous November combined with a newly booming economy, somehow the firework display had never been restarted. For the latter part of Wilson's governorship, he had, essentially, been a lame duck.

Now, four years after his ill-conceived presidential run and retired from electoral office, Wilson wanted to at least continue influencing the politics of his home state of California.

For a year now, the former governor had been stumping for a ballot initiative that would continue where the 1994 legislation on youthful offenders left off, in overhauling California's juvenile justice system. It was one of those loose ends that he'd never gotten a chance to tie up. As his term neared its conclusion, Wilson hoped that Dan Lungren would succeed him in the governor's mansion and make good on this. But Lungren had been defeated overwhelmingly by Gray Davis, receiving less than 40 percent of the vote to the Democrat's 58 percent. And even though Davis was fast proving himself as tough on crime as his predecessor, Wilson believed that it would take a popular upheaval as powerful as that which had generated Three Strikes six years before to ensure that violent teens, and gang members in particular, were punished in a manner befitting their crimes.

In the Gang Violence and Juvenile Crime Prevention Act, to be voted on as Proposition 21 in the March 2000 election, Wilson had found such a vehicle. For, despite the fact that teen crime and violence rates in California were tumbling, voters remained deeply fearful of the predatory gangs that had terrorized so many of the state's towns for so many years. Now here was legislation that would make it a felony for gangsters to recruit new members into their gang; that would mandate life sentences for carjackers, home invaders, shooters, and extortionists who committed their crimes under the rubric of a gang; that would extend the death penalty to specifically cover gang murders. Here was an initiative that upped the ante to make *un*armed robbery, *un*armed carjackings, and arson violent felonies. And it made any acts of vandalism that caused over four hundred dollars of damage, including graffiti painting, a felony offense punishable by up to three years in a state prison.

Perhaps most importantly, Proposition 21 removed violent teens fourteen years and older from juvenile court, from the institutions which had sentenced Billy Ochoa to Youth Authority camp four decades previously, and instead mandated their prosecution in adult courts. And, beyond that, it allowed for prosecutors to ask judges to try *any* gang-related offender as an adult. In so doing, it provided for the crimes of these teenagers to be counted as "strikes" under the policy Mike Reynolds had crafted six years earlier, thus raising the specter of troubled, but not necessarily murderous or irredeemable, teenage gang members striking out for life before they were even old enough to vote or to buy a pack of cigarettes.

The former governor not only put his name down as one of the proposition's sponsors; he also began aggressively campaigning in its favor.

On March 7, when voters went to the polls, Pete Wilson triumphed yet again. By huge margins, one precinct after another voted in favor of this overhauling of California's juvenile justice system. For the young gang members of the ghettos and barrios in the early years of the twenty-first century, there would no longer be the opportunity to work out their delinquent behavior inside camps and detention centers looking to rehabilitate them. Instead, the latter-day teenage Billy Ochoas were facing one-way tickets into adult prisons such as the one the older Billy was now incarcerated in after a lifetime of petty crime. Given the trajectory of Pete Wilson's career, the passage of Proposition 21 was as appropriate a coda as the aging ex-politician could have hoped for.

Prison was getting worse and worse for Ochoa. After the stabbing incident, and his time in Administrative Segregation, he'd been moved to the C Unit, far away from the B yard on which he had been stabbed. Still, he was always scared of being jumped by one of the young-punk prisoners. He chafed at the excessive restrictions on his movement. He dreamed of being transferred, but always he'd wake up still in CSP-SAC. In his mind, he sang golden oldies to himself, reminding himself of a happier time, when he was young and free, when Josie was still alive to comfort him. When he could, he telephoned Virginia, or his father William. They talked about the family, about local gossip. William told his son that he was thinking of buying some land up north and quitting L.A. altogether. His sister told him about family quarrels and tragedies. Her son, Arthur, had died a little over a year after Billy had gone to prison, and the prison hadn't given Billy permission to attend his funeral.

Sometimes Pat or Virginia or William sent him a care package. Some beef jerky, underwear, occasionally a few dollars to spend in the prison shops. So far, however, not a single friend or family member had visited him since his arrival more than three years earlier. Even if they had tried to, the Southern Hispanics were in lockdown so often that as likely as not his visitors would have been turned back by the paper-shufflers working the visits' admissions desk. That was one of the worst things for family members of prisoners. Driving all that way only to be told by an unsympathetic staffer that their son, or husband, or brother, or father was confined to his cell and forbidden from having any visits.

Over the summer of 2000 someone sent an anonymous note to the prison authorities. *Move the prisoners in cell C2-128 or they'll be shanked.* The fifty-six-year-old Ochoa was one of those living in C2-128. And so, in the topsy-turvy world of the prison, the guards entered Billy's cell one morning, when he was getting ready to head off to the yard for exercise and once again marched him through the huge concrete and barbed-wire complex to the Administrative Segregation units. *For your own protection*, they insisted to the irate old prisoner. After all, he couldn't be moved back to the B Unit, since he'd already been stabbed there. And he couldn't stay in C Unit, since someone was threatening to stab him. Hence there was nowhere else to move him apart from to Ad Seg. But Ochoa, who had seen the insides of so many prisons and jails over the years, didn't see it that way. After so many decades of in-again-out-again experiences, penal life was finally breaking down Ochoa's spirit. "I am in here because some inmate wrote a note to staff. My whole program was turned upside down," he scrawled plaintively. "I am in this hellhole without any of my property. So there is not much to do. I read whenever I can get hold of a book. They say this is not punishment, but I can't see it any other way. My property has been taken. I can't go out to any yard. I am handcuff [sic] everywhere I go. I really don't go anywhere, but to the shower three (3) times a week. All prevledges [sic] are taken away. I can't even make a phone call. You have nothing in your cell. They say this is not punishment; it's like after they have pissed on my feet, they say it just rained."[25] The only good news was that it got him away from his old cellmate, whose obsessive behavior had been grating on Ochoa's nerves: he had paced up and down the tiny cell all day, and because he refused to shower, Billy was beginning to find the smell in C2-128 somewhat nauseating. Now, in Ad Seg, he was housed with a new cellie, one with whom he got along just fine.

Prison policy dictated that inmates moved into Administrative Segregation couldn't take anything with them. Not even their prison blues clothing. And so, all through the summer, Ochoa spent his days locked up in a barren cell, wearing only white shorts and a white T-shirt. If he got cold, a prison-issue mustard yellow jumpsuit offered up one flimsy layer of extra protection. The jumpsuit didn't even have buttons. Instead, the front was tied shut with a series of cloth laces running up the chest. Ochoa's television and radio had been put into storage, and so he spent his hours talking with his Spanish-speaking cellmate, the two prisoners teaching each other new words in their respective languages: the cellmate inheriting English words from the older Ochoa, Ochoa trying to improve his somewhat rudimentary Spanish. When his companion was asleep—which was often—Billy would sit on his bed reading. He read cheap Westerns. He read *The Creature*. He devoured books from the "White Indian" series.

Three times a week, the prison let him out into the Ad Seg yard to exercise. But, in fact, calling it "exercise" was somewhat of an exaggeration. The guards would come to his cell, ask him to stand up against the inside of the door, and place his wrists next to the slot through which food was delivered. Then they would cuff him. Only when his arms were securely shackled would they open the door and lead him outside. They would take him to a small outdoor cell constructed of wire mesh, would lock him inside, and would then uncuff him. For the next couple hours, Ochoa was free to exercise, alone, in his outdoor coop. "Like a lion in a cage," he fulminated. *It's for your own safety*, the guards told him. *You're a protective custody inmate*. Only after a couple months of this, did Ochoa manage to convince the officials that he wouldn't be killed should they put him back on the general exercise yard in Ad Seg. Now, as the autumn advanced, while he remained isolated in Ad Seg, at least when he exercised he could do so in the presence of other inmates.

In late October, four years into his sentence, Billy met with the prison authorities one more time. *Please transfer me to another prison*, the broken-down prisoner begged. *Please let me get out of this hellhole*. This time around, his request was taken somewhat more seriously. After all, having been driven out of two of the three prison units by real, or threatened, acts of violence, there was nowhere else for the old addict to go. And, with the overcrowding as bad as ever, there were other, more dangerous prisoners who could be put in the Ad Seg cell that Ochoa was now occupying. "I was put up for transfer to one of two prison," he wrote with joy. "I may be transferred to Lancaster Prison in L.A. County, or Corcoran Prison; anyway these prisons are closer to Los Angeles and maybe my dad, sisters and cousin can come and visit me."[26]

Nothing happened, however. Through October, November, and

December, Ochoa remained in isolation out at New Folsom. Each time he wrote a letter, he convinced himself the move was just around the corner. "I believe all in all I am going to a better place," he wrote, almost like a condemned man about to be dispatched out of this life. "Whenever I can get to a level three prison I believe things will be much better for me." As the new year rolled around, Billy Ochoa was still sitting in his tiny cell, obsessively reading his books, staring at his blank concrete wall, waiting for the day when the guards would come and march him through the prison and onto a transport bus; waiting for the day when he would be driven back out down the road lined with all the motivational signs, down south to another prison where, once more, the steel doors would be locked shut and the elderly addict could more safely spend the remainder of his life.

Sitting in his orange prison jumpsuit, the paunchy little old man with the crooked teeth just waited. Waited. Waited.

Epilogue

In January of 2001, Billy Ochoa was finally transferred to another prison. His new home was the Substance Abuse Treatment Facility at Corcoran Prison, another supermax institution.

SATF was a treatment center in name only. In reality, it was home to hundreds of high-security prisoners brought to Corcoran from across California, removed from their previous prisons because of threats made against them, or because of violent acts they had committed against other inmates.

Ochoa had managed to get his status reclassified. No longer was he a "Southerner." Now, the prison bureaucracy labeled him a "National Mexican." It was a subtle distinction, but in the minutely controlled environment of the maximum-security prison, it meant the difference between being locked in one's cell twenty-three hours a day and having the right to go onto the exercise yard and take on work assignments. Ochoa's cellmate, however, was a Southerner, and had to spend all of his time inside their tiny cell.

In Corcoran, at least, Ochoa had a job. He worked in the prison library, sometimes two days a week, sometimes as many as five days a week, from eight-thirty in the morning until four in the afternoon. He found books for inmates—mainly legal materials needed by prisoners preparing their own court cases and appeals—and he photocopied forms. For this, Ochoa was paid eleven cents an hour. "If I work all month," he said, "I might get nineteen dollars if I'm lucky." But, with the exception of his work, Ochoa was finding Corcoran to be at least as unpleasant as was New Folsom. "Even though there's a lot of stabbing and cutting at Folsom, it was more comfortable over there," he remembered, with perhaps the rosy glow of nostalgia that distance places on one's memories. "I had more things, got out more. Maybe after six months it might loosen up here." He exercised on the yard, but, as he got older, he found his body let him down more often. Ochoa had colon problems, his body ached, he was frequently beset by pains.

Most days, when he finished working in the library, he returned to his cell, watched some television — the choice of channels in the Central Valley, in which Corcoran is located, is distinctly limited — and then went to sleep.

As the spring rains began falling over the Central Valley, Billy's stomach pains grew worse. He wanted to pass gas, but he couldn't. He played handball less now, and when he did, he often came off of the exercise yard sweating in agony. Sometimes, he'd see a swelling just above his belly button, and then it would vanish. *It's no big deal*, Ochoa kept telling himself, pepping himself up, not wanting to admit any weakness.

But then, one Sunday in late April, Ochoa practically collapsed. He spent the next twenty-four hours just hoping he could make it until the nurse came around the following day. When she did, Ochoa showed her what was by now a sizable bulge above his navel. It was clear that the old inmate had to see a doctor. And so, on Tuesday April 24, Ochoa was taken, under guard, to see the prison doctor.

Billy Ochoa, prisoner number D-35968, had, it turned out, a severe intestinal hernia, and the doctor realized it had been ignored for so long that the patient was now extremely close to death. Not having the facilities for a complex operation inside the prison, he ordered that Ochoa be immediately transferred to a hospital in the large town of Bakersfield. Late at night, Ochoa was driven out of the prison grounds and onto the freeways into town. Under normal circumstances, it would have been a rare adventure, of which the old heroin addict would have devoured every brief second. But now, he was in such great pain that, instead of savoring his brief sojourn into freedom, all he could think about was how people with terminal illnesses should be allowed to die. How life with such pain was just not worth living. Perhaps, in his haze, images of his mother, Josie, dying of diabetes complications a quarter century earlier, flickered up into his mind's eye.

In the hospital in Bakersfield, surgeons put him under anesthetic and, after prepping him for surgery, operated right away. "The doctor over there said my large intestine was decaying," Ochoa wrote a month later. "The part of the intestine that was decaying had to be cut out. They said another twenty-four hours I'd have probably been through."

When Ochoa woke up, he found himself already chained to the bed. The hospital he was in had given over the entire fifth floor to sick prisoners. "I had shackles on my feet with cable run through chained to the bed," Ochoa recalled of his first memories immediately after his surgery. Immobilized and in pain, Billy spent eight days in Bakersfield. An IV tube ran up his nose, down his throat and into his stomach. Out of it spewed the bile from his infected gut. To counter the infection, he had to take a strict regimen of antibiotics. If he wanted to go to the bathroom, he had to buzz someone to unlock his shackles and accompany him to the toilet.

When the eight days were up, Billy, still weak and in pain, was transferred back to the Corcoran prison hospital. There, as the April rains gave way to the May heat, he recuperated for another twelve days.

And so, Billy Ochoa survived his medical emergency. His prized prison library job, however, did not. In his absence, someone else had been assigned to take his place. Thus, as the summer rolled around — his fifth consecutive summer in a supermax prison — Billy found himself once more working as a porter, mopping up floors. He hated the work and resented the fact that, unlike the library job, it was unpaid. He'd set his sights, again, on getting himself transferred to another prison.

Despite the hopes that he'd nurtured before his transfer south, as winter gave way to spring and then to summer Ochoa still had not been visited by his father or his sisters. "It's a long ways to come," he explained somewhat defensively. And then, as if to reaffirm who it is who's in control, as if to stress that he does, indeed, still have some say over his destiny and over the choices made by his family and his captors, he added, "I got to write to the visiting center and see what's going on."

Bibliography

Abu-Jamal, Mumia. *Live from Death Row*. Reading, Mass: Addison-Wesley Publishing Company, 1995.

Addams, Jane. *Twenty Years at Hull House with Autobiographical Notes*. New York: Macmillan Company, 1912.

Adler, William. *Land of Opportunity: One Family's Quest for the American Dream in the Age of Crack*. New York: Atlantic Monthly Press, 1995.

American Friends Service Committee Booklet. *Struggle for Justice: A Report on Crime and Punishment in America*. New York: Hill and Wang, Inc., 1971.

Anderson, David C. *Crime and the Politics of Hysteria*. New York: Times Books (Random House), 1995.

Anslinger, Harry J., and William F. Tompkins. *The Traffic in Narcotics*. New York: Funk and Wagnalls, 1953.

Anthology. *"In Five Years They Will All Be Dead!": A Critical Analysis of Prostitution in Early Twentieth Century Chicago*. Chicago: Middlebury Press, date of publication unknown.

Badillo, Hermann, and Milton Haynes. *A Bill of No Rights: Attica and the American Prison System*. New York: Outerbridge and Lazard Inc., 1972.

Baum, Dan. *Smoke and Mirrors: The War on Drugs and the Politics of Failure*. Boston: Little, Brown and Company, 1996.

Beccaria, Cesare. *On Crimes and Punishment*. (translated by David Young for a modern republication, 1986). Indianapolis: Herskull Publishing Company.

Behr, Edward. *Prohibition: Thirteen Years That Changed America*. New York: Arcade Publishing, 1996.

Bellesiles, Michael A. (editor). *Lethal Imagination: Violence and Brutality in American History*. New York: New York University Press, 1999.

Bender, David L., Bruno Leone, and Bonnie Szumski (editors). *America's Prisons: Opposing Viewpoints*. Fourth edition of the opposing viewpoints series. St. Paul, MN: Greenhaven Press, 1985.

Bennett, William. *The Book of Virtues: A Treasury of Great Moral Stories*. New York: Simon & Schuster, 1993.

——. *The De-Valuing of America: The Fight for Our Culture and Our Children*. Second edition. New York: Touchstone Books, 1994. First published 1992; New York, Summit Books.

——. *The Index of Leading Cultural Indicators: Facts and Figures on the State of American Society*. New York: Broadway Books, 1999.

Bentham, Jeremy. *An Introduction to the Principles of Morals and Legislation*. First published in 1823. Modern edition published in New York by Hafner Publishing Company, 1948.

——. *The Correspondence of Jeremy Bentham*. Collected into a single edition published in London by Athlone Press, 1968.

——. *The Panopticon and Other Prison Writings*. First published 1791. Republished in London, New York by Verso, 1995.

Bourgois, Philippe. *In Search of Respect: Selling Crack in El Barrio*. Cambridge, New York: Cambridge University Press, 1995.

Branch, Taylor. *Parting the Waters: America in the King Years 1954–63*. New York: Simon & Schuster, 1988.

Browning, Frank, and John Garassi. *The American Way of Crime*. New York: Putnam, 1980.

Burns, Stewart. *Social Movements of the 1960s: Searching for Democracy*. Boston: Twayne Publishers, 1990.

Burton-Rose, Daniel, Dan Pens, and Paul Wright. *The Celling of America: An Inside Look at the U.S. Prison Industry*. Monroe, ME: Common Courage Press, 1998.

Butterfield, Fox. *All God's Children*. New York: Alfred A. Knopf, 1995.

Cable, George Washington. *The Convict Lease System in the United States*. New York: Scribner, 1883.

——. *The Silent South*. New York: Scribner, 1885.

California Department of Corrections. *Characteristic of Population in California State Prisons by Institution*. Sacramento: California Department of Corrections, 1999.

——. Report titled "California Prisoners and Parolees Report." 1996.

Caute, David. *The Great Fear: The Anti-Communist Purge Under Truman and Eisenhower*. New York: Simon & Schuster, 1978.

Chessman, Caryl. *Cell 2455, Death Row*. Revised edition. Englewood Cliffs, NJ: Prentice-Hall, Inc., 1960.

Clark, Norman H. *The Dry Years: Prohibition and Social Change in Washington*. Seattle: University of Washington Press, 1965.

Clark, Phyllis Elperin, and Robert Lehrman. *Doing Time: A Look at Crime and Prisons*. New York: Hastings House, 1980.

Cleaver, Eldridge. *Soul on Ice*. New York: Panther Books, 1968.

Clinton, Bill, and Al Gore. *Putting People First: How We Can All Change America*. New York: Times Books, 1992.

Coffey, Thomas M. *The Long Thirst: Prohibition in America: 1920–1933*. New York: W. W. Norton and Company, 1975.

Cummins, Eric. *The Rise and Fall of California's Radical Prison Movement*. Stanford, CA: Stanford University Press, 1994.

Currie, Elliott. *Crime and Punishment in America*. New York: Henry Holt and Company, Inc., 1998.

Davis, Angela. *An Autobiography*. New York: Random House, 1974.

Davis, Mike. *City of Quartz*. London, New York: Verso, 1990.

——. *Ecology of Fear: Los Angeles and the Imagination of Disaster*. New York: Metropolitan Books, 1998.

Dickens, Charles. *American Notes*. First published, 1842. Modern edition, New York: St. Martin's Press, 1985.

Donziger, Steven R. (editor). *The Real War on Crime: The Report of the National Criminal Justice Commission*. New York: HarperPerennial, 1996.

Duke, Steven B., and Albert C. Gross. *America's Longest War: Rethinking Our Tragic Crusade Against Drugs*. New York: Putnam, 1993.

Durham, Jennifer L. *Crime in America*. Contemporary World Issues Series, Santa Barbara, CA: ABC-CLIO, Inc., 1996.

Duster, Troy. *The Legislation of Morality: Law, Drugs, and Moral Judgment*. New York: The Free Press, 1970.

Dyer, Joel. *The Perpetual Prisoner Machine: How America Profits from Crime*. Boulder, Co: Westview Press, 2000.

Eddy, Paul, Hugo Sabogal, and Sara Walden. *The Cocaine Wars*. New York: W. W. Norton, 1988.

Ehrenhalt, Alan (editor). *Politics in America: The 100th Congress*. Washington D.C.: Congressional Quarterly Press, 1989.

Elias, Norbert. *The Civilizing Process: The History of Manners and State Formation and Civilization*. New York: Pantheon Books, 1982.

——. *The Civilizing Process: Sociogenetic and Psychogenetic Investigations*. New York: Pantheon Books, 1978.

Epstein, Edward Jay. *Agency of Fear: Opiates and Political Power in America*. New York: G. P. Putnam's Sons, 1977.

Erdoes, Richard. *Saloons of the Old West*. New York: Gramercy Books, 1979.

Escobar, Edward J. *Race, Police, and the Making of a Political Identity: Mexican Americans and the Los Angeles Police Department, 1900–1945*. Berkeley, CA: University of California Press, 1999.

Evans, Rowland, and Robert Novak. *The Reagan Revolution*. New York: E. P. Dutton, 1981.

Finnegan, William. *Cold New World*. New York: Random House, 1998.

Foucault, Michel. *Discipline and Punish: The Birth of the Prison*. New York: Pantheon Books, 1977.

——. *Madness and Civilization*. New York: Random House, 1965.

Friedman, Lawrence M. *Crime and Punishment in American History*. New York: Basic Books, 1993.

Gitlin, Todd. *The Sixties: Years of Hope, Days of Rage*. New York: Bantam Books, 1987.

Gordon, Diana R. *The Return of the Dangerous Classes: Drug Prohibition and Policing Politics*. New York: W. W. Norton and Company, 1994.

Gray, Mike. *Drug Crazy: How We Got Into This Mess and How We Can Get Out*. New York: Random House, 1998.

Greenberg, Martin Alan. *Prohibition Enforcement: Charting a New Mission*. Springfield, Il: Charles C. Thomas, 1999.

Hallinan, Joseph. *Going Up the River: Travels in a Prison Nation*. New York: Random House, 2001.

Harris, Bob. *Steal This Book: And Get Life Without Parole*. Monroe, ME: Common Courage Press, 1999.

Healey, Denis. *The Time of My Life*. New York: Michael Joseph imprint of Penguin Books, 1989.

Henstell, Bruce. *Los Angeles: An Illustrated History*. New York: Knopf, 1980.

Jackson, George. *Soledad Brother: The Prison Letters of George Jackson*. Revised edition published in Chicago by Laurence Hill Books, 1994.

Jonnes, Jill. *Hep-Cats, Narcs, and Pipe Dreams: A History of America's Romance with Illegal Drugs*. New York: Scribner, 1996.

Jordan, Hamilton. *Crisis: The Last Year of the Carter Presidency*. New York: G. P. Putnam's Sons, 1982.

Justice Policy Institute report published in Washington, D.C. titled "Second Chances: 100 Years of the Children's Court," 1999.

Kelling, George L., and Catherine M. Coles. *Fixing Broken Windows: Restoring Order and Reducing Crime in Our Communities*. First published in New York by Martin Kessler Books, 1996. Republished with a foreword by James Q. Wilson; New York: Touchstone Books, 1997.

Kennedy, Randall. *Race, Crime, and the Law*. New York: Pantheon Books, 1997.

Kessler, Lauren. *After All These Years: Sixties Ideals in a Different World*. New York: Thunder's Mouth Press, 1990.

Keve, Paul W. *Prisons and the American Conscience: A History of U.S. Federal Corrections*. Carbondale, IL: Southern Illinois University Press, 1991.

Kobler, John. *Ardent Spirits: The Rise and Fall of Prohibition*. New York: G. P. Putnam's Sons, 1973.

Kotkin, Joel, and Paul Grabowicz. *California Inc*. New York: Rawson, Wade Publishers, 1982.

Krajicek, David. *Scooped!* New York: Columbia University Press, 1998.

Kunstler, William M. (with Sheila Isenberg). *My Life As a Radical Lawyer*. Secaucus, NJ: Birch Lane Press, 1994.

Kyvig, David E. (editor). *Law, Alcohol, and Order: Perspectives on National Prohibition*. Westport, CT: Greenwood Press, 1985.

Lee, Henry. *How Dry We Were: Prohibition Revisited*. Englewood Cliffs, NJ: Prentice-Hall, Inc., 1963.

Loza, Steven. *Barrio Rhythms: Mexican American Music in Los Angeles*. Urbana, IL: University of Illinois Press, 1993.

Lusane, Clarence. *Pipe Dream Blues: Racism and the War on Drugs*. Boston: South End Press, 1991.

Mackay, Charles. *Extraordinary Popular Delusions and the Madness of Crowds.* (First published under the title *Memoirs of Extraordinary Popular Delusions*). First published in London: Richard Bentley, 1841. Modern edition published in New York by Three Rivers Press, 1980.

Manza, Jeff, and Christopher Uggen. Report titled "The Political Consequences of Felon Disenfranchisement Laws in the United States." National Science Foundation, University of Minnesota, 2000.

Marable, Manning. *Race, Reform and Rebellion: The Second Reconstruction in Black America, 1945–1990* (revised second edition). Jackson, MS: University Press of Mississippi, 1991.

Massing, Michael. *The Fix.* New York: Simon & Schuster, 1998.

Mauer, Marc, and Jenni Gainsborough. Report titled "Diminishing Returns: Crime and Incarceration in the 1990s." The Sentencing Project, 2000.

———. *Race to Incarcerate.* New York: New Press, 1999.

McGuigan, Patrick B., and Randall R. Rader (editors). *Criminal Justice Reform.* Chicago: Free Congress Research and Education Foundation, 1983.

Meier, Kenneth J. *The Politics of Sin: Drugs, Alcohol, and Public Policy.* Armonk, NY: M. E. Sharpe, Inc., 1994.

Merz, Charles. *The Dry Decade.* Garden City, NY: Doubleday, Doran and Company, 1930.

Miller, Jerome G. *Search and Destroy: African-American Males in the Criminal Justice System.* Cambridge, England and NY: Cambridge University Press, 1996.

Mollenhoff, Clark R. *The President Who Failed: Carter Out of Control.* New York: Macmillan, 1980.

Moore, Joan. *Homeboys: Gangs, Drugs and Prison in the Barrios of Los Angeles.* Philadelphia: Temple University Press, 1978.

Norris, Mikki, Chris Conrad, and Virginia Resner. *Shattered Lives: Portraits from America's Drug War.* El Cerrito, CA: Creative Xpressions, 1998.

Nyswander, Marie. *The Drug Addict as Patient.* Grüne & Stratton, 1956.

Parenti, Christian. *Lockdown America.* London, New York: Verso, 1999.

Phillips, Susan A. *Wallbangin': Graffiti and Gangs in L.A.* Chicago: University of Chicago Press, 1999.

Prejean, Helen. *Dead Man Walking.* New York: Random House, 1993.

Protess, David, and Rob Warden. *A Promise of Justice: The Eighteen-Year Fight to Save Four Innocent Men.* New York: Hyperion, 1998.

Rabinow, Paul (editor). *The Foucault Reader.* New York: Pantheon Books, 1984.

Ranney, Austin. *The American Elections of 1980.* Washington, D.C.: American Enterprise Institute for Public Policy Research, 1981.

Reynolds, Mike, Bill Jones, and Dan Evans. *Three Strikes and You're Out!: A Promise To Kimber.* Fresno, CA: Quill Driver Books, 1996.

Rhodes, Richard. *Why They Kill: The Discoveries of a Maverick Criminologist.* New York: Alfred A. Knopf, 1999.

Robinson, Paul H., and John M. Darley. *Justice, Liability, and Blame: Community Views and the Criminal Law*. Boulder, CO: Westview Press, 1995.

Rodriguez, Luis J. *Always Running—La Vida Loca: Gang Days in L.A.* Willmantic, CT: Curbstone Press, 1993.

Romo, Ricardo. *East Los Angeles: History of a Barrio*. Austin: University of Texas Press, 1983.

Rosenblatt, Elihu (editor). *Criminal Injustice: Confronting the Prison Crisis*. Boston: South End Press, 1996.

Rothman, David J. *The Discovery of the Asylum: Social Order and Disorder in the New Republic*. Boston: Little, Brown and Company, 1971.

Sanchez, George. *Becoming Mexican American: Ethnicity, Culture and Identity in Chicano Los Angeles: 1900–1945*. New York: Oxford University Press, 1993.

Skidmore, David. *Reversing Course: Carter's Foreign Policy, Domestic Politics, and the Failure of Reform*. Nashville: Vanderbilt University Press, 1996.

Smith, Joan, and William Fried. *The Uses of the American Prison: Political Theory and Penal Practice*. Lexington, MA: Lexington Books, 1974.

Solzhenitsyn, Alexander. *The Gulag Archipelago: 1918–1956*. New York: Harper & Row, 1973.

Summers, Anthony. *Official and Confidential: The Secret Life of J. Edgar Hoover*. London: Victor Gollancz, 1993.

Sykes, Gresham M. *The Society of Captives: A Study of a Maximum Security Prison*. Princeton, NJ: Princeton University Press, 1958.

Teeter, Negley K., and John D. Shearer. *The Prison at Philadelphia Cherry Hill: The Separate System of Penal Discipline: 1829–1913*. New York: For Temple University Publications by Columbia University Press, 1957.

Tonry, Michael. *Malign Neglect: Race, Crime and Punishment in America*. New York: Oxford University Press, 1995.

Trebach, Arnold S. *The Great Drug War: And Radical Proposals That Could Make America Safe Again*. New York: Macmillan Publishing Company, 1987.

Wicker, Tom. *A Time to Die*. New York: Quadrangle, 1975.

Wilson, James Q., and Joan Petersilia (editors). *Crime*. San Francisco: Institute for Contemporary Studies, 1996.

——., and Michael Tonry (editors). *Drugs and Crime*. Chicago: University of Chicago Press, 1990.

Wilson, James Q. (editor). *The Metropolitan Enigma: Inquiries into the Nature and Dimensions of America's Urban Crisis*. Cambridge, MA: Harvard University Press, 1968.

——. *The Moral Sense*. New York: Free Press, 1993.

——. *Thinking About Crime*. New York: Basic Books, 1975.

——. *Thinking About Crime* (revised edition). New York: Vintage Books, 1985.

Wilson, William Julius. *When Work Disappears: The World of the New Urban Poor*. New York: Alfred A. Knopf, Inc., 1996.

Wines, Enoch Cobb. *The State of Prisons and of Child-Saving Institutions*. New York: Cambridge University Press, 1880.

Young, Hugo. *The Iron Lady: A Biography of Margaret Thatcher*. New York: Farrar, Strauss, Giroux, 1989.

Zimring, Franklin E., and Gordon Hawkins. *Crime Is Not the Problem: Lethal Violence in America*. New York: Oxford University Press, 1997.

——, Sam Kamin, and Gordon Hawkins. *Crime & Punishment in California: The Impact of Three Strikes and You're Out*. Institute of Governmental Studies Press, University of California, Berkeley, 1999.

Notes

PROLOGUE

1. Information from this section is taken from the court records for this case. The case number is BA 108803. The files are stored in the Criminal Courts Building in downtown Los Angeles.
2. Author interviewed Ray Clark at his law office, 4050 Buckingham Road, on December 3, 1999.
3. Author interviewed Tamia Hope, January 11, 2000.

CHAPTER 1

1. Personal information surrounding Billy Ochoa's experiences was gathered from personal interviews with a large number of Ochoa's family members, from an extensive written correspondence between the author and Billy Ochoa, from reverse-charge phone calls which Ochoa made to the author from inside CSP-SAC prison, and from in-person meetings between the author and Ochoa in the prison visiting area. Where possible, the author attempted to verify memories by interviewing more than one person on a given issue. At other times, he had to rely on the memories of individuals.
2. Because Arthur was no longer alive when the author began researching this book, it was not possible to reconstruct all the interactions between uncle and nephew. Information about Arthur and Billy's relationship was garnered from Billy's memories, and from copies of letters between Arthur and Billy that Virginia Castaneda was kind enough to share with the author.
3. The circumstances of Billy Ochoa's arrest were reconstructed from various sources: interviews with Ochoa, court files, and reports written up by the probation office.
4. Ibid.
5. Told to the author by Ochoa during a visit at CSP-SAC prison, January 13, 2000.
6. Details on this case can be found in the court files, case number BA 074496. The files are stored in the basement Archives, in the Los Angeles Hall of Records Building.
7. The court files for both of Ochoa's welfare fraud cases contain printouts detailing Ochoa's criminal record. Supplementary information was provided by Ochoa himself.
8. Author interviewed Eastman at his office, February 14, 2000.
9. From transcripts of court proceedings, filed in Los Angeles Criminal Court Building.
10. Descriptions of Old and New Folsom are based on the author's personal observations. The tours of the prisons took place on January 14, 2000.
11. Statistics provided by the California Department of Corrections. The 1999 publication *Characteristic of Population in California State Prisons by Institution* lists 834 inmates, or 26.5 percent of CSP-SAC's population as being convicted in Los Angeles.
12. The October 1, 1999, California Department of Corrections Fact Sheet estimated that incarceration cost an average of $21,243 per year per inmate. Ochoa is in a supermax prison. It costs significantly more to hold someone in such an institution than to hold them in a lower-level prison.

13. Statistics here and over the following pages, on overall numbers in prison, were obtained from the Bureau of Justice Statistics and from The Sentencing Project's September 2000 report "Diminishing Returns: Crime and Incarceration in the 1990s." Authors Jenni Gainsborough and Marc Mauer.

14. Told to author during course of reporting on a 1999 article for the British newspaper *The Independent.*

15. Numbers provided by the California Department of Corrections, and the Texas Department of Criminal Justice.

16. According to researchers at Cambridge University and the United States Bureau of Justice Statistics, Americans convicted of burglary, robbery, and assault spend at least twice as long behind bars as do their British counterparts. David Farrington of Cambridge University and Bureau of Justice Statistics. Quoted by Elliot Currie in *Crime and Punishment in America.* Published by Henry Holt and Co. Inc., 1998.

17. Charles Mackay, *Extraordinary Popular Delusions and the Madness of Crowds*, first published in 1841 under the title *Memoirs of Extraordinary Popular Delusions.*

18. Lawrence M. Friedman, *Crime and Punishment in American History.* Basic Books, 1993, page 45.

19. Ibid., pages 24–33.

20. London's main court, the Old Bailey, sentenced over 10,000 criminals to be deported to the Colonies between 1717 and 1775. Columbia University historian Richard B. Morris estimated that, in total, Britain shipped over 50,000 convicts to America prior to the Revolution. France also sent hundreds of criminals, mainly convicted prostitutes, to the Louisiana Territories.

21. Frank Browning and John Garassi, *The American Way of Crime.* Putnam, 1980, page 133.

22. Ibid.

23. Fox Butterfield's book, *All God's Children*, Knopf, 1995, goes into more details on this phenomenon.

24. The historian of manners, Norbert Elias, writes of a civilizing process that had been going on in Western Europe since the fifteenth or sixteenth century. During this time, as society became more bureaucratized, as central governments began imposing order on unruly populaces, so increasingly courts began supplanting individuals in doling out justice. As a result, unsanctioned violence and bloodletting declined. This process was speeded up during the Industrial Revolution. By the end of the nineteenth century, a city like Amsterdam—which estimates indicate had a murder rate approaching 50 per 100,000 inhabitants in the fifteenth century—had murder rates of about two per 100,000 residents. The violent crime rate in areas of America such as Appalachia stood in stark contrast to these trends.

25. Lawrence M. Friedman, op. cit., page 44.

26. Richard Erdoes, *Saloons of the Old West.* Published by Gramercy Books, 1979. Quote from the chapter titled "His Honor (The Saloon Keeper) on His Bench (The Bar), or Saloon Law," pages 131ff.

27. Quoted by Lawrence Friedman, op. cit., page 77.

28. The French philosopher Michael Foucault wrote extensively on the history, and function, of punishment over the centuries. Although his theories fall somewhat outside the scope of this book, readers interested in learning more about punishment methods and goals are referred to *Discipline and Punish: The Birth of the Prison*, and also to *Madness and Civilization.*

29. For more details of this period in Philadelphia's penal history, see the *Prison at Philadelphia Cherry Hill: The Separate System of Penal Discipline: 1829–1913*, by Negley K. Teeters and John D. Shearer. Columbia University Press, 1957.

30. Prison records quoted in *The Prison at Philadelphia Cherry Hill: The Separate System of Penal Discipline: 1829–1913*, by Negley K. Teeters and John D. Shearer. Columbia University Press, 1957, pages 83–85.

31. Ibid., page 85.

32. Lawrence M. Friedman, op. cit., pages 77ff.

33. David J. Rothman, *The Discovery of the Asylum: Social Order and Disorder in the New*

Republic. Little, Brown & Co., 1971. Chapter 4, "The Invention of the Penitentiary," page 79.

34. Ibid, page 107.
35. Teeters and Shearer quote prison records that describe Dickens's visit.
36. Charles Dickens, *American Notes*, 1842. Quoted by Friedman.

CHAPTER 2

1. The text or Wilson's inaugural speech, and the press releases that his office issued in the days leading up to and following January 7, can be found in the California State Archives, Sacramento.
2. Sources for chapters on Pete Wilson's career include newspapers, journals, archived campaign material, and a variety of documents housed in the California State Archives, the Ronald Reagan Library, and the UCLA research libraries. The author also conducted interviews with some of the principals. Despite numerous requests, both written and by telephone, for an interview with Pete Wilson, the ex-governor declined to meet with, or communicate with, the author. By contrast, ex-Attorney General Dan Lungren, allowed the author to interview him in his home over the course of several hours.
3. July 1993 *California Journal.*
4. Information on the budget crisis comes from contemporary news reports, articles in the *California Journal*, and Thomas W. Hayes's oral history; Hayes was interviewed by Donald B. Seney, professor of government at California State University, Sacramento, as a part of the California State Archives, State Government Oral History Program. The interviews were conducted on August 29 and 30, 1995. The text is kept in the department of special collections of the Young Research Library, University of California at Los Angeles.
5. This poll was quoted in a June 1992 article by John Berthelson, titled "Room at the Inn," published in the *California Journal.*
6. Danielle Starkey and Vic Pollard. Article titled "The Prison Dilemma," published in the April 1994 issue of the *California Journal.*
7. A brief history of Wilson's political trajectory can be found in *Politics in America: The 100th Congress*, edited by Alan Ehrenhalt.
8. Campaign literature archived at the U.C.L.A. Young Research Library.
9. Information gathered from the Chicago Police Department and from a web page put up by Pete Wilson's first cousin, Michael Wilson, of Boynton Beach, Florida, in memory of his murdered grandfather.
10. Jane Addams. *Twenty Years at Hull House with Autobiographical Notes*, published by the Macmilian Company, 1912, pages 281–309.
11. These medicines are listed in a *New York Times* article from August 2, 1908, by Dr. J. Leonard Corning.
12. Information on prostitution in early twentieth-century Chicago compiled in the Middlebury anthology *"In Five Years They Will All Be Dead!"*; *A Critical Analysis of Prostitution in Early Twentieth Century Chicago."*
13. From the essay "Chicago in 1900—a Millennium Bibliography: Crime—Police, Criminals and Vice," published by the Chicago Public Library.
14. Statistic quoted in the Crime Control Commission's final report, 1981.
15. Quoted in the Executive Summary of the Commission's report, published in 1981.
16. Ibid., page 4.
17. Ibid., page 12.
18. Ibid., pages 16 and 17.
19. Letter from Edwin Meese III to Pete Wilson, dated November 2, 1981. Filed in the Ronald Reagan Presidential Library in Simi Valley.
20. White House staffing memorandum from August 18, 1982. Prepared by Richard Darman, assistant to the president. The memorandum is filed in the Ronald Reagan Library, in the town of Simi Valley. Document number 09489055 SP656.

21. The joint Baron and *National Journal* report found Wilson more conservative than 81 percent of the Senate on foreign policy issues, than 79 percent on economic issues, and than 64 percent on social issues. The following year, he was found to be more conservative than 86 percent of his colleagues on economics policy.

22. Wilson's voting record is listed in *Politics in America: The 100th Congress*, edited by Alan Ehrenhalt.

23. Wilson campaign literature, filed at U.C.L.A.'s Young Research Library.

24. Wilson letter to President Reagan, dated June 18, 1987. Filed in the Ronald Reagan library archives.

25. *Criminal Justice Reform*, edited by Patrick B. McGuigan and Randall R. Rader. Published by Free Congress Research and Education Foundation, 1983. Meese wrote Chapter 2, titled "Combating the American Epidemic." The quotes were taken from pages 17 to 19.

26. Information from Mike Gray's book *Drug Crazy: How We Got Into This Mess and How We Can Get Out*. Published by Random House, 1998.

27. Quoted on page 289 of Dan Baum's book *Smoke and Mirrors: The War on Drugs and the Politics of Failure*. Little, Brown & Co., 1996.

28. Statistics quoted by David Anderson, *Crime and the Politics of Hysteria*. Times Books, 1995.

29. Elliott Currie, *Crime and Punishment in America*. Henry Holt and Co., 1998.

30. Quoted by Dan Baum, in *Smoke and Mirrors: The War on Drugs and the Politics of Failure*. Little, Brown and Co., 1996.

31. Ibid. Page 226.

32. Michael Massing, *The Fix*. Simon & Schuster, 1998, page 32.

33. Frontline Documentary, titled "The War on Drugs," October 9 and 10, 2000.

34. Ibid., page 18. Anderson, who was on the *New York Times*'s editorial board during this period, describes how readers would write in demanding that criminals be detained in huge concentration camps, to be built either in the deserts of the Southwest, or, even further removed, in Alaska.

35. For more details on the circumstances surrounding this particular case, see David Anderson's book *Crime and the Politics of Hysteria*, op. cit. Anderson interviewed Horton and the Barneses during the writing of his book.

36. *National Journal*. January 15, 1983.

37. Richard Zeiger article in the October 1990 issue of the *California Journal*.

38. Figures taken from the October and November issues of the *California Journal*. The exact amount raised by the eight bond measures for prison building was $3.612 billion.

39. Letter sent out under Deukmejian's name to registered Republicans during the election campaign.

40. Page 33 of *Taking Charge of California's Future*. Of the manifesto's eighty-one pages, twelve are devoted to crime, more pages than are given over to any other single issue.

41. Statistic from the May 1991 issue of the *California Journal*. Fourteen of these prisons were completed during Deukmejian's term in office. The remaining eleven opened during Pete Wilson's tenure.

42. The California Department of Corrections Facts bulletin from March 1, 2000, estimates that California's prison population stood at 20, 345 in 1976, and that it passed 30,000 in 1982, the year Deukmejian was elected. Danielle Starkey writes in the March 1992 issue of the *California Journal* that by June 1991 the prison population had reached 101,658.

43. These numbers come from The Field Institute.

44. May 1991 *California Journal*. The increase was 13.2 percent.

45. The March 1992 issue of the *California Journal* extrapolated the numbers on welfare spending and prison spending for the coming fiscal year. The June 1992 issue explored the numbers working in the correctional system.

46. Information gathered from several *California Journal* articles published in 1993 and 1994.

47. Author interviewed Mike Reynolds at his house on January 17, 2000.

48. *Lockdown America*, published by Verso in 1999. On page 112, Parenti writes that the VCSU

teams went into operation in 1994. Parenti also writes that since then-Los Angeles police chief Daryl Gates developed the idea of the SWAT team in 1966, over 30,000 such teams have been deployed on the streets of America. Parenti writes that "tactical units have metastasized from urban emergency response specialists into a standard part of everyday policing."

49. Author interviewed Dan Lungren, May 30, 2000.
50. Quoted in Richard Zeiger article from the October 1990 issue of the *California Journal*.
51. Dan Lungren used this phrase in the May 30, 2000 interview.
52. Information on the Klaas case was gathered from news reports, and also from Polly Klaas's father, Marc Klaas, whom the author interviewed on December 1, 1999. The California State archives' files on Pete Wilson's speeches and public appearances also provided much valuable information for this section.
53. Information provided by Marc Klaas.
54. Charles August Junior was kidnapped from the Lindberghs' home in New Jersey on March 1, 1932. Ten weeks later, the twenty-month-old's body was found. Two years after that a carpenter named Bruno Richard Hauptmann was arrested for the crime. He was executed in 1936.
55. Quotes from transcripts kept in the California State Archives.
56. Author interviewed Marc Klaas on the Three Strikes law in September 1999.
57. Information provided by Mike Reynolds during interview with the author, January 12, 2000.
58. See Uniform Crime Report statistics.

CHAPTER 3

1. Information on Anthony Williams was provided to the author during telephone interviews and face-to-face interviews with Nazimova Varick during April 2000. Anthony Williams also phoned the author from prison several times.
2. Uniform Crime report statistics, as written about by Michael Massing, in his book *The Fix*. Published by Simon & Schuster, 1998.
3. Quoted by Massing, op. cit., page 126.
4. Congressmen Robert Steele (R., Connecticut) and Morgan Murphy (D., Illinois) had toured Vietnam in April 1971 and reported back to Congress that they found 10 to 15 percent of the soldiers there to be addicted to heroin.
5. *The Real War on Crime: The Report of the National Criminal Justice Commission*, edited by Steven R. Donziger. Published by HarperPerennial, 1996, pages 64–65.
6. Center for Media and Public Affairs Study, 1995. Quoted in Joel Dyer's book *The Perpetual Prisoner Machine: How America Profits From Crime*. Westview Press, 2000.
7. The exact number, as of December 31, 1999, was 2,351 Third Strikers sentenced for crimes against the person, a mere 39.9 percent of the total number of Three Strikes convictions. Figures provided by Families to Amend California's Three Strikes (FACTS), based on numbers from the Data Analysis Unit of the Department of Corrections.
8. Ibid.
9. Information on Steven White, and on several other suicides related to the Three Strikes law, was gathered from Families to Amend California's Three Strikes, and from interviews conducted with lawyers during the course of author's reporting of an article on the U.S. prison system, published in the British newspaper *The Independent* in June 1999.
10. Author interviewed Lillie Blevins over the telephone in the spring of 1999 for the abovementioned article he was writing for the British newspaper *The Independent*.
11. Information contained in the *Frontline* documentary "The War on Drugs," aired on PBS October 9 and 10, 2000.
12. The statistics in this section come from the Bureau of Prisons.
13. This number is quoted in Enoch Cobb Wines's *The State of Prison and Child-Saving Institutions*, Cambridge University Press, 1880. In 1871 Wines had been appointed as a commissioner with the authority to organize an international prison congress in London. His book grew out of the studies he pursued while working in this capacity.

14. George Washington Cable, *The Silent South*. Scribner, 1885. Quote from page 92.
15. The exact numbers, according to Cable, were: South Carolina, 406 Black prisoners and 25 white; and in Georgia, 1,083 Black prisoners and 102 white. Cable's numbers are widely accepted as being definitive.
16. George Washington Cable, essay titled *The Convict Lease System in the United States*, first published in 1883.
17. Ibid.
18. George Washington Cable, *The Silent South*. Quotes from pages 27 and 93.
19. Official Proceedings of the Constitutional Convention of the State of Alabama, May 21, 1901, to September 3, 1901, page 8. This is quoted in a *Progressive Magazine* article on felony disenfranchisement, and was also used as evidence in a 1985 lawsuit challenging the constitutionality of Alabama's disenfranchisement laws.
20. More details on the use of prisons as tourist sites can be found in Paul W. Keve's book *Prisons and the American Conscience: A History of U.S. Federal Corrections*. Southern Illinois University Press, 1991.
21. Frank Browning and John Garassi, *The American Way of Crime*. Putnam, 1980. This quote is from the introduction.
22. Manning Marable, *Race, Reform and Rebellion: The Second Reconstruction in Black America, 1945–1990 (revised second edition)*. Published by University Press of Mississippi, 1991, page 207.
23. *Pipe Dream Blues*, by Clarence Lusane. South End Press, 1991, page 16.
24. *Race, Reform and Rebellion*, op. cit., page 183.
25. Ibid., page 193.
26. World Health Organization statistics, quoted by Elliott Currie in *Crime and Punishment in America*.
27. 1993 Op-ed in *New York Times*. Quoted by Elliott Currie, op. cit.
28. Amnesty International documents the racially discriminatory impact of the implementation of justice in the U.S. in several reports. *Rights for All* contains much of this information.
29. Author visited St. Clair Prison in February 1999, in the course of researching the above-mentioned article for *The Independent*. He spoke to Bonner, McElroy, and Norris for several hours in the visiting area of the prison. Unlike the prisons in California, St. Clair let the author in as a journalist, and allowed him to take notes and to tape-record the interviews. The interview with Helen Bonner was carried out over the telephone.
30. Telephone interview, February 1999.
31. Mike Davis uses the term "carceral Keynesianism" on page 416 of his book *Ecology of Fear* (Metropolitan Books, 1998). Davis terms the current rush to incarcerate "utterly incoherent as criminal justice policy, but wonderful as a stimulus to the kind of carceral Keynesianism" that politicians today have embraced as a way of bringing employment to areas suffering from the effects of industries relocating and small farms being driven out of business.
32. Author visited Corcoran, and was taken on a tour of the prison by Bruce Gomez, in early 1999.
33. Page 18 of *The New York Times*, July 6, 2000.
34. The RAND study, titled *Projecting California's Fiscal Future*, was published in 1995. Its authors were Stephen Carroll, Eugene Bryton, C. Peter Rydell, and Michael Shores. The study estimated that by 2005, as the prison expansion continued to eat up state revenues, the University of California system would have to turn away the equivalent of 135,000 full-time students, and the state's community colleges, 180,000 students.
35. According to a 1996 study carried out by the federally funded National Assessment of Educational Progress. Quoted by Nicholas Lemann in his November 1997 *Atlantic Monthly* article titled "The Reading Wars."
36. The author visited Pelican Bay in the spring of 1999. As part of the standard procedure he had to sign a document stating his awareness of the fact that the prison would not negotiate for his release should he be taken hostage. Prison guards work under the same rule: all know that other staff members are forbidden to negotiate with prisoners should a guard be seized.

Senior staffers, in a position to give orders, automatically lose all authority to issue instructions to other guards, once seized by inmates. The policy is designed to minimize the risk of escape through hostage-taking.

CHAPTER 4

1. The author Luis J. Rodriguez, who grew up in East L.A. about a decade after Ochoa, writes about this culture in his book *Always Running—La Vida Loca: Gang Days in L.A.* Published by Touchstone Books, 1993.
2. Ibid., page 20.
3. Ibid., page 41.
4. For more details on the East L.A. music scene from this period, see Steven Loza's book *Barrio Rhythms: Mexican American Music in Los Angeles*. University of Illinois Press, 1993.
5. Joan Moore's book *Homeboys: Gangs, Drugs and Prison in the Barrios of Los Angeles*. Published by Temple University Press, 1978. Moore's research is quoted in depth by the Chicano historian Edward J. Escobar, in his book *Race, Police, and the Making of a Political Identity: Mexican Americans and the Los Angeles Police Department, 1900–1945*. Published by University of California Press, 1999.
6. Ibid, page 131.
7. Ibid., page 170. On education discrimination, Escobar writes that "The Los Angeles School District, for example, underfunded the Mexican schools, not providing such basic facilities as cafeterias, playgrounds, and auditoriums, and dumping second-rate teachers on the Mexican schools."
8. Ibid., pages 179ff.
9. Ibid., page 187.
10. For information on the look of the zoot suit, the author is indebted to the descriptions offered by Edward Escobar, op. cit., page 178.
11. Ibid., page 178.
12. A discussion of the numbers wearing zoot suits can be found in Beatrice Griffith's book *American Me*. Greenwood Press, 1943.
13. Quoted by Edward Escobar, op. cit., page 201.
14. Another headline, this one in the *Los Angeles Herald and Express*, expressed its sympathies with the headline, "Sailor Taskforce Hits L.A. Zooters."
15. Carey McWilliams, *North from Mexico*. J. B. Lippincott Co., 1949.
16. The California Department of Corrections "California Prisoners and Parolees" report, 1996. The exact statistics given for 1996 were 34.1 percent Hispanic and 31.4 percent Black. Page 44.
17. 1998 Sentencing Project study. And year 2000 Uggen and Manza study, titled "The Political Consequences of Felon Disenfranchisement Laws in the United States."

CHAPTER 5

1. Information compiled in the April 1994 *California Journal*. The specific statistics can be found in Danielle Starkey and Vic Pollard's article "The Prison Dilemma."
2. Ibid.
3. Wilson's weekly radio address, 10/2/93.
4. Speeches in the fall of 1993.
5. The memos and files from which these quotes are taken are contained in the Wilson speech files of the California State Archives. These memos are contained in the file dated September 29, 1993, the day the bill was actually signed by Wilson.
6. Speech to California Republican Party Convention, September 18, 1993. Records of this meeting can be found in the California State Archives.
7. MARC was led by Clark and Lin Squires, whose fifteen-year-old son, Marc, had been shot dead on Thanksgiving Day, 1990. Wilson had first met the Squires on September 30, at the Devonshire Division Police Station.
8. Speech notes on the November 10 meeting, filed in the California State Archives.

9. Address to the California Narcotics Officers Association, Harrah's, Lake Tahoe. November 11, 1993.
10. See Note 5 above.
11. Much of the information on the chronology of Wilson's anticrime rhetoric can be found in the California State Archives. Wilson's speeches, and information on meetings he attended, are catalogued in chronological order.
12. Lewis wrote this shortly after the 1994 election.
13. Wilson speech to California Republican Party convention at the Anaheim Hilton Hotel, Saturday September 18, 1993.
14. Bill Clinton and Al Gore. *Putting People First: How We Can All Change America.* Times Books, 1992. Pages on crime policy: 71–74.
15. Bureau of Justice statistics. As of December 31, 1992, BOJ estimated 850,566 in prison and 441,781 in jail. As of December 31, 1993, BOJ estimated 909,000 in state and federal prison and another 456,000 in jail. A year later the state and federal prison population had risen by another 83,294 and the jail population had also increased.
16. Bureau of Justice Statistics Bulletin, published in August 2000. Report compiled by Dr. Allen J. Beck, one of the BOJ's resident statisticians.
17. Quote from a White House briefing on President Clinton's State of the Union speech in 1996.
18. Quoted in *The New York Times*, September 14, 1994. Article by David Johnston and Steven A. Holmes, titled "Experts Doubt Effectiveness of Crime Bill."
19. Quoted by the Associated Press, September 15, 1996.
20. Death penalty statistics published in the Bureau of Justice Statistics annual bulletins.
21. The exact number of executions in 1997 was 74; the total number of people on California's Death Row at year's end was 486.
22. According to Jay Hein and John Clark of the Hudson Institute, in their report titled "The Political Economy of Welfare Reform in the United States." The authors state that the total spent on AFDC in 1994 (in constant 1996 dollars) was $24.802 billion.
23. The 40 percent lead figure is given in *The New York Times*, October 20, 1994, page A25. Article by Jason DeParle titled "The 1994 Campaign: The Welfare System."
24. Ibid.
25. Quoted by Katharine A. Seelye, in her *New York Times* article "The 1994 Campaign: The Republicans; With Fiery Words, Gingrich Builds His Kingdom."
26. This speech was well-documented. In response, *New York Times* columnist Anthony Lewis wrote "Slash and burn, knife and smear: The Gingrich instincts are unrelenting. Herb Block got it right in his *Washington Post* cartoon when he had Mr. Gingrich crawling out of the same sewer where he portrayed Richard Nixon years ago."
27. Reported in 1994 campaign literature filed in UCLA's Young Research Library.
28. CCPOA financial records show that the union donated $50,000 to the Three Strikes You're Out Criminal Justice Committee on November 23, 1993.
29. Pages 35ff of *Three Strike and You're Out: A Promise to Kimber.* By Mike Reynolds, Bill Jones, and Dan Evans. Quill Driver Books, 1996.
30. Mike Davis in *The Ecology of Fear* quotes the author Mary Comerio as estimating that 437,000 housing units were damaged in the earthquake. Page 31.
31. Quoted in Mike Davis's book *The Ecology of Fear: Los Angeles and the Imagination of Disaster.* Metropolitan Books, 1998, page 7.
32. Quoted in the Mike Reynolds, Bill Jones, and Dan Evans book *Three Strike And You're Out: A Promise To Kimber,* op. cit., page 198. They source the quote to a March 4, 1994, article in the *Victor Valley Daily Press.*

CHAPTER 6

1. From list of Ochoa's prior convictions, compiled by probation department at time of Ochoa's 1995 trial.
2. Information provided to author by Ochoa's cousin, referred to in this book as Jamie.

3. Ochoa told probation officer Whisenant about his use of Seconal and downers, while on trial for burglary in 1980. Court records stored in Los Angeles's Hall of Records.
4. Ibid.
5. Specific details in this chapter were provided to the author over the course of numerous interviews conducted with members of Ochoa's family throughout 1999 and 2000.
6. For more details of America's indigenous opium production, see Clarence Lusane's book *Pipe Dream Blues: Racism and the War on Drugs*. Published by South End Press, 1991.
7. For more details on the medical morphine trade, see Troy Duster's book *The Legislation of Morality: Law, Drugs, and Moral Judgment*. Published by The Free Press, New York, 1970.
8. Clarence Lusane. Page 32.
9. Marie Nyswander provides this estimate in *The Drug Addict as a Patient*. Published by Grune & Stratton, 1956.
10. Ibid., page 7.
11. Ibid., page 8.
12. For more details on this event, see Mike Gray's book *Drug Crazy: How We Got Into This Mess and How We Can Get Out*, published by Random House, 1998.
13. Ibid., page 53ff.
14. Clarence Lusane, *Pipe Dream Blues*, op. cit., page 33.
15. Quoted on page 57 of Mike Gray's book *Drug Crazy*.
16. Ibid., page 16.
17. For the exact chronology of events leading up to President Woodrow Wilson's signature of the Volstead Act, see Henry Lee's history, *How Dry We Were*. Published by Prentice-Hall, Inc., 1963.
18. Details of this growing anti-alcohol movement, and the dates of the relevant nineteenth-and early-twentieth-century legislation, can be found in Charles Merz's *The Dry Decade*, published by Doubleday, Doran and Company, 1930; and in the collection of essays, edited by David E. Kyvig, titled *Law, Alcohol, and Order: Perspectives on National Prohibition*. Published by Greenwood Press, 1985.
19. Thomas M. Coffey, *The Long Thirst: Prohibition in America: 1920–1933*. Published by W. W. Norton and Co., 1975, page 7.
20. Ibid., page 3.
21. Henry Lee, *How Dry We Were*, op. cit., page 58.
22. The number of Prohibition Bureau agents is quoted in Martin Alan Greenberg's book *Prohibition Enforcement: Charting a New Mission*. Published by Charles C. Thomas, 1999, page 157.
23. Charles Merz, *The Dry Decade*, op. cit., page 135.
24. Ibid., page 146. Merz writes that 42,223 were arrested in 1921, and that the number of arrests peaked in 1924, with 68,116.
25. Mike Gray, *Drug Crazy: How We Got Into This Mess and How We Can Get Out*, op. cit., pages 72–73.
26. Harry Anslinger and William F. Tompkins, *The Traffic in Narcotics*. Published by Funk and Wagnalls, 1953.
27. Mike Gray, *Drug Crazy*, op. cit., page 83.
28. Ibid.
29. *The Traffic in Narcotics*, page 11.
30. Ibid., pages 295 and 296.
31. For more information, see Mike Gray's book *Drug Crazy*.

CHAPTER 7
1. Well into the 1960s, LSD was used, legally, by psychiatrists, army doctors conducting what many considered to be mind-control experiments, and a growing legion of casual users. The author Ken Kesey created an LSD-influenced troupe named the Merry Pranksters, which toured America on a psychedelic bus. Into the second half of the decade, mass ingesting of LSD occurred quite openly at large events known as Acid Tests.

2. Todd Gitlin, *The Sixties: Years of Hope, Days of Rage*. Bantam Books, 1987. Page 81.
3. For information on Ochoa's appearance, I am indebted to Virginia Castaneda, who permitted me to delve through the family photo albums and to borrow photos that I needed for the purpose of describing Billy Ochoa during decades past.
4. Information provided to author during meeting with Ochoa at CSP-SAC, October 1, 2000.
5. Author could not track down the woman written about here. Therefore, her real name has been changed to protect her identity. Information on this relationship provided by Billy Ochoa, William Ochoa, and court records from the time.
6. Quoted on page 164 of Elliott Currie's book *Crime and Punishment in America*. Published by Henry Holt & Co., Inc., 1998.
7. Quoted on page 11 of Dan Baum's book *Smoke and Mirrors: The War on Drugs and the Politics of Failure*. Published by Little, Brown and Co., 1996.
8. Ibid., page 6.
9. Ibid.
10. This information is found on page 19 of Christian Parenti's book *Lockdown America*. Published by Verso, 1999. Parenti cites a survey titled "The National Crime Information Center, a Special Report."
11. Ibid., page 26.
12. Roper polls, quoted on page 55 of *Smoke and Mirors: The War on Drugs and the Politics of Failure*.
13. Information from pages 142 to 144 of Edward Jay Epstein's book *Agency of Fear: Opiates and Political Power in America*. Published by G.P. Putnam and Sons, 1977.
14. Nixon's "national emergency" is discussed in *Agency of Fear*. The relevant information can be found from page 138 onwards.
15. Ibid., page 165.
16. Information on Del La Reyas was provided by William Ochoa Sr. during the course of several interviews in 1999 and 2000.
17. Letter to author from Billy Ochoa, dated September 18, 2000.
18. Story told to author by Ochoa during visit to CSP-SAC, Ocober 1, 2000.
19. These examples are given by Dartmouth College sociologists Joan Smith and William Fried, in their book *The Uses of the American Prison*. Published by Lexington Books, 1974.
20. Specific details on the structure of the California Rehabilitation Center are written about by Troy Duster, in his book *The Legislation of Morality: Law, Drugs, and Moral Judgement*. Published by The Free Press, 1970. Duster worked at the center in the late 1960s.
21. Letter to author from Billy Ochoa, July 2000.
22. Troy Duster, *The Legislation of Morality*, op. cit., page 143.
23. Michael Massing. *The Fix*. Published by Simon & Schuster, 1998, page 109.
24. Ibid.
25. Quoted in Joan Smith and William Fried's book *The Uses of the American Prison*, op. cit., page 23.
26. Information contained in court records, filed in the Los Angeles Hall of Records, from Ochoa's subsequent burglary trials.

CHAPTER 8

1. The trajectory of the Carter Administration's policies toward drugs, as well as information on the marijuana decriminalization laws are well summarized in Michael Massing's book *The Fix*, published by Simon & Schuster, 1998. Bourne would eventually have to resign after newspapers ran articles alleging that he had written out a phony prescription for a female staffer of his to obtain Quaaludes and had used drugs at a NORML gathering.
2. From conversation author had with Billy Ochoa at CSP-SAC, Sunday October 1, 2000.
3. Court testimony during the 1980 trial.
4. Information on this particular burglary was compiled from court records and transcripts filed in the Los Angeles Hall of Records. Case number A559436. General information on house

burglary techniques come from interviews with Billy and Jamie conducted by the author in 1999 and 2000.

5. Opinion polls quoted by Austin Ranney, in his book *The American Elections of 1980*. Published by the American Enterprise Institute for Public Policy Research, 1981, page 30.

6. Hamilton Jordan, *Crisis: The Last Year of the Carter Presidency*. Published by G. P. Putnam's Sons, 1982, page 37.

7. *The Real War on Crime: The Report of the National Criminal Justice Commission*, edited by Steven R. Donziger, quotes Uniform Crime Reports and National Crime Victimization Survey numbers indicating these increases. Using figures gathered by the U.S. Department of Justice, the Bureau of Justice Statistics and the FBI, the authors found crime in these years rose, briefly, to a level that would not be reached again until the late 1980s.

8. By 1990, 138 mainly low-level "mules" had been so sentenced under this Michigan law.

9. More details on the Attica rebellion and its bloody denouement can be found in Tom Wicker's book *A Time to Die*, published by Quadrangle, 1975; and in Herman Badillo and Milton Haynes' book *A Bill of No Rights: Attica and the American Prison System*, published by Outerbridge and Lazard, Inc., 1972.

10. Quoted in Badillo and Haynes' book, op. cit., page 88.

11. Gallup Poll, October 2, 1980. The author researched Gallup poll data from this period in the Ronald Reagan Presidential Library in Simi Valley, California.

12. Quoted by Todd Gitlin, in *The Sixties: Years of Hope, Days of Rage*. Published by Bantam Books, 1987, page 217.

13. Rowland Evans and Robert Novak, *The Reagan Revolution*. Published by E. P. Dutton, 1981.

14. James Q. Wilson, *Thinking About Crime*. Published by Basic Books, 1975. Revised edition, Vintage Books, 1985, pages 33, 46, and 48.

15. Described by Senator Paula Hawkins (R., FL) in her essay "Drugs and Crime: Possibilities for Reform," published as a chapter in *Criminal Justice Reform*, Free Congress Research and Education Foundation, 1983.

16. Information contained in pretrial letter sent by Captain Robert Grimm to Judge Ricardo A. Torres of the Pasadena Superior Court. Dated May 1, 1980.

17. Motion filed by Ochoa before the court on May 8, 1980.

18. Told to author by Ochoa in conversation at CSP-SAC, October 1, 2000.

19. William Julius Wilson, *When Work Disappears: The World of the New Urban Poor*. Published by Alfred A. Knopf, Inc., 1996, page 156.

20. Dennis Healey, *The Time of My Life*. Published by the Michael Joseph imprint of Penguin Books, 1989, page 463.

21. Gallup polling data from November 1980 and March 1981.

22. Gallup poll from April 4, 1982.

23. Rolling survey; data provided in Gallup Poll, September 18, 1986.

24. National Punishment Survey, 1987. Quoted on page 27 of Diana R. Gordon's book *The Return of the Dangerous Classes: Drug Prohibition and Policy Politics*. Published by W. W. Norton and Co., 1994.

25. Dan Baum, *Smoke and Mirrors: The War on Drugs and the Politics of Failure*. Published by Little, Brown and Co., 1996, page 286.

26. Ibid., page 33.

27. Op. cit., page 33.

28. Bureau of Justice Statistics, as quoted in 1990 study on state drug laws by the National Criminal Justice Association.

29. Figure quoted by Manning Marable, in *Race, Reform and Rebellion: The Second Reconstruction in Black America, 1945–1990*. Published by University Press of Mississippi, 1991; revised second edition, page 193.

30. Ibid., page 211.

31. Dan Baum, *Smoke and Mirrors*, op. cit.

32. Quoted by Baum, page 266.

33. Ibid.
34. Joel Dyer quotes this on page 242 of his book *The Perpetual Prisoner Machine: How America Profits from Crime.* Westview Press, 2000. He sources this information to *The Corrections Yearbook: Adult Correction.* South Salem, NY: Criminal Justice Institute, 1981–90.
35. Joel Dyer, op. cit., pages 249ff.
36. Ibid., page 259.
37. Ochoa told these details to the author during a conversation at CSP-SAC, October 1, 2000.

CHAPTER 9
1. Arnold S. Trebach, *The Great Drug War: And Radical Proposals That Could Make America Safe Again.* Published by Macmillan Publishing Company, 1987.
2. Ibid., page 15.
3. The October 2000 PBS *Frontline* documentary on the drug wars argued that these government statistics implied money should have been channeled into treatment programs for the addicts rather than into law-enforcement and interdiction efforts.
4. William J. Bennett, *The De-Valuing of America: The Fight for our Culture and our Children.* Published by Touchstone Books, 1992, page 92.
5. Ibid., page 47.
6. Quoted in the *Frontline* documentary.
7. After he left office, Bennett detailed these ideas in *The De-Valuing of America: The Fight for our Culture and Our Children*, op. cit.
8. Ibid., pages 115 and 116. Bennett boasted of this event on several subsequent occasions. At a National Press Club meeting shortly afterward, he told the journalists that "This war is not for delicate sensibilities. This is tough stuff. We need to get tough, we need to get tough as hell, we need to do it right now."
9. Ibid., page 148.
10. Michael Massing, in his book *The Fix,* published by Simon & Schuster, 1998, writes that in 1981 the federal antidrug budget hit $1.5 billion; and by 1997 it had already reached $17 billion.
11. Wilson testified in front of the Senate Appropriations Committee, chaired by Senator Robert Byrd (D., WVA), June 22, 1994.
12. Information contained in Wilson press releases and speeches stored in California State Archives, Sacramento.
13. Wilson speech, March 14, 1994, at "Law Enforcement Legislative Day" event at the Hyatt Regency Hotel, Sacramento.
14. Public filings made by the California Correctional Peace Officers Association's Political Action Committee.
15. According to CCPOA records, Wilson was given $533,572.33, and Lungren $92,500.
16. The file containing all the background material on Nixon's eulogy, including the various drafts of this speech, are stored in the California State Archives. Wilson speeches, 4/27/94 file.
17. Law Enforcement in California Statistics, faxed to Wilson's aides during 1994 and filed among background papers to Wilson speeches.
18. Joseph McNamara, "Runaway Crime and the End of Dreams," *California Journal,* October 1995 issue.
19. Wilson address to California Federation of Republican Women, Sacramento Convention Center, April 13, 1994.
20. Wilson announced these budget cuts at a press conference in room 1190 of the Capitol Building on June 13, 1994.
21. Bill Stall article titled "Poll Finds Gap Closing, Wilson, Brown Nearly Even." Stall specifically identified the governor's highly visible attendances at the funerals of slain police officers as having contributed to his recovery.
22. Text of advert filed with Wilson's papers in the California State Archives.

23. Reported in the December 1994 issue of the *California Journal*.
24. November 22, 1994. Speech delivered at the Williamsburg Lodge. The event was sponsored by the Republican Governors Association.
25. January 26, 1995.

CHAPTER 10
1. Author interviewed Trehune, January 12, 2000.
2. Information sheet on California Department of Corrections Y2K efforts.
3. CSP-SAC institution profile.
4. Statistics on the prison provided by California Department of Corrections statistics. Taken from the CSP-SAC institution profile.
5. California Department of Corrections Facts Bulletin, March 2000.
6. The author was taken on a tour of the prison on January 14, 2000. Because of California laws restricting access to inmates, he was not allowed to interview Ochoa while on this tour or to see his cell. He returned to the prison another day and interviewed Ochoa in the visiting room.
7. The author visited a prison technology trade show in Denver, Colorado, in August 1999. The companies selling similar antennae to high-security prisons across America were also under contract to protect American nuclear installations and the Israeli border regions.
8. Estimate quoted by Ted Koppel in a *Nightline* special on solitary confinement in Texas. ABC news, 1999.
9. The author visited Estelle Unit prison and interviewed Larry Fitzgerald in early 1999, while reporting an article for *The Atlantic Monthly*. Fitzgerald's quotes were originally printed in this article, titled "When They Get Out," and published in the June 1999 issue. The author personally saw the immediate aftermath of one inmate having slashed the arteries in his hand. Regarding escapes, in late 1999, one inmate did force his way out of Estelle. He was, however, shot during the escape, and his body was found on prison grounds a few days afterward.
10. Quoted by Kevin Johnson, *USA Today*, as reprinted in *The Detroit News*, August 8, 1997. The article is titled "American Journal: New Prisons Isolate Worst Criminals."
11. Virginia Castaneda provided the authors with photocopies of the letters her brother wrote to her during the first three years of his incarceration at CSP-SAC.
12. This information came out when author was interviewing Ochoa at CSP-SAC, October 1, 2000.
13. Information provided author by Lieutenant Billy Mayfield, CSP-SAC's public information officer, when author toured prison.
14. California Department of Corrections Fact Sheet, March 1, 2000. The CDC estimated 56,440 of its inmates came from L.A. County, which has a population of under three million. This was an incarceration rate nearly five times the national average.
15. The congressional vote was on February 9, 1995. Judge Keep's decision was handed down on February 13.
16. Quoted in Townhall.com and in *Mother Jones Magazine*, January 1995 issue, in an article by Will Saletan titled "Phil's Felon."
17. Speech to Republican National Committee, July 1995.
18. Quoted in October 1995 newsletter put out by the National Drug Sentencing Network.
19. Memo dated May 7, 1995.
20. June 5, 1995.
21. On April 30, 1995, Gayle Wilson had told a crowd at the Lincoln Club of California that phone banking had raised $8 million for her husband, along with pledges for another $15 million.
22. June 27, 1995.
23. Wilson speech to National District Attorneys' Association, summer conference, MGM Grand Hotel, Las Vegas. July 17, 1995.

24. LCC meeting, October 24, 1995. CPOA meeting, Silverado Hotel, Napa, November 13, 1995.
25. Letter to author, dated September 18, 2000.
26. Letter from Ochoa to author, dated October 23, 2000.

Index

Addams, Jane, 35
affirmative action, 236–37
African Americans, xii–xiii, xvi, 9, 51–52,
    76, 79–81, 103, 156–57, 181–85
  discrimination against, 101, 106, 157
  disenfranchisement of, xiii, 80–81, 106
  drugs and, 43, 77, 84–85, 139–41, 146–
    47
  and history of crime and punishment,
    19–21, 25, 80–81
  and history of prison system, 79–80
  homicides among, 84, 195
  Horton case and, 46
  Johnson and, 156
  Nixon on, 157
  at Pelican Bay prison, 90
  poverty among, 190
  prison violence and, 182–84, 222
  Rockefeller laws and, 66
  unemployment among, 83
  Wilson's presidential campaign and,
    236–37
Agency of Fear (Epstein), 160
Aid to Families with Dependent
    Children (AFDC), 51, 118, 123–24,
    156, 220
Alabama, 81
  drug busts in, 76, 85–86
  prison system of, xii–xiii, 196
Alcatraz prison, 75, 82, 145, 227

alcohol, 138, 140–47
All God's Children (Butterfield), 18–19
Alston, Gilbert C., 189
Ambrose, Myles, 159, 168
American Way of Crime, The (Browning
    and Garassi), 18, 24
Andal, Dan, 125
Anderson, David, 43–44
Anslinger, Harry, 146–51, 156, 203, 207
Anti-Drug Abuse Act, 13, 202
anti–hate crime legislation, 127
Anti-Saloon League of America, 138, 143
Anti-Violent Crime Strategy (AVCS), 120
Appalachia, 17–18, 74
Appleton, Ray, 54
Archambault, David, 90
Asian Americans, 51–52
Attica prison, 145, 182–84, 188
Auburn prison, 24–27, 77
Austin, Charlotte, 113–14
Ayres, Edward Duran, 101

Barnes, Angela and Cliff, 45
Baron Report, 39
Basin's Rebellion, 17
Baum, Dan, 44, 131, 157, 194
Bean, "Judge" Roy, 22
Benedict, Paul, 3–5
Bennett, William, 46, 195–96, 203–4
Benson, Russell, 73–74

Bentham, Jeremy, 22, 89, 228
Bias, Len, 44
Bird, Rose, 122
Blackbeard (Edward Teach), 20, 70
Blevins, Lillie, 75–76, 85–86
Boggs, Hale, 67, 148–50, 164, 203
Bonner, Helen, 86
Bonner, William Steve, 86
Bowler, Larry, 125
Brown, Jerry, 117, 122, 209, 217, 234
    Reynolds and, 52–53
    senatorial campaign of, 38–39
Brown, Kathleen, 117
    gubernatorial campaign of, 32, 113,
        129, 205–6, 208–10, 213, 215–16,
        218
Brown, Willie, 59, 127, 216
Browning, Frank, 18, 20, 24, 82
Buckner, Alan, xviii–xix, 9–10, 20–21, 28–
    30, 72
Bureau of Narcotics, 145–48, 156
Bureau of Narcotics and Dangerous
    Drugs (BNDD), 156, 159
Bureau of Prisons, 144–45
Bush, George, 39, 120, 195, 202–4
    crime and, 6, 13, 46, 63, 202–3
    economy under, 30
    L.A. riots and, 32
    and War on Drugs, 42
    Wilson's gubernatorial campaigns and,
        50
Bush, George W., 122
Butterfield, Fox, 18–19

Cable, George Washington, 79–80, 82
California, 13–14, 30–34, 133
    affirmative action in, 236–37
    CAMP in, 42
    capital punishment in, 122–23, 182–84
    criminal justice system of, 36, 48–51,
        117, 154, 212

economy of, 30–33, 40, 48–49, 51, 88,
    108, 113, 213–14, 218–19, 235, 237,
    239
history of, 98–100
illegal immigrants in, 205–7, 211, 213–
    14, 235
Klaas case and, 116
Lungren and, 57–58
One-Strike law in, 214–17
prison system of, xii, xvi, 7, 14, 48–51,
    57–58, 73, 75, 87–91, 106, 112–13,
    116–17, 196, 207–9, 211, 221–33,
    235, 237–38, 240–47
Reynolds and, 52–53
Three Strikes law and, xx, 6–7, 13, 30,
    59–63, 71–74, 112, 116, 119, 125–
    26, 128–30, 206, 208–10, 214–15,
    234, 239–40
welfare system of, 118, 205–8, 213,
    216, 219–20
Wilson's gubernatorial campaigns in,
    32, 48–51, 62–63, 113–15, 118, 126,
    129, 205–19, 237, 239
Wilson's political career in, 33–34, 36–
    38, 208, 210, 234
Wilson's senatorial campaigns and, 38–
    40, 47–48, 186–87
Wilson's senatorial tenure and, 39–41,
    46–47, 49–50, 122
    see also Propositions, California
California Correctional Peace Officers
    Association, 63, 87, 126, 210
California Institute for Women, 166, 171–
    72
California Men's Colony prison, 73
California Narcotics Officers Association,
    115
California Peace Officers Association, 61,
    116, 129, 217, 237–38
California Rehabilitation Center (CRC),
    163–69

Ochoa's commitment to, 163–66, 169, 171, 173, 190, 198

California State Prison, Sacramento (CSP-SAC), 221
  Administrative Segregation (AD Seg) at, 29, 226–27, 241–44
  eating at, 229–30
  labeling system of, 12–13, 230–31
  Ochoa's imprisonment at, 11–13, 28–29, 75, 87, 97, 155, 224–26, 228–33, 241–44, 246
  Ochoa transported to, 11, 232
  physical description of, 11–12, 224–30
  security at, 231
  violent tensions in, 12–13, 29, 230–33, 241, 243, 246

California State Sheriffs' Association, 214

California Youth Authority (CYA) camps, 217, 222
  Ochoa's detention at, 92–93, 95–96, 133, 240
  at Ontario, 95, 133

Callaghan, James, 191

Callahan, Michael Dennis, 34–36, 50, 140

Campaign Against Marijuana Production (CAMP), 42

capital punishment, 120–25, 182–84
  Clinton and, 120–21, 205
  for drug-related crimes, 149
  Gingrich and, 124, 236
  Reagan and, 192
  statistics on, 122–23
  Wilson on, 49–50, 122, 125, 128–29, 212–13, 215

Capone, Al, 144–45

Carrington, Michael, 113–14

Carswell Federal Medical Center, 75, 85

Carter, Jimmy, 36, 41, 175, 179–80, 184, 190–91, 193

Carter, Melvin, 208–9

Casriel, Tom, 112

Castaneda, Arthur, xvii, 3–4, 241

Castaneda, Virginia Ochoa, xvii–xviii, 3–4, 110, 133, 135–37
  brother's drug addiction and, 4, 135, 137
  brother's imprisonment and, 230–33, 241, 243, 247

Catholic Church, 15–16, 19

Center for Media and Public Affairs, 69–70

Central Intelligence Agency (CIA), 42, 159

Chessman, Caryl, 182

Chicago, Ill., 103, 155
  drugs in, 34–35, 50, 74, 83

China, 148, 207
  and history of drug use, 139
  prison system of, xii

Chino prison, xviii, 5, 189–90, 217

civil rights movement, 151–52, 182, 185

Civil War, 147–49, 156
  drug use during, 137
  and history of crime and punishment, 18–20
  and history of prison system, 78–80, 82–83

Clark, Ray, xviii–xix, 8–10

Clinton, Bill, 13, 118–21, 213–14, 234, 237
  crime strategy of, 119–21, 205
  illegal immigrants and, 207

cocaine, 34–35, 41–42, 44, 50, 150, 190, 198
  federal drug busts and, 77
  history of, 137–41, 143, 146–47
  Rockefeller laws and, 66
  and War on Drugs, 42
  White case and, 72
  Wilson on, 41
  see also crack

Coffey, Thomas, 143
Common Cause, 48
Comprehensive Crime Control Act, 48, 57
congregate system of incarceration, 25–26
Congress, U.S., 63, 68, 170, 207–8, 218, 220
  alcohol banned by, 142
  crime and, 120–22, 158
  drugs and, 42, 44, 46–47, 57, 139, 145–49, 158–59, 168, 186–87, 195
  Gingrich and, 123–24
  illegal immigrants and, 207, 213, 235
  Lungren and, 57–58
  prison system and, 24, 81–82, 228
  welfare system and, 123
  Wilson's campaigns for, 38–40, 47–48, 186–87
  Wilson's tenure in, 39–41, 46–47, 49–50, 122
Connecticut, prison system of, 196
Constitution, U.S., 81, 158
  Eighteenth Amendment to, 142–43
  Twenty-first Amendment to, 145
Contract with America, 124–25
Corcoran prison, 12, 87–90, 224, 243
  Ochoa's imprisonment at, 245–47
  violence at, 221–22
Corning, J. Leonard, 140
Costa, Jim, 126, 129
crack, xiv, 42–44, 64, 193–95, 202–3
  Bennett on, 203
  Blevins case, 76
  Ochoa's addiction to, 198–200
  wars over, 70, 74, 194–95
crime, criminals, criminal justice system, 67–84, 112–31, 154–60, 180, 192–96, 202–9
  Benson case and, 73–74
  Blevins case and, 76
  Bush and, 6, 13, 46, 63, 202–3

  of California, 36, 48–51, 117, 154, 212
  Clinton on, 119–21, 205
  comparison between sin and, 16
  CSP-SAC prisoners and, 224
  Davis and, 234–35, 239
  and discrimination against Mexican Americans, 100–101, 104–6
  federal, 76–79
  Gingrich and, 124–25, 236
  goals of, 166–68, 170, 186, 195
  in Great Britain, 15, 17, 21–23, 71, 192
  hysteria over, 68–71, 75
  history of, 14–27, 68–70, 74, 78, 80–82
  in inner cities, 83–84
  Johnson on, 155–56
  juvenile, see gangs
  Lungren and, 57–58
  Nixon on, 41, 115, 131, 157–60, 166–70, 175, 213
  in presidential campaigns, 41, 45–46, 63, 119, 235–39
  Reagan on, 41–42, 185–86, 192–93
  reforms in, 163–64
  relationship between drugs and, xii–xv, 6, 13–14, 41–44, 69–71, 140–41, 147–50, 167–68, 175, 193–96, 205
  Reynolds and, 52, 54–56
  statistics on, xiii, 43, 84, 195, 212, 223
  welfare system and, xx, 3–10, 13, 118, 125
  White case and, 72
  Wilson on, 6–7, 34, 36–40, 46–51, 62–63, 71, 112–19, 125–30, 189, 205–9, 211–20, 234–40
  see also War on Crime
Crime and Punishment in American History (Friedman), 16
Crime Control Commission, San Diego, 36–38
Crime Summit, 115, 126–29
Cummings, Homer S., 144–45

Cuomo, Mario, 123, 196, 212, 218
Current Affair, A, 69
Currie, Elliott, 43

Davis, Gray, 223, 234–35, 239
Davis, Jo, 54–56, 112
Davis, Richard Allen, 60–61
debtors, imprisonment of, 23
Del La Reyas, Tony, 160–61
DeParle, Jason, 123
Detroit, Mich., 74, 180
Deukmejian, George, 53, 234
   on prison system, 48–49, 57–58, 196
De-Valuing of America, The (Bennett),
   203
Dickens, Charles, 27
Dillinger, John, 134, 146
Discovery of the Asylum, The (Rothman),
   26–27
District Attorney's Association of Los
   Angeles, 10
Dole, Bob, 236, 238
Donovan, Maureen, 45
Draft Riots, 20
Dreser, Herr, 138
drive-by killers, 113–14
Drug Crazy (Gray), 141
Drug Enforcement Administration
   (DEA), 159, 170
drugs, drug users, 64–77, 83–87, 108,
   133–53, 156–75, 180–82, 184–87,
   192–205, 223–24
   Bennett on, 195, 203–4
   Benson case and, 73
   Blevins case, 76
   Bush and, 202–4
   California gubernatorial campaigns
      and, 49–50
   Clinton and, 205
   communism associated with, 148–49
   comparisons between witches and, 15–
      16

CSP-SAC prisoners and, 224
federal busts for, 76–77, 85, 141
federal prison system and, 83–84
Gingrich on, 236
history of, 34–35, 137–41, 145–50,
   175, 193
Johnson and, 156
Just Say No campaign on, 193–94
life sentences for, 85–87, 180, 194
Mexican-American gangs and, 96
New York prison system and, 84–85
Nixon on, 68, 157–60, 167–70
Ochoa's addiction to, xviii–xix, 4–6, 8,
   28, 92, 96–97, 133–35, 137, 139,
   152–53, 160–63, 166, 170–75, 178,
   187, 190, 197–201, 243–44, 246
popularity of, 153, 159, 182
Reagan and, 185–86, 192–93, 202, 205
regulation of, 138–41, 145–50
relationship between crime and, xii–xv,
   6, 13–14, 41–44, 69–71, 140–41,
   147–50, 167–68, 175, 193–96, 205
Reynolds and, 52, 54
state laws on, 34–35, 65–68, 170
Three Strikes law and, 71–72
treatment for, 163–69, 171, 173
welfare system and, 118
White case and, 72
Williams's sentence and, 64–66
Wilson on, 41, 46–47, 113, 115, 212
see also cocaine; crack; War on Drugs
Drug War Bond Act, 47
Dukakis, Michael, 6, 13, 49, 119, 205,
   216
   Horton case and, 45–46, 63
Duster, Troy, 138–39, 166

Eastern Penitentiary (Cherry Hill), 21,
   25, 77, 82
Eastman, Don, 9
Education Department, U.S., 204
Edwards, Dick, 184

Ehrlichman, John D., 158, 167
Eisenhower, Dwight D., 131, 149, 151–52, 157–58
elderly, 69
energy crisis, 179–80, 185
Epstein, Edward, 160
Erdoes, Richard, 22
Escobar, Edward J., 100–101, 104
Europe, 75
    and history of crime and punishment, 15–16, 21–22
    and history of drug use, 139–40
    immigrants in Los Angeles from, 99–100
Evans, Rowland, 186

Federal Bureau of Investigation (FBI), 120, 146, 156, 168, 212
Feinstein, Dianne, 49–50
felony disenfranchisement laws, xii–xiii, 80–81, 106
Ferguson, Colin, 121
Field Foundation, 83
Fitzgerald, Larry, 227
Florence, Colo., federal prison in, 88–89, 224
Florida, xii–xiii, 42, 69
Ford, Gerald, 41, 68, 180
Fox TV, 69–70
France, 17, 23, 139
Fraternal Order of the Police, 121
Freud, Sigmund, 138
Fried, William, 169
Friedman, Milton, 191–92
frontier, 21–22, 70

Gallego, Gil, 121
gangs, xiv, 6, 38, 43, 74, 84, 180, 194–95
    California initiative on, 239–40
    Clinton and, 120
    crack epidemic and, 70

Fresno police and, 55
    and history of crime and punishment, 21–22
    Latino, 12–13, 93–96, 105, 136, 230–31
    Lungren and, 58
    Nixon and, 159
    prison system and, 12–13, 90, 222, 226, 230–31
    Prohibition and, 144
    Three Strikes law and, 240
    Wilson and, 113, 116, 128, 212, 239
Gang Violence and Juvenile Crime Prevention Act, 239–40
Garassi, John, 18, 20, 24, 82
Gates, Darryl, 42
Georgia, 13, 79
Gilligan, John, 5–6
Gingrich, Newt, 123–25, 195, 208, 220, 236
Gitlin, Todd, 151
Giuliani, Rudolph, 123
Gomez, Bruce, 87
Goodman, Leslie, 236
Gordon, Diana, 194
Gore, Al, 46, 119
Gould, Russ, 31–32, 213–14
Gramm, Phil, 84, 195, 235–36
Grant, Ulysses S., 78
Gray, Mike, 141, 144, 148
Great Britain:
    criminal justice system in, 15, 17, 21–23, 71, 192
    economy of, 191–92
    and history of drug use, 139
    homicide rates in, 84
Great Depression, 32, 87, 101–2, 145, 147, 219
Greene, Leroy, 129
Grimm, Robert T., 188–89
Grundy, Ben, 89

Haas, Thomas, 86–87
Hannigan, Maury, 217
Hard, William, 35
Harrison Narcotic Act, 140, 143, 146
Hawkins, Paula, 42
Hayakawa, Sam, 38
Healey, Denns, 191
Helms, Jesse, 195
Heritage Foundation, 218–19
Heston, Charlton, 47–48
High Desert prison, 89
Hinckley, John, 192
Hiss, Alger, 158
History of a Barrio (Romo), 99
Hobson, Richmond Pearson, 141
Holland, Jimmy, 177
Hoover, J. Edgar, 146, 156
Hope, Tamia, xix–xx, 9–10, 30
Horton, Willie, 44–46, 63, 209
Huffington, Michael, 63, 126
Human Rights Watch, 84
Humphrey, Hubert, 155, 185, 237
Hunt, Ed, 52, 55–56, 212
Huntsville prison, 90, 227

illegal immigrants, Wilson on, 40, 118–
    19, 205–7, 211, 213–14, 216, 218–
    20, 235–37
Illinois:
    drugs and, 35, 168
    prison system of, 88–89
Inmates Bill of Rights, 116–17, 125, 217–
    18, 234
Innocent VIII, Pope, 15
Interior Department, U.S., 78
Irish Americans, 19–20
Italy, 15, 21–23

Jaffe, Jerome, 168, 170
James, Jesse, 70, 134
Jeffers, Kenneth, 200

Johnson, Lyndon, 41, 118, 152, 155–56,
    167, 233
Jones, Bill, 126, 129
Jordan, Hamilton, 180
Judiciary Act, 24
Justice Department, U.S., 57, 78, 120
Just Say No campaign, 193–94

Keep, Judith, 235
Kennedy, Bobby, 87, 154–55
Kennedy, John F., 41, 96, 151, 155, 167,
    182
Keynes, John Maynard, 87, 191
Khomeini, Ayatollah, 179
King, Martin Luther, Jr., 58, 151–52,
    154, 181–82, 237
King, Rodney, 32
Klaas, Marc, 62–63, 214
Klaas, Polly, 60–63, 69, 112, 115–16,
    121, 127, 205, 214
Knox, John, 81
Krajicek, David, 69
Krogh, Egil, 167, 169

LaGuardia, Fiorello, 147
Laidig, Samuel L., 187
Larry King Live, 204
Latinos, 9, 51, 84–85
    Attica uprising and, 182–83
    discrimination against, 101, 106
    drugs and, 43, 85, 147
    imprisonment of, xii, 12–13, 230–31
    see also Mexican Americans
Law Enforcement Assistance
    Administration (LEAA), 156, 158
Leavenworth prison, 82, 145
Leonard, Bill, 125, 217
Lewis, Anthony, 118
Lincoln, Abraham, 78
Lindbergh, Charles, 61
Liss, Peter, 73

Long Island Railroad massacre, 69, 121, 205
Los Angeles, Calif., 133, 153–55, 235
  CRC residents from, 164
  discrimination against Mexican Americans in, 99–101, 104
  drugs in, 74, 83
  earthquake in, 126–27
  economy of, 83, 108, 110
  history of, 98–105, 108–10
  Mexican-American gangs in, 94–96
  Ochoa's birth in, 97, 102
  Ochoa's fruit and vegetable business in, 106–7
  race riots in, 32, 59, 103–5, 154, 207
  violent crime in, 43
  Wilson's Crime Summit in, 115, 126–29
Los Angeles County Central Jail, xviii, 154–55, 160, 162, 187–89
Los Angeles Police Department (LAPD), 130, 134, 154
  and discrimination against Mexican Americans, 100–101, 105
  Zoot Suit Riots and, 207
Los Angeles Times, 99, 104–5, 128, 214, 222
Louisiana, 18, 67, 80, 141
Lungren, Dan, 7, 56–59, 127, 210, 217–18, 234–35, 239
Lusane, Clarence, 137–38

McCarthy, Joseph, 148, 150, 158
McCollum, Bill, 228
McGrath, Joe, 89–91
Mackay, Charles, 15
McNamara, Joseph, 212
McVeigh, Timothy, 120–21
McWilliams, Carey, 105
Mafia, 71, 144–45, 158
mandatory minimum sentences, 13, 44, 65–68, 170, 196, 202

Manson, Charles, 57, 87–88, 162, 166, 214
Manza, Jeff, 106
Marable, Manning, 83
Marpet, Jane, 200
Massachusetts, 45, 63, 142
  history of crime and punishment in, 16, 19
Massing, Michael, 168
Maxwell, Richard, 206
Mayeda, Jon M., 6
media, 121, 128–30, 133, 213–15
  Attica uprising and, 183–84
  and banning of alcohol, 143
  and discrimination against Mexican Americans, 100, 104–5
  drugs and, 43–44, 140, 168
  and history of crime and punishment, 17–18
  images of crime in, xiii–xiv, 6, 69–71, 196, 213
  Nixon and, 157
  Three Strikes law and, 112, 129–30
  on welfare system, 123
  Wilson's Crime Summit and, 128
  Wilson's gubernatorial campaigns and, 214–15, 219
Meese, Edwin, III, 37–38, 41–42, 46, 202
Mexican Americans, 98–106
  at CRC, 164
  discrimination against, 99–101, 104–6
  gangs of, 93–96, 105, 136, 230
  in history of L.A., 98–105, 108–9
  L.A. race riots and, 103–5
Midget Dukes, 93–95, 230
Minnesota, 196
Moore, Joan, 96
Moyer, William, 82
Murphy, Bobbi, 113–14
Murphy, Morgan, 167
Murray, Charles, 186

Narcotic Drug Control Act, 149
Nation, Carrie, 138
National Crime Information Center
    (NCIC), 158
National Criminal Justice Commission,
    69
National Drugs and Crime Emergency
    Act, 195–96
National Journal, 48
National Policy Forum, 219
National Rifle Association, 47–48, 63,
    126
Native Americans, 19, 146–47
New Folsom Prison, see California State
    Prison, Sacramento
New York, 103, 108, 115, 180, 218
    banning of alcohol in, 142, 144
    capital punishment in, 123, 212
    drugs and, 34–35, 74, 83, 139, 147
    history of crime and punishment in,
        17–20, 24–27
    homicides in, 84, 195
    mandatory minimum sentences in, 13,
        65–68, 170
    panics over crime in, 69–71
    prison system of, 24–27, 64–66, 68, 77,
        84–85, 145, 182–84, 188, 196
    welfare system of, 123
    Williams case in, 64–65
New York Times, 18, 43, 118, 123, 183
Nidorf, Barry J., 8
Nixon, Richard, 6, 30–31, 53, 120, 148,
    151, 155–60, 185, 205, 239
    anti-communist campaign of, 158
    on crime, 41, 115, 131, 157–60, 166–
        70, 175, 213
    death of, 210–11
    demise of, 41, 169–70, 175
    on drugs, 68, 157–60, 167–70
Noonan, Peggy, 211
Norris, Rex David, 86
North Carolina, 18, 20, 80

North County Correctional Facility in
    Wayside, xviii, 8
Norworth, Jack, 1
Novak, Robert, 186

Ochoa, Cruz William, 98, 102, 135
Ochoa, Gloria, xvii, 110, 133–37
    brother's drug addiction and, 135, 137,
        173
Ochoa, Josephine Cata "Josie," xvii, 4–5,
    28, 92–93, 97, 102, 107–11, 133–37,
    170, 172–76, 241, 247
    death of, 174–76, 197
    home life of, 107–8, 110–11, 133
    son's drug addiction and, 173–74
Ochoa, Kenneth, 4, 107–8, 110, 133,
    172, 174–75
Ochoa, Rudy, 106–7, 110, 135, 231–32
Ochoa, Victoria St. Onge, 98, 102
Ochoa, William Cruz, Jr. "Billy," xv–xx,
    3–13, 52, 92–98, 101–3, 133–37,
    150, 152–55, 170–78
    adolescence of, 92–97, 105, 110–11,
        134, 153, 201
    aliases of, 3–5, 197–98, 201
    arrests of, xvii–xviii, 3–7, 133–34, 154,
        162–63, 171–72, 177–78, 197–98,
        200
    birth of, 97, 102–3
    books read by, 242–43
    burglaries of, 4, 6, 8, 92, 111, 125, 135–
        36, 154, 160–62, 172, 176–78, 189,
        197–98, 200–201
    childhood of, 107–11
    drug addiction of, xviii–xix, 4–6, 8, 28,
        92, 96–97, 133–35, 137, 139, 152–
        53, 160–63, 166, 170–75, 178, 187,
        190, 197–201, 243–44, 246
    education of, 95, 109–11, 134, 165
    finances of, xvii, xx, 4–5, 29, 94, 96–
        97, 135, 137, 153, 161–62, 170, 172–
        73, 198–201, 245

Ochoa, William Cruz, Jr. (*continued*)
  gang membership of, 93–95, 105, 136, 230
  girl kidnapped by, 8, 95
  guitar played by, 111
  heritage of, 12–13, 93, 97–98, 102, 230–31, 241, 245
  illnesses and injuries of, 29, 95, 111, 135, 161–63, 188–89, 232–33, 241, 246–47
  imprisonment of, xviii–xix, 3–6, 8, 10–13, 24, 28–29, 73, 75, 87, 92–93, 95–97, 133–34, 154–55, 160–66, 169, 171, 173–76, 187–90, 198, 217, 224–26, 228–33, 240–47
  infancy of, 102
  mother's death and, 174–75
  nickname of, 95
  perjury committed by, 4
  physical appearance of, xviii, 6, 28, 92, 108, 110–11, 133, 152–53, 160, 168–69, 197, 199–200, 244
  pigeons raised by, 110
  plea bargain of, 5–6
  in prison protests, 188–89
  psychiatric treatment of, 164–66
  romances of, 153–54, 160–61, 163, 170–73
  sense of humor of, 28
  sentences of, xviii–xx, 9–10, 20–21, 28–29, 64, 66–67, 71–72, 189, 194, 201, 227, 230, 240
  Three Strikes law and, xx, 6–10, 30, 62, 72–73, 125
  trials of, xvii–xx, 5–6, 8–10, 125
  welfare fraud crimes of, xx, 3–10, 13, 125
  womanizing of, 5, 199–200
Ochoa, William Cruz, Sr., xvii, 4–5, 93–94, 97–98, 102–11, 133–35, 160–61, 170, 172
  fruit and vegetable business of, 106–7, 110, 133

  son's imprisonment and, 241, 243, 247
  Zoot Suit Riots and, 103–5
Office of Drug Abuse Law Enforcement (ODALE), 159, 168
Old Folsom Prison, 12, 224–26, 229
Omnibus Drug Bill, 44
One Strike and You're Out law, 7, 116, 128, 214–17
Open Letter to the People of California on Affirmative Action, 237
Operation Hold The Line, 207
opiates, history of, 137–39, 148
Organized Crime Control Act, 158
Otis, Harrison Gray, 99

Pacific Capital Group (PCG), Inc., 233
Palacios, Mario, 5
panopticons, 89, 228
Parenti, Christian, 55
Pataki, George, 123
Paxton Boys, 19
Pelican Bay prison, 12, 75, 89–91, 221, 224
Pennsylvania:
  history of crime and punishment in, 17, 19, 21–25
  prison system of, 88–89
Perlstein, John, 10
Perry, Charles, 5
Person, Suzanne, xviii
Philadelphia, Pa.:
  history of crime and punishment in, 17–19, 21–22, 24–25, 27, 78, 82
  panics over crime in, 69–71
Pipe Dream Blues (Lusane), 137–38
piracy, 20, 74
politics, politicians:
  and discrimination against Mexican Americans, 100
  and history of crime and punishment, 17, 20, 23
  radicalization of, 181–84

Rockefeller laws and, 66

tough-on-crime, xiii–xv, 6–7, 13

see also Congress, U.S.

Presley, Elvis, 94, 153

prisoners-rights movement, 182–84, 188

prisons, prisoners, prison system, 44–45,
71–91, 122

   Administrative Segregation (AD Seg)
in, 27, 29, 226–27, 241–44

   Bennett and, 204

   Benson case and, 73

   of California, xii, xvi, 7, 14, 48–51, 57–
58, 73, 75, 87–91, 106, 112–13, 116–
17, 196, 207–9, 211, 221–33, 235,
237–38, 240–47

   Clinton and, 119–20, 205

   disenfranchisement of, xii–xiii, 80–81,
106

   drugs and, 13, 83–85, 149

   federal, 76–85, 88–89, 120, 145

   finances of, 87–88, 91

   Gingrich and, 125

   goals of, xvi, 20–27, 57, 162–64, 195,
228

   high-tech, 87, 89, 224

   history of, 20–27, 77–83

   illegal immigrants in, 207, 211, 235

   Johnson on, 155

   Lungren and, 57–58

   maximum-security, 65, 75, 85–87, 145,
162, 165, 183, 224, 227, 230, 232,
245, 247

   medium-security, 189, 224

   mental health programs in, 90, 164–66

   minimum-security, 229

   of New York, 24–27, 64–66, 68, 77, 84–
85, 145, 182–84, 188, 196

   and panics over crime, 71

   prisoner-leasing in, 79–80

   Prohibition and, 144–45

   Reagan and, 185, 192

   reform movement in, 78–80

   Reynolds and, 56

   Rockefeller laws and, 66

   Secure Housing Units (SHUs) in, 27,
88–90

   silence and isolation of, 25–27, 227–28

   size of, xii–v, 13–14, 44, 48–51, 60,
68, 73–75, 78, 82–83, 87–88, 91,
112–13, 119–20, 149, 160, 162, 175,
196, 204, 221–23, 235

   as symbol of national pride, 26–27

   Three Strikes law and, 60, 71–72

   violence in, 12–13, 29, 89–90, 182–84,
188, 221–22, 226, 230–33, 241, 243,
246

   White case and, 72

   Wilson and, 48–51, 57–58, 112–13,
116–17, 209, 214–15, 217–18, 221–
22, 237–38

   Y2K and, 221, 223, 233

Prohibition, 142–46

Propositions, California, 13, 33, 38–39,
208 21, 239–40 139, 50 184, 7, 119,
206, 208, 218, 187, 119, 206, 208, 218

Public Safety Rally, 214–16

Puritans, 14–17, 22, 68

Putting People First, 119

Quakers, 16, 23, 78

Rainey, Richard, 126

Rand Drug Policy Research Center, 77

Reagan, Nancy, 39, 193

Reagan, Ronald, 6, 30–31, 36–40, 48,
120, 123, 184–86, 189, 202–5, 211,
236

   on crime, 41–42, 185–86, 192–93

   economy under, 83, 190, 192–93

   federal prison system and, 83

   Lungren and, 57

   Reynolds and, 52

   welfare system and, 83

   Wilson's senatorial tenure and, 39

Real War on Crime, The, 69
Reconstruction, 79–80
Rector, Ricky Ray, 119
Reefer Madness hysteria, 69
Regulator Movement, 18
Reynolds, Kimber Michele, 53–56, 58–
    59, 62, 112, 209
Reynolds, Mike, 52–56, 214
    death of daughter of, 53–56, 58–59,
        62, 112
    Three Strikes law and, 30, 59, 61–63,
        112, 119, 125–26, 206, 209–10, 240
    Wilson and, 30, 53, 212
Reynolds, Sharon, 53–54, 56
Robinson, Jean, 7
Rockefeller, Nelson D., 65–68
    Attica uprising and, 183
    and panics over crime, 71
    tough-on-crime rhetoric of, 67–68,
        115
    Williams case and, 67
Rockefeller Drug Laws, 65–68, 170
Rodota, Joe, 113
Rodriguez, Luis, 93, 97
Romo, Ricardo, 99, 102
Roosevelt, Franklin D., 118, 156, 186
    and history of drug use, 147
    Prohibition and, 142, 145
Rose, Carol, 215
Rothman, David J., 26–27

St. Clair prison, 85–87
Salem witch trials, 16
San Diego, Calif.:
    Stamp Out Crime Council in, 47
    Wilson as mayor of, 33–34, 36–38, 40
San Quentin prison, 145, 182, 225
    Ochoa's imprisonment at, 10–11
Scooped (Krajicek), 69
Senate Drug Enforcement Caucus, 42,
    186–87
Sentencing Commission, 57

Sentencing Project, 106
Shays, Daniel, 19
Singapore, 234
slavery, 19–20, 79
Smith, Arlo, 58
Smith, Brent, 5
Smith, Joan, 169
Smith, Susan, 121, 124, 208
Smoke and Mirrors (Baum), 44, 131, 157
Society for the Suppression of Disorders,
    The, 17
South:
    disenfranchisement of African
        Americans in, 81
    history of crime and punishment in,
        18–19, 80–81
    and history of drug use, 140
    prison system in, 79–83
South Carolina, 18, 79
South Florida Task Force, 42
Soviet Union, 184–85, 193
    collapse of, 30, 195
    prison system of, xii, 80
Special Action Office for Drug Abuse
    Prevention (SAODAP), 168, 170
Steele, Robert, 167
Supreme Court, U.S., 122, 235

Taking Charge of California's Future
    (Wilson), 50
Tate, Doris, 57, 216
Tate, Sharon, 57, 214
Taxation of Marijuana Act, 147
Tehachapi prison, 174–76
Tennessee, 26, 79–80
Texas, 102
    history of crime and punishment in,
        22
    parole abolished in, 13
    prison system of, xii, xvi, 88, 90, 227
Thatcher, Margaret, 191–92
Thompson, Tommy, 123

Three Prison Act, 82
Three Strikes and You're Out law, 6–10,
106, 149, 196
ballot initiative on, 7, 119, 206, 208–
10, 218
in California, xx, 6–7, 13, 30, 59–63,
71–74, 112, 116, 119, 125–26, 128–
30, 206, 208–10, 214–15, 234, 239–
40
citizens' crusade for, 63, 112, 209–10
and Davis, 234
drafting of, 59, 126
federal, 120
and Klaas case, 61–63
legislation for, 125–26, 129–30
people imprisoned under, 60, 71–72
unfairness of, 62, 72–74
and Wilson, 7, 30, 59, 61–63, 112,
116, 119, 128–30, 208–10, 214–15,
239
Tocqueville, Alexis de, 26
Traffic in Narcotics, The (Anslinger), 147
Treasury Department, U.S., 140, 145
Trebach, Arnold S., 202
Trehune, Cal, 221–23, 233
truth-in-sentencing statutes, 13, 119–20,
125, 196
20/20, 112

Uggen, Christopher, 106
"Unprecedented Progress in the War on
Violent Crime" (Wilson), 217

Valens, Ritchie, 94
Varick, Nazimova, 64–67
Victims' Rights movement, 127, 129
Vietnam War, 152, 154–55, 167, 179–80
Vigilance Committees, 18
Villaluazo, Patty, xvii, 28–29, 136, 176–
77, 241, 243
Violent Crime Control and Law
Enforcement Act, 120–21

Virginia, 19, 26, 122
Volstead Act, 142–43

Walker, Douglas, 54–56
Walker, Sandra, 5
Walnut Street Prison, 23–25, 78
War of Independence, 19, 21, 23, 98
War on Crime, xiv, 152, 170
and drugs, 41–42
history of, 146
and Lungren, 57
and Reagan, 186
and Three Strikes law, 59
and Wilson, 36–37, 50, 116–17, 127,
129, 189
War on Drugs, xiv, 41–42, 44, 84, 119,
122, 152, 170
arrests as priority in, 195
history of, 140–41, 145–48
and history of crime and punishment,
15–16, 18
and Lungren, 57
mandatory prison sentences in, 44
military participation in, 47, 202, 204
Nixon on, 68, 157, 159, 167
and prison system growth, 13
and Reagan, 186, 193
Wilson-sponsored legislation in, 46–47
Washington, D.C., 13, 74, 167
Washton, Arnold, 43
Watergate scandal, 41, 68, 175, 210
Weingart Center, 3
Weld, William, 236
welfare system, 50–52, 83, 123–25, 153,
180, 185–86
Gingrich and, 124–25
Johnson and, 156
Ochoa's fraudulent claims and, xx, 3–
10, 13, 125
public opinion on, 123
Reagan and, 185
Reynolds and, 52

welfare system, (*continued*)
  Wilson on, 50–51, 118–19, 205–8,
    213, 216, 219–20, 235–37
West, history of crime and punishment
  in, 21–22
White, Steven, 72–73
Wicker, Tom, 183–84
Williams, Anthony, 64–67
Williams, Charles, 20–21, 25
Wilson, Gayle Edlund, 39, 219, 237
Wilson, James Q., 74, 128, 186
Wilson, Pete Barton, xv–xvi, 30–42, 53,
    205–22, 233–40
  agribusiness support for, 40, 48, 207
  background of, 210–11
  California's economy and, 30–33, 40,
    51, 113, 214, 218–19, 237, 239
  on capital punishment, 49–50, 122,
    125, 128–29, 212–13, 215
  conservativism of, 38–40, 48, 63
  on crime, 6–7, 34, 36–40, 46–51, 62–
    63, 71, 112–19, 125–30, 189, 205–9,
    211–20, 234–40
  federal drug busts and, 77
  fund-raising of, 48, 210, 238
  gubernatorial campaigns of, 32, 48–51,
    62–63, 113–15, 118, 126, 129, 205–
    19, 237, 239
  honors and awards of, 47
  on illegal immigrants, 40, 118–19, 205–
    7, 211, 213–14, 216, 218–20, 235–
    37
  illnesses of, 237
  inaugural addresses of, 31, 219–20
  Klaas case and, 61–63, 112, 115–16
  L.A. earthquake and, 127
  L.A. riots and, 32
  Lungren and, 57–58

Nixon's death and, 210–11
Ochoa's sentencing and, 66–67
physical appearance of, 47, 112
political ambitions of, 30–32, 37–39,
  48, 218–20, 235–36, 239
pragmatism of, 40
presidential campaign of, 235–39
on prison system, 48–51, 57–58, 112–
  13, 116–17, 209, 214–15, 217–18,
  221–22, 237–38
Public Safety Rally of, 214–16
retirement from electoral politics of,
  233–34, 239–40
as San Diego mayor, 33–34, 36–38, 40
senatorial campaigns of, 38–40, 47–48,
  186–87
senatorial tenure of, 39–41, 46–47, 49–
  50, 122
shooting of grandfather of, 34–36, 50,
  140
Three Strikes law and, 7, 30, 59, 61–
  63, 112, 116, 119, 128–30, 208–10,
  214–15, 239
Wilson, William Julius, 190
Wilson, Woodrow, 142
Wilson-Hunt Amendment, 47
Wisconsin, 123
witches, witchcraft, 15–16
World War I, 140–42, 156
World War II, 101–6, 108–10, 135, 147–
  48, 156, 164, 191
  Zoot Suit Riots and, 103–5
Wright, Hamilton, 139–40
Wright, Thomas, 74

Zepeda, Sylvia, 5
zero-tolerance laws for drugs, 13
Zoot Suit Riots, 103–5, 207